BUDGETING

PRINCIPLES OF BUDGETING AND DRAFTING BUDGETS

Qualifications and Credit Framework

Level 4 Diploma in Accounting

British Library Cataloguing-in-Publication Data

A catalogue record for this book is available from the British Library.

Published by
Kaplan Publishing UK
Unit 2, The Business Centre
Molly Millars Lane
Wokingham
Berkshire
RG41 2QZ

ISBN 978-0-85732-372-9

We are grateful to the Association of Accounting Technicians for permission to reproduce past assessment materials and example tasks based on the new syllabus. The solutions to past answers and similar activities in the style of the new syllabus have been prepared by Kaplan Publishing.

We are grateful to HM Revenue and Customs for the provision of tax forms, which are Crown Copyright and are reproduced here with kind permission from the Office of Public Sector Information.

CONTENTS

Introduction   v

Unit guide   vii

The assessment   xix

Study skills   xxi

STUDY TEXT AND WORKBOOK

Chapter		Study text	Workbook Activities Answers
1	Forecasting and planning	1	253
2	Dealing with fixed overheads	49	258
3	Preparing budgets	73	263
4	Budgetary control – flexing budgets	117	283
5	Investigating and reporting variances	149	292
6	Performance indicators	175	299
7	Budgeting – other considerations	217	305
Mock Examination Questions		317	
Mock Examination Answers		333	
Index		I.1	

INTRODUCTION

HOW TO USE THESE MATERIALS

These Kaplan Publishing learning materials have been carefully designed to make your learning experience as easy as possible and to give you the best chance of success in your AAT assessments.

They contain a number of features to help you in the study process.

The sections on the Unit Guide, the Assessment and Study Skills should be read before you commence your studies.

They are designed to familiarise you with the nature and content of the assessment and to give you tips on how best to approach your studies.

STUDY TEXT

This study text has been specially prepared for the revised AAT qualification introduced in July 2010.

It is written in a practical and interactive style:

- key terms and concepts are clearly defined

- all topics are illustrated with practical examples with clearly worked solutions based on sample tasks provided by the AAT in the new examining style

- frequent activities throughout the chapters ensure that what you have learnt is regularly reinforced

- 'pitfalls' and 'examination tips' help you avoid commonly made mistakes and help you focus on what is required to perform well in your examination

- practice workbook activities can be completed at the end of each chapter.

WORKBOOK

The workbook comprises:

Practice activities at the end of each chapter with solutions at the end of the text, to reinforce the work covered in each chapter.

The questions are divided into their relevant chapters and students may either attempt these questions as they work through the textbook, or leave some or all of these until they have completed the textbook as a final revision of what they have studied.

ICONS

The study chapters include the following icons throughout.

They are designed to assist you in your studies by identifying key definitions and the points at which you can test yourself on the knowledge gained.

 Definition

These sections explain important areas of Knowledge which must be understood and reproduced in an assessment

 Example

The illustrative examples can be used to help develop an understanding of topics before attempting the activity exercises

 Activity

These are exercises which give the opportunity to assess your understanding of all the assessment areas.

UNIT GUIDE

Budgeting is divided into two units, but for the purposes of assessment, these units will be combined.

Principles of Budgeting (Knowledge)

3 credits

Drafting Budgets (Skills)

4 credits

Purpose of the units

The AAT has stated that the creation of these two core units at level 4 is recognition of the importance of financial planning in every organisation. Budgets are an essential tool in planning, coordinating, authorising and cost control. Much of the 'Principles of Budgeting' unit consolidates knowledge required at level 3. However, 'Drafting Budgets' requires new skills to create appropriate forecasts and budgets for a wide range of activities and circumstances; to agree the budgets with other functional managers, to monitor results against budget and trigger suitable management interventions.

Learning objectives

In the Principles of Budgeting unit, learners develop an understanding of how and why budgets are prepared. Assessment candidates need to display the necessary knowledge to prepare revenue forecasts and a range of budgets for different circumstances, and be able to tailor them to meet organisational requirements. They must understand the component parts of budgetary procedure to aid organisational planning and control.

In the 'Drafting Budgets' unit, learners develop their forecasting and budgeting skills. Assessment candidates need to demonstrate their ability to prepare budgets, analyse variances and make recommendations for improving organisational performance. They must also be able to guide managers in planning and control.

Learning Outcomes and Assessment criteria

Each unit includes three learning outcomes comprised of a number of assessment criteria.

Principles of Budgeting (knowledge)

- Demonstrate an understanding of the impact of internal and external business factors on budgets
- Understand why budgets are used
- Understand the skills needed in budget preparation.

Drafting Budgets (skills)

- Prepare forecasts and budgets
- Understand the impact that changes in the economic environment will have on the budget
- Use budgetary control to ensure organisational targets are met.

Knowledge

To perform this unit effectively you will need to know and understand the following:

		Chapter
1	**Demonstrate an understanding of the impact of internal and external business factors on budgets**	
1.1	Explain the structure of the organisation; responsibility centres and the relationships between the departments and functions	1
1.2	Identify internal and external sources of information on costs, prices, demand, availability of resources and availability and cost of finance, to include Government statistics, trade associations, financial press quotations and price lists	1
1.3	Describe the impact of the external environment and any specific external costs on budgets	1

KAPLAN PUBLISHING

		Chapter
1.4	Describe the internal charges made to attribute indirect costs to production	2
2	**Understand why budgets are used**	
2.1	Explain the behavioural aspects of budgeting	7
2.2	Justify the uses of budgetary control for planning, co-ordinating, authorising and cost control	1,3, 4
2.3	Identify the correct budget to prepare, according to the organisational requirements	1,3
2.4	Explain the relationship between budgetary control, product lifecycles, and forecasts and planning	1
2.5	Explain the significance of budget variances	5
2.6	Recognise the effect that capacity, production and sales constraints have on budgets	3,4
3	**Understand the skills needed in budget preparation**	
3.1	Explain the principles of standard costing	3,4
3.2	Describe the purpose of revenue and costs forecasts and how they link to budgets	1,3,4
3.3	Identify when to use the following techniques : Indexing, Sampling, Moving averages, Linear regression and Seasonal trends.	1
3.4	Recognise expenses as different types of costs	2,3,4
3.5	Identify the sources of relevant data used in budget proposals	1

Skills

To perform this unit effectively you will need to be able to do the following.

Chapter

1 Prepare forecasts and budgets

1.1	Identify relevant data for forecasting income and expenditure from internal and external sources	1
1.2	Correctly code, classify and allocate cost and revenue data to responsibility centres	1,2
1.3	Forecast future income from relevant internal and external data	1
1.4	Schedule the required production resources to meet forecasts	3
1.5	Budget in accordance with the organisation's costing systems stating any assumptions made	3
1.6	Prepare accurate cash flow forecast to facilitate the achievement of organisational objectives	3
1.7	Prepare draft budgets from forecast data	1,3
1.8	Break down budgets into time periods according to organisational needs	3
1.9	Plan and agree draft budgets with all parties involved	1,3

2 Understand the impact that changes in the economic environment will have on budget

2.1	Calculate the effect that variations in capacity on costs, production and sales will have on budgeted costs and revenues.	3,4
2.2	Prepare an accurately flexed budget	4
2.3	Analyse critical factors affecting costs and revenues and draw clear conclusions	3,4
2.4	Identify and evaluate options and solutions to increase profitability or reduce financial losses or exposure to risk	3,4,6

Chapter

3   Use budgetary control to ensure organisational targets are met

3.1   Set clear targets and performance indicators to enable budgets to be monitored   6

3.2   Check and reconcile budget figures on an ongoing basis

3.3   Review and revise the validity of budgets in the light of any significant anticipated changes   5

3.4   Identify variances between budget and actual income/expenditure   5

3.5   Analyse the variances and explain the impact this will have on the organisation   5

3.6   Inform management of any significant issues arising from budgetary control

3.7   Present any recommendations with a clear rationale to the appropriate people   5,6,7

Delivery guidance

The AAT have provided delivery guidance giving further details of the way in which the unit will be assessed.

Principles of budgeting

Demonstrate an understanding of the impact of internal and external business factors on budgets

1.1   Explain the structure of the organisation; responsibility centres and the relationships between the departments and functions
Candidates must understand that the structure of a budget needs to be appropriate to the organisation. For instance, if there is a production department, a marketing department and an administration department, the organisation's budget will need to include a production budget, a marketing budget and an administration budget. Appropriate profit centres, cost centres and investment centres will need to be defined and the budget must be structured accordingly. The budget responsibility of managers must be consistent with their authority. Candidates can be assessed on their ability to propose or critique the structure of a budget; to describe the purpose of departments and functions and to describe

the responsibility of senior managers for preparing budgets and delivering performance.

1.2   Identify internal and external sources of information on costs, prices, demand, availability of resources and availability and cost of finance, to include Government statistics, trade associations, financial press quotations and price lists

Budget data is drawn from a wide variety of sources within the organisation and externally. Candidates must be able to suggest an appropriate, reliable source for each piece of information required in budget construction. They will not be expected to have a detailed knowledge of, for instance, every government statistical publication, but must be able to demonstrate that they know which external source or which member of the organisation to go to for any specified data.

1.3   Describe the impact of the external environment and any specific external costs on budgets

The external environment has a direct impact on sales demand, prices, availability of resources and costs. Some external costs, including taxes, are not within the organisation's control. Realistic budgets are prepared in this context. Candidates must be able to review budget proposals and comment on their achievability.

1.4   Describe the internal charges made to attribute indirect costs to production

Indirect costs may be attributed to production through apportionment to departments and the use of overhead recovery rates, or through activity based costing, etc. The budget needs to be consistent with the method of attribution that will be employed to calculate the actual results. Candidates need to be able to propose appropriate methods of attribution and recognise the distortions that can be created by inappropriate methods.

Understand why budgets are used

2.1   Explain the behavioural aspects of budgeting

The purpose of a budget is to drive improved performance for the organisation. It should be motivational. A budget is both a plan and a performance measure. Poor budgeting can be extremely demotivating. Each element of a budget must be owned by an appropriate manager. Candidates must be able to describe the relationships between budgets and accountability, between authority and responsibility, and between planning and control, and make recommendations to ensure that budgets promote the right behaviour.

2.2 Justify the uses of budgetary control for planning, co-ordinating, authorising and cost control

Budgetary control fulfils these four apparently diverse functions and a balance needs to be maintained. For instance, over-emphasis on cost control can constrain business growth. Also, high level planning targets can conflict with detailed co-ordination activity. Candidates must be able to describe each of these functions and demonstrate an understanding of the potential for conflict.

2.3 Identify the correct budget to prepare according to the organisational requirements

Candidates must know the purpose and content of each of the following budgets: Income and expenditure, Production, Material and Labour (employees and other resources). They must also be able to explain the distinction between Capital and Revenue. They must be able to describe the circumstance under which Flexible budgets are appropriate and when it is better for budgets to be fixed. Finally they need to be able to explain the purpose and construction of a Cash budget and how it links to other budgets.

2.4 Explain the relationship between budgetary control, product lifecycles, and forecasts and planning

Many organisations prefer the term financial plan to budget. The budget is an integral part of an overall plan for the business. Forecasting is an essential part of determining realistic data and assumptions upon which the plan is based. Statistical projections are useful aids to forecasting (see assessment criterion 3.3 below) but judgement and knowledge of the market and the products is essential. Candidates must be able to describe budgetary control, product lifecycles, and forecasts and make appropriate recommendations to ensure that budgets are soundly based.

2.5 Explain the significance of budget variances

Variances can be caused by better or worse than expected performance within the organisation or by unforeseen external factors. They can also be due to unrealistic or inaccurate budgeting. A significant variance requires a management response, which could, for instance, be to investigate poor performance and take corrective action. Candidates need to be able to demonstrate an understanding of how variances should be investigated and the range of management actions that could be appropriate.

2.6 Recognise the effect that capacity, production and sales constraints have on budgets

To be realistic budgets have to be based on what is practically possible. Every business has a budget factor (limiting factor), which could, for instance, be a production bottleneck, possible market share or access to finance. Candidates must be able to identify budget factors and describe how to create a budget that maximises the potential contribution.

Understand the skills needed in budget preparation

3.1 Explain the principles of standard costing

Standard costing and budgetary control are powerful management tools that can be used separately but naturally combine into a seamless system of planning and control. They share the approach of setting targets, measuring actual performance, analysing variances and initiating management action to correct or improve future performance and set new targets. This creates a cycle of continuous improvement. Candidates must be able to describe the principles of standard costing and variance analysis, explain the main variances and identify possible causes of each.

3.2 Describe the purpose of revenue and cost forecasts and how they link to budgets

Some aspects of business performance are within the control of the organisation and can be planned. Others are subject more or less to external factors that must be forecast. For example, budgeted revenue may be calculated from forecasts of market demand and market share. Cost budgets may be influenced by forecasts of world markets and national inflation. These forecasts are used to develop the planning assumptions on which budgets are based. These assumptions must be clearly stated so that variances from budget can be analysed and understood. Candidates must be able to distinguish between forecasts and plans, and describe how each forecast fits into the planning process. They must also be able to recommend techniques for dealing with the uncertainty inherent in forecasts. These techniques include planning models, regular re-forecasting and flexible budgets.

3.3 Identify when to use the following techniques: Indexing, Sampling, Moving Averages, Linear Regression and Seasonal Trends

These techniques have been learned in previous units. Detailed explanations of each technique are not required at this level but candidates must be able to recognise the circumstances in which each technique could be appropriate, explain why, and describe limitations to their use.

3.4 Recognise expenses as different types of costs

Cost budgets include both direct and indirect (overhead) costs (see assessment criterion 1.4 above) and the budget construction must be consistent with the organisation's costing and accounting systems. Candidates must be able to explain how to budget for underlying indirect costs and for their attribution into product costs (cost objects). They must also be able to describe the appropriate methodology for raw materials, direct labour and other direct costs.

Various cost behaviours are recognised such as variable, semi-variable and stepped. Not all costs fit these textbook profiles, of course. Labour is usually described as variable when, in practice, basic wages are often a fixed cost and overtime is a variable at a higher rate that only applies when basic hours are utilised. Candidates need to be able to recognise cost behaviours and recommend appropriate methods of budget calculation and performance measurement.

3.5 Identify the sources of relevant data used in budget proposals

Budgets are compiled from a wide range of sources: market forecasts, current performance data and planning assumptions. Candidates must be able to clearly state these sources in appropriate footnotes to the budget or covering correspondence.

Delivery guidance: Drafting budgets (skills)

Prepare forecasts and budgets

1.1 Identify relevant data for forecasting income and expenditure from internal and external sources

Candidates must be able to recognise the relevance of data available for forecasting and extract the appropriate items.

1.2 Correctly code, classify and allocate cost and revenue data to responsibility centres

The creation of an appropriate accountability structure (investment centres, profit centres and cost centres) is fundamental to planning, coordination and control. Candidates must be able to recommend suitable structures and to classify and allocate cost and revenue data accordingly.

1.3 Forecast future income from relevant internal and external data

Candidates must be able to prepare income forecasts from relevant internal and external data using appropriate forecasting techniques and judgement and present the results clearly, stating assumptions.

1.4 Schedule the required production resources to meet forecasts

Candidates must be able to prepare the underlying 'physical' plans upon which budgets are calculated. This involves calculating the requirements for materials, labour and production facilities and correctly adjusting for stock levels, wastage, available staff hours and production facility hours, etc.

1.5 Budget in accordance with the organisation's costing systems stating any assumptions made

Candidates must be able to prepare budgets for production costs (consistent with the organisation's costing systems) based on 'physical plans' for materials, labour and other production resources, and present the results clearly, stating assumptions.

1.6 Prepare accurate cash flow forecast to facilitate the achievement of organisational objectives

Cash flow forecasts must be consistent with all other aspects of the budget. Candidates must be able to prepare a cash flow forecast from the budget data and update it as actual performance results become available. Forecasts must be presented clearly, stating assumptions.

1.7 Prepare draft budgets from forecast data

Candidates must be able to prepare budgets for income, material costs, labour (employees and other resources), other production resources, other overheads (including depreciation), capital expenditure and cash and assemble these results into a master budget. Budgets must be presented clearly, stating assumptions.

1.8 Break down budgets into time periods according to organisational needs

Candidates must be able to break down budgets into weeks, months or quarters, etc, to facilitate regular reporting and monitoring of performance.

1.9 Plan and agree draft budgets with all parties involved

Communication is a key requirement of the budgeting process and candidates must be able to demonstrate their ability to read and understand the planning data available; check their understanding with appropriate managers; set out the results of their work in a clear, understandable and professional manner; understand the impact of these results on the organisation and provide management with clear written explanation and advice.

2 Understand the impact that changes in the economic environment will have on the budget

2.1 Calculate the effect that variations in capacity on costs, production and sales will have on budgeted costs and revenues

Candidates need to be able to deal with budget limiting factors (constraints in capacity and limitations on costs and sales) in two ways. Firstly, preparing or revising a budget to fit within the constraint and, secondly, producing a budget that optimises contribution.

2.2 Prepare an accurately flexed budget

Candidates must be able to flex a budget, adjusting each element of the budget correctly according to the original budget data and stating assumptions about cost behaviour. They must also be able to present the flexed budget clearly and explain the changes from the original.

2.3 Analyse critical factors affecting costs and revenues and draw clear conclusions

Candidates must be able to identify critical factors affecting costs and revenues, such as market conditions, staffing levels, material availability, etc, and explain their impact on the budget. They must be able to advise on the consequences of changes to key planning assumptions.

2.4 Identify and evaluate options and solutions to increase profitability or reduce financial losses or exposure to risk

Candidates must be able to calculate the impact on the budget of alternative strategies and provide sound advice based on their evaluation of profitability and exposure to risk

3 Use budgetary control to ensure organisational targets are met

3.1 Set clear targets and performance indicators to enable the budgets to be monitored

Candidates must be able to identify suitable physical and financial measures, consistent with the key planning assumptions, to use as performance measures. They must be able to calculate these measures for the budget and for actual performance and provide clear advice to enable budgets to be achieved. Examples of physical measures include quality indicators such as reject rates; efficiency indicators such as the number of products made per labour hour or idle time ratios, and capacity measures, such as machine utilisation rates. Financial measures include Return on Capital Employed, Net Profit Margin, Asset Turnover and subsidiary ratios to these.

3.2 Check and reconcile budget figures on an ongoing basis

Candidates must ensure that budget data is reported accurately and consistently.

3.3 Review and revise the validity of budgets in the light of any significant anticipated changes

Budgets need to be reviewed regularly in the light of actual performance and by updating the underlying forecasts. Candidates need to be able to review the planning assumptions, recalculate budgets and offer appropriate guidance to management.

3.4 Identify variances between budget and actual income/expenditure

Candidates must be able calculate variances in absolute and percentage terms, accurately comparing like with like and present the results clearly.

3.5 Analyse the variances and explain the impact that this will have on the organisation

Candidates must be able to analyse variances, in the context of any operational information available, to identify possible causes and provide suitable management advice. This advice might explain how performance could be improved or suggest appropriate further investigation. Candidates also need to explain how any variance impacts on overall performance and the possible consequences for the organisation.

3.6 Inform management of any significant issues arising from budgetary control

Issues that arise can include changes in planning assumptions or underlying forecasts; significant variance from budget; inaccuracies in the budget; organisational issues and problems with accountability or motivation. Candidates must be able to clearly describe the issue to the appropriate manager(s) and offer constructive advice.

3.7 Present any recommendations with a clear rationale to appropriate people

Communication is a key constituent of an effective planning and control system. Candidates must be able to present forecasts, budgets and control reports clearly, highlighting key issues for attention and providing relevant and focused recommendations to initiate management action.

KAPLAN PUBLISHING

THE ASSESSMENT

The format of the assessment

The assessment will be divided into two sections, one section for Planning and one section for control.

Section 1 – Planning consists of six tasks which will include the research of available data, forecasting, production scheduling, financial budgeting and splitting plans and budgets in accounting periods. It also includes relevant communication.

Section 2 – Control consists of two task which cover budget flexing, variance analysis and reporting plus relevant communication. The focus of this section will be on understanding and communicating the significance of results.

Learners will normally be assessed by computer-based assessment (CBA), which will include extended writing tasks. Learners will be required to demonstrate competence in both sections of the assessment. As this CBA will require both computer and human marking, results will normally be available approximately 6 weeks after the assessment.

Time allowed

The time allowed for this assessment is **two hours and 30 minutes.**

STUDY SKILLS

Preparing to study

Devise a study plan

Determine which times of the week you will study.

Split these times into sessions of at least one hour for study of new material. Any shorter periods could be used for revision or practice.

Put the times you plan to study onto a study plan for the weeks from now until the assessment and set yourself targets for each period of study – in your sessions make sure you cover the whole course, activities and the associated questions in the workbook at the back of the manual.

If you are studying more than one unit at a time, try to vary your subjects as this can help to keep you interested and see subjects as part of wider knowledge.

When working through your course, compare your progress with your plan and, if necessary, re-plan your work (perhaps including extra sessions) or, if you are ahead, do some extra revision / practice questions.

Effective studying

Active reading

You are not expected to learn the text by rote, rather, you must understand what you are reading and be able to use it to pass the assessment and develop good practice.

A good technique is to use SQ3Rs – Survey, Question, Read, Recall, Review:

1   **Survey the chapter**

    Look at the headings and read the introduction, knowledge, skills and content, so as to get an overview of what the chapter deals with.

2   **Question**

    Whilst undertaking the survey ask yourself the questions you hope the chapter will answer for you.

3   Read

Read through the chapter thoroughly working through the activities and, at the end, making sure that you can meet the learning objectives highlighted on the first page.

4   Recall

At the end of each section and at the end of the chapter, try to recall the main ideas of the section / chapter without referring to the text. This is best done after short break of a couple of minutes after the reading stage.

5   Review

Check that your recall notes are correct.

You may also find it helpful to re-read the chapter to try and see the topic(s) it deals with as a whole.

Note taking

Taking notes is a useful way of learning, but do not simply copy out the text.

The notes must:

- be in your own words
- be concise
- cover the key points
- well organised
- be modified as you study further chapters in this text or in related ones.

Trying to summarise a chapter without referring to the text can be a useful way of determining which areas you know and which you don't.

Three ways of taking notes

1   Summarise the key points of a chapter

2   Make linear notes

A list of headings, subdivided with sub-headings listing the key points.

If you use linear notes, you can use different colours to highlight key points and keep topic areas together.

Use plenty of space to make your notes easy to use.

3   Try a diagrammatic form

The most common of which is a mind map.

To make a mind map, put the main heading in the centre of the paper and put a circle around it.]

Draw lines radiating from this to the main sub-headings which again have circles around them.

Continue the process from the sub-headings to sub-sub-headings.

Highlighting and underlining

You may find it useful to underline or highlight key points in your study text – but do be selective.

You may also wish to make notes in the margins.

Revision phase

Kaplan has produced material specifically designed for your final examination preparation for this unit.

These include pocket revision notes and a bank of revision questions specifically in the style of the new syllabus.

Further guidance on how to approach the final stage of your studies is given in these materials.

Further reading

In addition to this text, you should also read the "Student section" of the "Accounting Technician" magazine every month to keep abreast of any guidance from the examiners.

Forecasting and planning

1

Introduction

This chapter provides general background information to the context of budgeting as a key element of management accounting. It is essential background knowledge and should be useful in answering tasks in the exam.

Using time series analysis in order to forecast future figures in a budget is a favourite examination topic. You only need to use the time series techniques to forecast future trends.

You should be able not only to use the time series techniques to forecast future trends and seasonal variations but also understand the weaknesses of time series analysis and the problems of using historical data to predict the future.

Sampling and index numbers are also important topics and are covered in this chapter.

KNOWLEDGE

- Explain the structure of the organisation; responsibility centres and the relationships between the departments and functions (Element 1.1)

- Identify internal and external sources of information on costs, prices, demand, availability of resources and availability and cost of finance, to include Government statistics, trade associations, financial press quotations and price lists (Element 1.2)

- Describe the impact of the external environment and any specific external costs on budgets (Element 1.3)

CONTENTS

1   Planning, budgeting and forecasting

2   Principal budgetary factors

3   The budget preparation and coordination process

4   Internal sources of information

5   External sources of information

6   Forecasting techniques: time series

7   Forecasting with time series analysis

8   Forecasting techniques: sampling

9   Forecasting techniques: index numbers

- Justify the uses of budgetary control for planning, co-ordinating, authorising and cost control (Element 2.2)

- Explain the relationship between budgetary control, product lifecycles, and forecasts and planning (Element 2.4)

- Identify when to use the following techniques : Indexing, Sampling, Moving Averages, Linear Regression and seasonal trends (Element 3.3)

- Identify the sources of relevant data used in budget proposals (Element 3.5)

SKILLS

- Identify relevant data for forecasting income and expenditure from internal and external sources (Element 1.1)

- Correctly code, classify and allocate cost & revenue data to responsibility centres (Element 1.2)

- Forecast future income from relevant internal and external data (Element 1.3)

- Prepare draft budgets from forecast data (Element 1.7)

- Plan and agree draft budgets with all parties involved (Element 1.9)

1 Planning, budgeting and forecasting

1.1 Introduction

Given the increasing complexity of business and the ever-changing environment faced by firms it is doubtful whether any firm can survive by simply continuing to do what it has always done in the past. If the firm wishes to earn satisfactory levels of profit in the future, it must plan its course of action in order to attempt to improve its performance.

In a management accounting context, the budgeting process is part of the overall planning process.

1.2 The concept of corporate planning

Planning is an important concept in all walks of life, including your preparation for examinations. A **plan** is a series of actions to be carried out if objectives and goals are to be met.

In a business context, the term corporate planning is often used. **Corporate planning** is a long run, on-going activity which seeks to determine the direction in which the firm should be moving in the future. 'Where do we see ourselves in ten years time'.

A frequently asked question in formulating the corporate plan is:

(a) the reason why the company exists (its **mission**)

(b) what it wants to achieve (its corporate **objectives**)

(c) how it intends to get there (its business **strategy**)

(d) what resources will be required (its **operating plans**)

(e) how well it does in comparison to the plan (**control**).

These areas are discussed below.

Mission is a broad statement of the overall aims of the organisation.

A clearly defined mission, which is widely publicised within and outside the organisation, will guide it in its decision making. Most organisations now prepare and publish their mission in a document known as a mission statement.

Examples of real world mission statements are:

*   'To be the industry leader in the vehicle interior trims market by offering excellent quality, flexibility and value, by proactively partnering our customers in a joint mission to create a world class service.'

- Our mission: 'To make Hampshire safer' (Hampshire Fire Brigade).

- 'Our Corporate Mission Statement is for Fly Magic to become the largest pleasure flying organisation in the UK.'

Note that mission statements give an overall aim or goal which is not time specific and not quantified. You should contrast this with the concept of objectives dealt with below.

Corporate objectives are quantified, time-limited statements of what a firm wishes to achieve. Traditionally it was assumed that all firms were only interested in the maximisation of profit (or the wealth of their shareholders). Nowadays it is recognised that for many firms profit is only one of many objectives pursued.

Examples of other objectives include:

(a) maximisation of sales (whilst earning a 'reasonable' level of profit)

(b) growth (in sales, asset value, number of employees, etc)

(c) survival

(d) research and development leadership

(e) quality of service

(f) contented workforce

(g) respect for the environment.

For corporate planning purposes it is essential that the objectives chosen are quantified and have a timescale attached to them. It has been suggested that objectives should be SMART:

- **S**pecific
- **M**easurable
- **A**chievable
- **R**elevant
- **T**ime limited

A statement such as maximise profits and increase sales would be of little use in corporate planning terms. The following would be far more helpful:

(a) achieve a growth in profit of 5% per annum over the coming ten-year period

(b) obtain a turnover of $x million within six years

(c) launch at least two new products per year, etc.

Some objectives may be difficult to quantify (e.g. contented workforce) but if no attempt is made there will be no yardstick against which to compare actual performance.

Strategy is the course of action, including the specification of resources required, that the company will adopt to achieve its specific objective.

Strategy formulation usually involves:

(a)   an analysis of the environment in which the firm operates, a review of the strengths and weaknesses of the company and a consideration of the threats and opportunities facing it

(b)   the results of the firm's existing operations are then projected forward and compared with stated objectives

(c)   any differences between projected performance and objectives ('gaps') are identified.

To bridge these gaps the firm will either change its objectives (because they are too optimistic) or attempt to change the firm's direction to improve performance. This change of direction is strategy formulation.

Formulation of strategy is largely a creative process, whereby the firm will consider the products it makes and the markets it serves. Typical strategies include:

- market penetration (sell more of existing products to existing customers)

- product development (new products sold to existing customers)

- market development (continue in existing markets, develop new ones)

- diversification (develop new products and sell them to new customers).

These strategies might be followed either:

- internally – for example, the company develops its own products

- by acquisition – the company buys another which currently has the product range it wants.

Operating plans are the short-term tactics of the organisation.

A strategic plan might call for expansion in a particular market; whereas the operating plan will detail how the extra products are to be made and how much is to be spent on advertising. Military analogy is useful here – strategy is how to organise to win the war, operating plans (or tactics) are how to fight individual battles.

Control is the comparison of the results of the plans and the stated objectives to assess the firm's performance, and the taking of action to remedy any differences in performance.

This is an essential activity as it highlights any weakness in the firm's corporate plan or its execution. Plans must be continually reviewed because as the environment changes so plans and objectives will need revision. Corporate planning is not a once-in-every-ten-years activity, but an 'on-going' process which must react quickly to the changing circumstances of the firm.

Overview of the planning process

The overall planning and control process is summarised in the diagram that follows.

You will note that the bottom section of the diagram introduces the word budget.

We saw earlier the concept of a plan and mentioned the example of students having a plan to help them to achieve their objective of passing examinations. You, as an individual, might take the view that you can afford to buy this (essential and invaluable) textbook, but you may not be able to afford to attend a series of expensive seminars held in upmarket hotels where leading experts discuss management accounting topics in great detail. By taking this view, you are, in effect turning your plan to pass the examination into a budget.

The classic concept of a budget is that it takes a plan, which might be in terms of, say hours, number of units of sales etc and turns it into MONEY terms.

A budget is a plan in monetary terms.

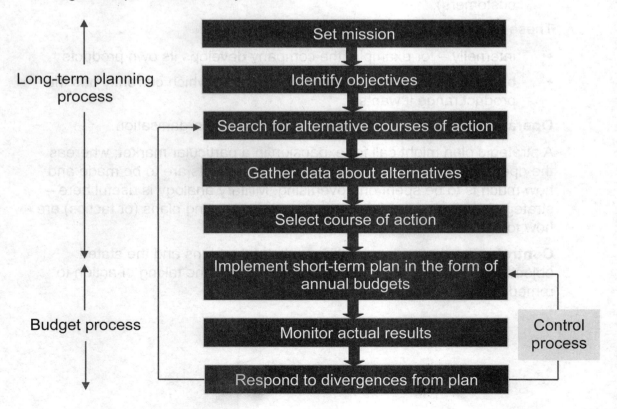

The eight stages are explained below:

(a) **Set mission**

This involves establishing the broad overall aims and goals of the organisation – these may be both economic and social.

(b) **Identify objectives**

This requires the company to specify objectives towards which it is working. These objectives may be in terms of:

- economic targets
- type of business
- goods/services to be sold
- markets to be served
- market share
- profit objectives
- required growth rates of sales, profits, assets.

(c) **Search for possible courses of action**

A series of specific strategies should be developed dealing particularly with:

- developing new markets for existing products
- developing new products for existing markets
- developing new products for new markets.

(d) **Gathering data about alternatives and measuring pay-offs**

This is an information-gathering stage.

(e) **Select course of action**

Having made decisions, long-term plans based on those decisions are created.

(f) **Implementation of short-term plans**

This stage signals the move from long-term planning to short-term plans in the form of annual budgeting. The budget provides the link between the strategic plans and their implementation in management decisions. The budget should be seen as an integral part of the long-term planning process.

(g) **Monitor actual outcomes**

This is the particular role of the cost accountant, keeping detailed financial and other records of actual performance compared with budget targets (variance accounting).

(h) **Respond to divergences from plan**

This is the control process in budgeting, responding to divergences from plan either through budget modifications or through identifying new courses of action.

Before we leave this section we should relate together some of the most important features of management accounting, and of your examination syllabus, which we have now seen:

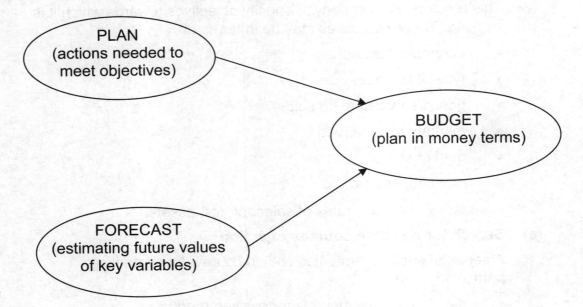

This indicates that the preparation of a budget, the subject matter of this and the next few chapters in this book needs a plan to be in place AND requires relevant forecast information to be available. Planning and forecasting are seen to be essential preliminary steps in the budgetary process.

1.3   Influences on planning and control systems

The planning and control system in all organisations should follow the general structure set out above. However, the detail of the process will be influenced by a number of factors and therefore will vary from one organisation to another.

The principal factors which will influence the process in a given organisation will include:

- organisational structure
- corporate objectives
- administrative procedures
- the nature of the activities of the business.

KAPLAN PUBLISHING

1.4   Why prepare budgets?

The simple reason why organisations spend considerable time and resources on budgeting is very simple – the organisation is taking the view that the benefits of budgeting outweigh the costs involved.

The costs involved in budgeting are mainly costs of setting up systems and procedures to implement the budgetary process. (We shall suggest in a later chapter that there may also be hidden costs of budgeting if the processes involved adversely influence behaviour in the organisation.)

The principal benefits of a sound budgeting system can be dealt with under the following headings:

1   planning and co-ordination

2   authorising and delegating

3   evaluating performance

4   identifying trends

5   communicating and motivating

6   control.

7   Planning and co-ordination

Success in business is closely related to success in planning for the future. In this context the budget serves three functions:

(a)   It provides a formal **planning framework** that ensures planning does take place.

(b)   It **co-ordinates** the various separate aspects of the business by providing a master plan (the master budget is dealt with later) for the business as a whole. This is particularly important in a large organisation engaged in making several different products, where otherwise it is too easy for individual managers to concentrate on their own aspects of the business.

(c)   Though not all decisions can be anticipated, the budget provides a **framework of reference** within which later operating decisions can be taken.

Authorising and delegating

Adoption of a budget by management explicitly authorises the decisions made within it. This serves two functions:

(a)   the need continuously to ask for top management decisions is reduced

(b)   the responsibility for carrying out the decisions is delegated to individual managers.

Evaluating performance

One of the functions of accounting information is that it provides a basis for the measurement of managerial performance. By setting targets for each manager to achieve, the budget provides a benchmark, against which his actual performance can be assessed objectively.

Note, however, that before a budget can successfully be used for this purpose, it must be accepted as reasonable by the individual manager whose area of responsibility it covers and whose performance is to be evaluated.

Identifying trends

It is important that management should be made aware as soon as possible of any new trends, whether in relation to production or marketing. The budget, by providing specific expectations with which actual performance is continuously compared, supplies a mechanism for the early detection of any unexpected trend.

Communication and motivating

The application of budgeting within an organisation should lead to a good communications structure. Managers involved in the setting of budgets for their own responsibility need to have agreed strategies and policies communicated down to them. A good system of downward communication should itself encourage good upward and sideways communication in the organisation. Budgets that have been agreed by managers should provide some motivation towards their achievement.

Control

Budgets provide a yardstick against which actual performance can be measured and variances analysed. Action can then be taken to adjust performance or targets.

2 Principal budgetary factors

Before we move on to deal with the budget preparation process in detail, we need to look at the important topic of the principal budgetary factor also known as the key factor or limiting factor.

Definition The principal budgetary factor is a factor that places a limit on the activities of the organisation.

Consider the details below of two companies:

	COMPANY A	COMPANY B
Maximum output Per annum (note 1)	100,000 units	300,000 units
Maximum customer Demand per annum (note 2)	150,000 units	200,000 units

Notes

(1)   The customer demand figures here would be derived from a forecasting exercise of the type we dealt with in an earlier chapter.

(2)   The output is limited as a result of a limited number of labour hours being available to each company.

In the case of Company A there is no point in budgeting to produce 150,000 units (customer demand) as the company cannot produce this amount. The principal budgetary factor here is production capacity, or, more specifically, labour hours. This is the figure Company A will start with in preparing its budgets.

Turning to Company B, there is no point here in budgeting to produce 300,000 units, even though it has the labour capacity to do so. If 300,000 units were produced, 100,000 of them would go unsold – a waste of resources! Here, the principal budgetary factor is market demand – this is the figure which Company B should take as the starting point for its budget preparation process.

In short, the principal budgetary factor is that factor (usually market demand or an internal resource) which places a limit on the activities of the organisation. For most companies the principal budgetary factor is likely to be market demand or an internal resource. In the public sector it is more likely to be cash or the availability of skilled staff. For example, hospitals and schools will be limited in the service which they can offer by the amount of funding available or the number of skilled doctors or teachers. This becomes the starting point for the budget preparation process.

3 The budget preparation and coordination process

This section looks at how an organisation should go about setting up a budgetary system and, once set up, how that system should operate. This is largely a descriptive part of the syllabus which may produce written questions in an examination paper.

3.1 Setting up a budgetary control system

Before a budgetary control system can be introduced, it is essential that:

(a) key executives are committed to the proposed system

(b) the long-term objectives of the organisation have been defined

(c) there is an adequate foundation of data on which to base forecasts and costs

(d) an organisation chart should be drawn up, clearly defining areas of authority and responsibility. The organisation can then be logically divided into budget centres, such that each manager has a budget for, and is given control information about, the area which he can control. This is the essence of responsibility accounting

(e) a budget committee should be set up and a budget manual produced

(f) the principal budgetary factor is identified.

3.2 Stages in the budgetary process

These may be identified as follows:

(a) **Communicating policy guidelines to preparers of budgets**

The long-term plan forms the framework within which the budget is prepared. It is therefore necessary to communicate the implications of that plan to the people who actually prepare the budget.

(b) **Determining the factor which restricts output**

Generally there will be one factor which restricts performance for a given period. Usually this will be sales, but it could be production capacity, or some special labour skills. This is, as we already know, the principal budget factor.

(c) **Preparation of a budget using the principal budgetary factor**

On the assumption that sales is the principal budget factor, the next stage is to prepare the sales budget. This budget is very much dependent on forecast sales revenue – we draw on the forecasting techniques which we looked at in an earlier chapter.

(d) Initial preparation of budgets

Ideally budgets should be prepared by managers responsible for achieving the targets contained therein. This is referred to as participative budgeting. The role of the finance specialists should be to assist in turning physical budget forecasts into financial budgets.

(e) Co-ordination and review of budgets

At this stage the various budgets are integrated into the complete budget system. Any anomalies between the budgets must be resolved and the complete budget package subject to review. At this stage the budget income statement, balance sheet and cash flow must be prepared to ensure that the package produces an acceptable result.

(f) Final acceptance of budgets

All of the budgets are summarised into a master budget, which is presented to top management for final acceptance.

(g) Budget review

The budget process involves regular comparison of budget with actual, and identifying causes for variances. This may result in modifications to the budget as the period progresses.

3.3 Information for budgeting

When producing a budget in accordance with guidelines drawn up by the senior management of an organisation the usual starting point is the previous year's actual results. In some cases the budgeting process merely takes the form of adding to last year's income statement a general allowance for changes in volume and prices. This 'incremental' approach to budgeting is not regarded as an effective means of providing useful information for planning and control. Any inefficiency that has occurred in the current year will be perpetuated in future years. Nevertheless, the current income statement provides useful information.

In addition to previous year information, figures in budgets can come from three other sources.

Other internal sources

Information about the state of repair of non-current assets, training needs of staff, long-term requirements of individual large customers, etc. can be obtained by talking to individual junior managers. Likely costs of new products or services can be estimated using work study techniques or the services of the research and development team, quantity surveyors or sales team.

Statistical techniques

Figures such as sales forecasts or estimates of the fixed and variable elements of semi-variable costs can be produced with the aid of techniques such as linear regression. Other techniques can help determine optimal inventory levels and optimal ways of organising large construction projects.

External sources

The obvious external source of budgetary information will be suppliers' price lists both for materials and for services. It is important for a firm to try to establish how long those prices are likely to last and the size of any price rises. In addition external, market, rates of pay should be established so as to determine a sensible level of wage rises.

The production of an annual budget is not a precise science, figures in it are always subject to uncertainty. It is said that a budget is more than just a forecast of future costs and revenues that may be incurred or received, it is a statement of what management feels should be paid or received. Nevertheless, firms operate in an uncertain economic climate.

3.4 Budget committee

A **budget committee** is a group of managers and employees drawn from a range of departments within the organisation with responsibility for the budgetary process.

A typical budget committee comprises the chief executive, the management accountant (acting as budget officer) and functional heads. The functions of the committee are to:

(a)   agree policy with regard to budgets

(b)   co-ordinate budgets

(c)   suggest amendments to budgets (e.g. because there is inadequate profit)

(d)   approve budgets after amendment, as necessary

(e)   examine comparisons of budgeted and actual results and recommend corrective action if this has not already been taken.

The budget officer (usually a management accountant) is secretary to the committee and is responsible for seeing that the timetables are adhered to and for providing the necessary specialist assistance to the functional managers in drawing up their budgets and analysing results.

3.5 Budget manual

A budget manual is a document which sets out standing instructions governing the responsibilities of persons, and the procedures, forms and records relating to the preparation and use of budgets. It sets out the procedures to be observed in budgeting, the responsibilities of each person concerned, and the timetable to be observed.

Nowadays much of the budget manual is likely to be distributed as blank computer files (particularly spreadsheet files) for managers to complete. In this way the management accountant or the finance director can ensure that information is received from the various sources in a form that is easy to consolidate into a master budget.

4 Internal sources of information

Internal information may come from various sources.

4.1 Accounting system

The accounts system will collect data from source documents such as invoices, timesheets and journal entries. The data will be sorted and analysed by the coding system by type of expense, department, manager and job. Reports of direct and indirect costs compared to budgets may be produced at regular intervals to help managers plan and control costs. Ad hoc reports may be produced to help managers make specific decisions.

Consider the examples listed below – you can probably think of many others from your own experience.

- Sales analysed by product will help management to assess the patterns of demand for each product.

- This same information will help plan production and inventory levels.

- In turn, production information will enable the organisation to plan its requirements for raw materials, labour and machine hours.

- Information on material, labour and other costs will allow the organisation to set estimated costs for its products. This will be the basis for a budgetary control and standard costing system, as we shall see in a later chapter.

- In the context of long-term, strategic decision making, the sales analysis given above may help management to assess future product strategies – expand output of those for which demand is increasing, reduce output of those for which demand is falling.

- An aged receivables report would provide the basis for debt collection decisions taken by a credit control manager.

- Figures for wastage rates or product reject rates may allow management to reach decisions on the product quality aspect of the organisation's operations.

4.2   Payroll system

The payroll system may provide information concerning detailed labour costs. Hours paid may be analysed into productive work and non-productive time such as training, sick, holiday and idle time. Labour turnover by department or manager may be analysed and may help management to assess the employment and motivation policies.

4.3   Strategic planning system

The strategic planning system may provide information relating to the organisation's objectives and targets. Assumptions relating to the external environment may be detailed. Details of the organisation's capital investment programme and product launch programme may also be recorded here. Some of this information will be very commercially sensitive and only accessed by very senior managers in the organisation.

5   External sources of information

Businesses are finding it increasingly difficult to succeed if they ignore the external environment which will influence their activities. The process known as environmental scanning or environmental monitor is becoming a more important part of the role of the management accountant. These terms are used to describe the process whereby data is collected from outside, as well as from inside, the organisation and used in the decision-making process.

The main sources of external information which we shall consider here are:

- government sources

- business contacts – customers and suppliers

- trade associations and trade journals

- the financial and business press and other media.

These are dealt with in more detail below. A word of warning first, however. Internal information is produced by the company itself so they are aware of any limitations in its quality or reliability. External information is not under the control of the organisation – they may not be aware of any limitations in its quality – this point should always be considered. Even government produced statistics have been known to contain inaccuracies!

5.1 Government sources

There is a wealth of published statistical data covering many aspects of the nation's economy: population, manpower, trade, agriculture, price levels, capital issues and similar matters. Most, but not all of this is produced by national governments.

The primary purpose of this data is to provide information for economic planning at the national level. The data serves the secondary purpose of providing industry with useful background information for deciding on future policies such as raising new finance or recruiting specialised labour. The data is only published in general terms (e.g. for a particular industry or geographical area).

The following list shows some (there are many others) of the main sources of this type of information in the UK. Other countries will usually have similar information available. Copies are generally available in reference libraries and on government websites – have a look to see the type of data published.

Title	Frequency of publication	Main topics covered
Employment Gazette	Monthly	Earnings, basic wage rates, unemployment, indices of wholesale and retail prices.
British Business	Weekly	Wholesale and retail prices, production for specific sectors of industry, capital expenditure.
National Income and Expenditure Blue Book	Annually	Personal income and expenditure, gross national product.
Financial Statistics	Monthly	Money supply, interest rates, hire purchase liabilities, building societies.
Bank of England Quarterly Bulletin	Quarterly	Both summarise many of the above statistics.
Monthly Digest of Statistics	Monthly	

Economic Trends	Monthly	Similar coverage to Monthly Digest, but given information stretching back over a long period.
Annual Abstract of Statistics	Annually	
Price Indices for Current Cost Accounting	Annually, but updated by monthly supplement	Retail price index, also industry specific and asset specific price indices.

All the above publications relate to the UK. Publications concerned with statistics relating to the European Union include *European Economy Annual Statistical Yearbook*, *Eurostat* (monthly) and *OECD Main Economic Indicators* (monthly). Information on the World Economy is available from the United Nations (*Demographic Yearbook* and *Statistical Yearbook*), the International Labour Organisation (*Yearbook of Labour Statistics*) and UNESCO (*Statistical Yearbook*).

5.2 Business contacts

Government produced information will be broadly based and general, dealing with the economy as a whole or particular sectors or industries. An organisation may be looking for information more focused on its own position. Its day-to-day business contacts, customers and suppliers, can be a useful source of this information – and often it is available free.

Customers can provide information on such matters as:

– the product specification which they require

– their quality requirements

– requirements for delivery periods

– preference for packaging and distribution methods

– feedback on the above and on general aspects of customer service.

Suppliers may be able to provide information on:

– quantity discounts and volume rebates which may help the organisation to decide on order size

– availability of products and services

– alternative products or services which may be available or may become available

– technical specifications of their product.

5.3 Trade associations and trade journals

Most major industries have their own trade association. The role of these organisations includes:

- representing their member firms in legal and other disputes

- providing quality assurance schemes for customers of member organisations

- laying down codes of practice to be followed by their member organisations

- publishing trade journals and other information useful for the management and development of their businesses.

There follows a very brief list of just a small selection of trade associations operating in the UK – it is taken from an alphabetical listing of associations and shows the first few starting with the letter A. There are hundreds more!

- *Agricultural Industries Confederation*

- *Airport Operators Association*

- *Association for Payment Clearing Services APCS*

- *Association for Road Traffic Safety & Management*

- *Association of Art and Antique Dealers*

- *Association of British Fire Trades Ltd.*

Many of these organisations publish their own industry or trade journals which will contain useful news and other information for organisations operating in that industry. Trade journals are also published by many publishing organisations. In the UK one of the best known of these journals is *The Grocer* aimed at the food and drink retail sector. Again, many others exist.

5.4 The financial press, business press and other media

In the UK, *The Financial Times*, the *Guardian*, *The Times* and the *Daily Telegraph* together with some regional newspapers provide statistics and financial reviews as well as business and economic news and commentary. These include:

- the FTSE 100 Index, the stock market index of the 100 leading shares

- the FT Actuaries All-share Index – an index of all share prices quoted on the stock exchange.

Such information is now also widely available via electronic media. Digital television services available on satellite or cable systems carry specialist business and financial channels and programmes (such as Bloomberg TV) which give both national and world-wide coverage. There is also the internet as a widely available source of up-to-date financial information.

6 Forecasting techniques: time series

6.1 Introduction

The process of forecasting will inevitably involve some analysis of historic data (sales, costs, share prices, etc) in order that future values may be predicted.

The data may concern the economy as a whole, the particular industry with which the organisation is involved (or wants to be) or the organisation itself.

Definitions

A **time series** is a set of values for some variable (e.g. monthly production) which varies with time. The set of observations will be taken at specific times, usually at regular intervals. Examples of figures which can be plotted as a time series are:

- monthly rainfall in London;

- daily closing price of a share on the Stock Exchange;

- monthly sales in a department store.

Time series analysis takes historic data and breaks it down into component parts that are easier to extrapolate (predict future values of). In particular, it will isolate the underlying trend.

6.2 Plotting the graph of a time series

The basic pattern of a time series can be identified by plotting the recent points of the values on a graph, such as below.

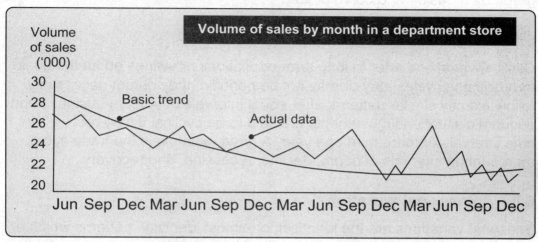

In such a graph time is always plotted on the horizontal x axis. Each point is joined by a straight line hence the typically 'jagged' appearance. Don't

Try to draw a smooth curve which will pass through all the points on a time series graph. You will find it practically impossible and, in any case, it is incorrect to do so. The only reason for joining the points at all is to give a clearer picture of the pattern, which would be more difficult to interpret from a series of dots.

On the graph above you will see that, having completed the time series graph, we have sketched in a 'basic trend' line. But what does it tell us? We need to look in more detail at what factors are at play in a time series.

6.3 Characteristic time series components

Analysis of time series has revealed certain characteristic movements or variations, the components of the time series. Analysis of these components is essential for forecasting purposes.

The four main types of component are as follows:

* basic trend (long-term);
* cyclical variations (not so long-term);
* seasonal variations (short-term);
* irregular or random variations (short-term).

6.4   Basic trend

The basic trend refers to the general direction in which the graph of a time series goes over a long interval of time once the short-term variations have been smoothed out. This movement can be represented on the graph by a basic trend curve or line.

6.5   Cyclical variations

Cyclical variations refer to long term oscillations or swings about the basic trend. These cycles may or may not be periodic; they do not necessarily follow exactly similar patterns after equal intervals of time. In business and economic situations movements are said to be cyclical if they recur after time intervals of more than one year. A good example is the trade cycle, representing intervals of boom, decline, recession, and recovery.

6.6   Seasonal variations

Seasonal variations are the identical, or almost identical, patterns which a time series follows during corresponding intervals of successive periods. Such movements are due to recurring events such as the sudden increase in department store sales before Christmas. Although, in general, seasonal movements refer to a period of one year, this is not always the case and periods of hours, days, weeks, months, etc may also be considered depending on the type of data available.

Having isolated the trend we need to consider how to deal with the seasonal variations. We will look at two models – the additive model and the multiplicative model.

The additive model is the simplest model and is satisfactory when the variations around the trend are within a constant band width. If, as is more usual, the variations around the trend increase as the trend itself rises, it is better to use the multiplicative model.

The additive model – finding the seasonal variations

The additive model we will use expresses variations in absolute terms with above and below average figures being shown as positive or negative.

The four components of a time series (T = trend; S = seasonal variation; C = cyclical variation; R = random variation) are expressed as absolute values which are simply added together to produce the actual figures:

Actual data (time series) = T + S + C + R

For unsophisticated analyses over a relatively short period of time cyclical variations (C) and random variations (R) are ignored. Random variations are ignored because they are unpredictable and would not normally exhibit any repetitive pattern, whereas cyclical variations (long-term oscillations) are ignored because their effect is negligible over short periods of time. The model therefore simplifies to:

Actual data = T + S

The seasonal variation+ is therefore the difference between the computed trend figure and the original time series figure. Thus:

S = Actual – T

 Example

The seasonal variations can be extracted by subtracting each trend value (using the moving averages method) from its corresponding time series value.

Solution

Quarter	Original time series	Underlying trend	Seasonal variation (S)
	(a)	(b)	(a) – (b)
3	94	100	(6)
4	127	102	25
1	84	106	(22)
2	106	111	(5)

6.7 Random variations

Random variations are the sporadic motions of time series due to chance events such as floods, strikes, elections, etc.

By their very nature they are unpredictable and therefore cannot play a large part in any forecasting, but it is possible to isolate the random variations by calculating all other types of variation and removing them from the time series data. It is important to extract any significant random variations from the data before using them for forecasting.

Random variations will not concern you in your examination.

6.8   Isolating the trend

There are three ways of isolating the trend:

- drawing a scattergraph;

- using moving averages;

- using linear regression.

Scattergraph – sketching a basic trend line

A basic trend line was drawn in on the time series graph shown earlier in this chapter. Indeed one way of isolating the trend is simply to draw it in freehand on the graph. This is called a 'scattergraph'.

This is actually a very helpful method. Once a time series has been prepared as a graph, it is usually a fairly simple matter to sketch in a basic trend line which manages to echo the overall long-term trend of the time series. There are some advantages to doing it this way:

- It is quick and easy.

- It allows one to interpolate a value easily. If you have monthly data for, say, Months 1, 3, 5, 7, 9 and 11 only, plotting those values and sketching a trend line will allow you to see what the likely value for the even-numbered months might have been. On the graph below you will see that we have interpolated the values of £125,000 for Month 6 of 20X4, and £175,000 for Month 12 of 20X4.

- It is possible to extrapolate a figure past the end of the data available (see the dotted line on the graph below). It is always worth bearing in mind, however, that data cannot be extrapolated very far ahead. Common sense suggests, for instance, that the trend line in the graph below is unlikely to continue in a horizontal line for very long – it is bound either to rise or fall. So the extrapolation of £175,000 for Month 7 in 20X5 is not unreasonable, but it would not be helpful to extrapolate the line and make the same prediction for, say, Month 1 of 20X6.

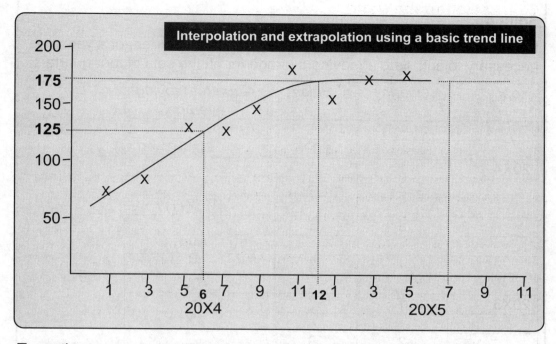

Two other common methods for isolating the trend are as follows:

Moving averages

By using moving averages, the effect of any seasonal variation in a time series can be eliminated to show the basic trend. This elimination process will only work if the moving average is calculated over the correct number of values (being the number of values in one complete cycle). For instance, if a seasonal variation present in a time series is repeated every fourth period, then moving averages with a cycle of four should be used.

This will become clearer as you follow through this simple example.

 Example

The following time series shows a set of sales figures for eight quarters which are clearly increasing. At first sight, however, this increase appears to be quite erratic. We can however produce this trend by the use of moving averages.

Year	Quarter	Sales £000
20X4	1	3
	2	5
	3	5
	4	5
20X5	1	7
	2	9
	3	9
	4	9

Solution

Because we are told that the sales figures are for quarters of a year, it is necessary to calculate a moving average for all the sets of four quarters.

Year	Quarter	Sales	4-quarter moving average
		£000	£000
20X4	1	3	
	2	5	
			4½ (W1)
	3	5	
			5½
	4	5	
			6½
20X5	1	7	
			7½
	2	9	
			8½
	3	9	
	4	9	

Workings

The moving average for the first four quarters is calculated as

$$\frac{3+5+5+5}{4} = 4½$$

Each moving average value is calculated and then placed in the centre of the numbers that were used in the calculation. For example, the first 4value moving average is calculated as the average of the first four numbers, and then placed mid-way between the 2nd and 3rd quarter values of 2004

The moving average of four values captures the steadily increasing basic trend.

It will usually be fairly obvious which is the appropriate order in an examination question due to the way in which the data are presented, e.g. in 'quarters' (order 4) or days of the working week (order 5).

Be sure that you have understood the positioning of the moving averages in the above table. Each average has been written exactly opposite the middle of the figures from which it has been calculated. This results in the moving averages for even numbers of values (four in this case) being suspended halfway between two of the original figures.

Where you have a moving average for an even number of values, it is necessary to realign the moving averages so that they fall opposite the original values by calculating a centred moving average for every two moving average values.

Year	Quarter	Original time series	Moving average (4 values)	Centred moving average order 4
20X4	1	3		
	2	5		
			4½	
	3	5		5 (W)
			5½	
	4	5		6
			6½	
20X5	1	7		7
			7½	
	2	9		8
			8½	
	3	9		
	4	9		

As you can see by the centring process, the centred moving average is the basic trend.

(W) (4½ + 5½) ÷ 2 = 5

Example

The following data represents the sales for TS Limited for the eight quarters shown.

	Quarter			
	1	2	3	4
Year 1	74	100	94	127
Year 2	84	106	120	141

Calculate the trend using moving averages.

Solution

Year	Qtr	Value	4-quarter moving total	4-quarter average	Trend
1	1	74			
	2	100			
			395	99	
	3	94			100
			405	101	
	4	127			102
			411	103	
2	1	84			106
			437	109	
	2	106			111
			451	113	
	3	120			
	4	141			

Disadvantages of moving averages

- Values at the beginning and end of the series are lost – therefore the moving averages do not cover the complete period.

- The moving averages may generate cycles or other variations that were not present in the original data.

- The averages are strongly affected by extreme values. To overcome this a 'weighted' moving average is sometimes used giving the largest weights to central items and small weights to extreme values.

Linear regression

The third way of isolating a trend is to use a mathematical technique called 'linear regression'. Only a broad understanding of linear regression is required in the context of producing a trend for a time series.

Regression analysis is a technique for estimating the line of best fit, given a series of data. It is essentially a statistical technique, and the description that follows is only a working guide for applying the technique.

Regression analysis is based on the concept of 'drawing the line that minimises the sum of the squares of the deviations of the line from the observed data' (so it is sometimes referred to as the least squares method). The regression line of *y* on *x* is used when an estimate of *y* (the **dependent** variable) is required for a given value of *x* (the **independent** variable).

The general equation for the regression line is given as:

$y = a + bx$

Where:

x is the independent variable

y is the dependent variable

a is the fixed element

b is the variable element

You do not have to understand how this equation is calculated, but you do need to be able to use it.

In particular, you must understand that the independent variable (x) in some way causes the dependent variable (y) to have the value given by the equation.

Thus, if we were calculating the value of umbrellas sold for given amounts of monthly rainfall, the rainfall would be the independent variable (x) and the sales value would be the dependent variable (y) (rainfall causes umbrella sales and not vice versa).

Example

X Ltd is forecasting its sales for the four quarters of 20X5. It has carried out a linear regression exercise on its past sales data and established the following:

   a = 20

   b = 0.7

The equation of the regression line is therefore:

   y = 20 + 0.7x

When x is number of the quarter and y is the sales value in £000s. Calculate the sales for each of the quarters in 20X5. Solution

		£000
Quarter 1	y = 20 + (0.7 × 1) =	20.7
Quarter 2	y = 20 + (0.7 × 2) =	21.4
Quarter 3	y = 20 + (0.7 × 3) =	22.1
Quarter 4	y = 20 + (0.7 × 4) =	22.8

Regression analysis is based on sample data and if we selected a different sample it is probable that a different regression line would be constructed. For this reason, regression analysis is most suited to conditions where there is a relatively stable relationship between cost and activity level.

Assumptions we are making:

* The relationship is a linear one.
* The data used is representative of future trends.

7 Forecasting with time series analysis

7.1 Introduction

Earlier we noted that the analysis of a time series into its component parts would make extrapolation easier for forecasting future values for planning purposes.

In general, for short-term forecasts, only the trend and seasonal variations will be used; the cyclical variations will only have a significant effect over quite a long period of time and the random variations are, by their *very* nature, unpredictable.

Thus the approach to forecasting will be to:

- extrapolate the trend to the appropriate future time; and

- adjust the extrapolated trend value by the appropriate seasonal variation.

7.2 Extrapolating the trend

There is no unique method for extrapolation of the basic trend, as it will very much depend upon its particular shape (if, indeed, it has a discernible one).

In practice, computers will be of great help in producing various possible equations for the trend, which can be rapidly tested against the data available to determine which fits best.

If the moving averages method has been used, a certain amount of judgement will be necessary. Possible approaches include the following:

- Plot the trend values on a graph and extrapolate by eye. (In fact, an initial sketch graph can be useful anyway to get a visual impression of the trend, before using one of the following methods to predict it.)

- Look at the increments between each trend value for any approximate pattern (e.g. roughly equal, which makes the trend approximately linear or steadily increasing) and continue this pattern to the future time required.

- If the increments appear to vary randomly, an average increment for the period may be calculated and used in the forecast.

- If the pattern of the trend appears to change significantly over the period, you may restrict your prediction technique to later data values only, as being more representative of future values.

Example

We will now use the time series analysis from paragraph 5.2 to forecast the sales value for quarter 4 of year 3, given that the time series figures are the quarterly sales in £000.

Solution

The trend values obtained by moving averages have been plotted on a graph (unless specifically required, it is unlikely that you would have time to do this in an examination).

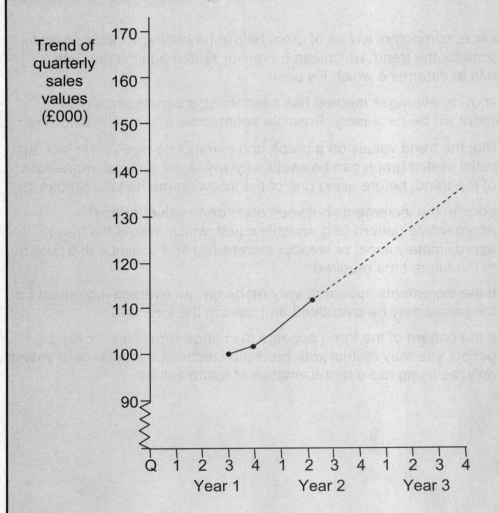

The graph shows an upward sloping trend, very approximately linear, but which becomes increasingly steep.

If we were to use the graphical approach to extrapolation, one approach would be to extend the line using the later, steeper gradient (although it should be noted that the earlier part of the curve shows that this may, in fact, revert to a shallower gradient). This approach may be over-optimistic. Perhaps it would be more prudent to assume that the earlier gradient will continue. The dashed line on the above graph shows a compromise between the two and produces a forecast for *Q4* of *Year 3* of approximately *135*, indicating a trend value for sales of *£135,000*.

Now consider the increments (the differences between each successive pair of trend values). Note that you do not need to work these out exactly; they will just be used to detect any pattern or change.

| From previous quarter to | | Trend | Approximate increment |
Year	Quarter		
1	3	100	–
	4	102	2
2	1	106	4
	2	111	5

There is no clear pattern, so some average increment may be used. The average increment over the whole period is $(111 - 100)/3 \cong 3.67$

(Note that we divide by the number of increments (3), not the number of trend values; we are averaging the 'gaps'.)

This would result in a forecast trend value for year 3, quarter 4 (which is six increments on from the last trend value) of 111 (the last trend value) + (6 × 3.67) = 133, or trend sales of £133,000.

Now we must adjust the trend value for the expected seasonal variation.

This is a lot more straightforward! We already have the seasonal variations for each quarter, the relevant one here being that for quarter 4: +25

This means that we expect quarter 4 values to be £25,000 above the trend value. Thus, seasonally-adjusted predictions for quarter 4, year 3 would be:

£133,000 + £25,000 = £158,000 (using the incremental method); or

£135,000 + £25,000 = £160,000 (using the graphical method)

depending upon which trend value was used.

In an examination, you should only make one prediction, justifying the approach used. There will rarely be one 'correct' way, so do not spend too long deciding how you are going to do it.

7.3   Seasonal variations and the multiplicative model

In some examinations you may be given the trend figures and seasonal variations but, instead of the seasonal variations being given in absolute figures as in the additive model that we have used so far, the seasonal variations may be given as percentage figures. This is the case if the multiplicative model is used for the time series analysis.

In order to find the forecast figures in this case, simply multiply the trend figure by the seasonal variation percentage and either add it to the trend or deduct it from the trend.

 Example

Given below are the estimated trend figures for a company's sales for the next four quarters:

20X3	Trend
	£
Quarter 1	560,000
Quarter 2	580,000
Quarter 3	605,000
Quarter 4	632,000

The seasonal variations using the multiplicative model have been calculated as:

Quarter 1	+ 15%
Quarter 2	+ 10%
Quarter 3	− 5%
Quarter 4	− 20%

Calculate the forecast sales figures for each of the next four quarters.

Solution

Quarter 1	£560,000 + (560,000 × 0.15) =	£644,000
Quarter 2	£580,000 + (580,000 × 0.10) =	£638,000
Quarter 3	£605,000 − (605,000 × 0.05) =	£574,750
Quarter 4	£632,000 − (632,000 × 0.20) =	£505,600

7.4 Problems with forecasting

There are a number of problems with using time series analysis in order to estimate or forecast future results.

- The main problem is the inherent weakness of extrapolation. In order to estimate the trend for the future the trend line is extended on the graph and the figures read off. However, although the time series has moved in that particular manner in the past, it does not necessarily mean that it will continue to do so in the future.

- The seasonal adjustments used to find the forecast for the future are again based upon historic figures that may well already be out of date. There is no guarantee that the seasonal variations will remain the same in the future. If the time series has a large residual or random variation element, then this will make any forecasts even less reliable.

8 Forecasting techniques: sampling

8.1 Introduction

As we have seen, the purpose of the management information system and the management accountant is to provide useful information to the management of the business. In order to do this the management accountant will have to collect the information in the first place. However, before collecting information, it will be necessary to determine what the population is that we are interested in.

🔍 Definition

The population is simply all of the items of information that the collector is interested in. For example, if the management accountant wanted to know the proportion of defective units produced by a machine in a day then the population would be all of the units of product produced by the machine in the day.

8.2 Census or sampling approach

If information is required about a particular topic then there are two main approaches to obtaining the information, the census approach or the sampling approach.

The question here is whether we examine every item in the population, the census approach, or take a sample of the population. In business contexts it is rare to use the census approach so some form of sampling technique will be used. When sampling is used only a small number of items in the population are examined or tested.

Care must be taken when selecting a sample as the reliability of the results will be dependent upon how unbiased the sample is.

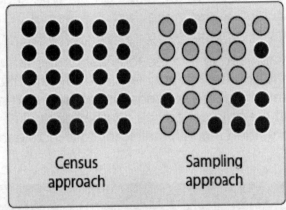

The census approach examines every item in the population

8.3 Random sampling

Random sampling is the best method of producing a totally unbiased sample; each item in the population has an equal chance of being included in the sample. In order for random sampling to be used each item in the population must be known and must have a consecutive number assigned to it. The sample is then chosen by random numbers taken from random number tables or a random number generator.

It is rare in practice for all items of the population to be known and for pure random sampling to be used. Therefore there are a number of other quasi-random methods of sampling that could be used:

- systematic sampling;
- stratified sampling;
- multi-stage sampling.

8.4 Systematic sampling

Systematic sampling is a simpler method of random sampling where again all of the items in the population must be known and each item must have a consecutive number assigned to it. Under systematic sampling the first item in the sample is chosen using a random number. Thereafter, every nth item in the population is taken to make up the sample. For example, the 14th item followed by every 50th item would produce a sample of 20 items from a population of 1,000 items.

8.5 Stratified sampling

Stratified sampling can be used if the population falls into distinct layers or groups. The population is split into these groups and the sample is then chosen from each group in proportion to the size of the group compared to the total population.

8.6 Multi-stage sampling

Again this is a method that can be used if the population naturally fall into fairly large groups or areas. Initially a number of groups or areas are selected randomly. The next stage is to take each group that has been selected and to split them into smaller groups from which again a sample is chosen randomly. This can be done any number of times until the final sample has been chosen.

8.7 Non-random sampling methods

In some instances it may not be cost effective to carry out random sampling techniques and therefore some form of non-random sampling is used. These methods will not produce such accurate results as the random sampling methods but the information collected can still be useful. Typical non-random sampling methods that can be used are:

- quota sampling;
- cluster sampling.

8.8 Quota sampling

This is particularly useful when market research is being carried out. Quota sampling can be used when there are a number of different groups in the population, for example men under 30, women over 30, etc. The number of sample members required from each group is determined and these samples are taken on a non-random basis from the group until the required number has been reached.

8.9 Cluster sampling

Cluster sampling is where one or more areas of the population are determined to be representative of the population as a whole and therefore the sample is taken from that group alone. For example, if a business was carrying out market research into the buying habits of supermarket shoppers countrywide then it may be decided that customers shopping at three different supermarkets in Birmingham are representative of nationwide supermarket shoppers and the sample can then be taken from shoppers at these three supermarkets only.

9 Forecasting techniques: index numbers

9.1 Introduction

We have seen that the trend of income or costs can be estimated using time series analysis. However, this method is quite complex and time-consuming. There are other methods of indicating the trend of figures for income or costs and one of these is to use index numbers.

9.2 Use of index numbers

A time series of figures for costs or income can be easily converted into an index. This is done firstly by choosing a base year and allocating to this year's figure an index of 100. Each subsequent period's figure is then converted into a relevant index number using the formula:

$$\text{Index} = \frac{\text{Current year' s figures}}{\text{Base year figure}} \times 100$$

 Example

The materials costs for a business for the last six months have been as follows:

	£
March	427,000
April	442,000
May	460,000
June	433,000
July	447,000
August	470,000

If the index for March is 100, what are the index numbers of the costs for each of the subsequent months and what do these index numbers tell us?

Solution

Month		Index
March		100.0
April	$\dfrac{442,000}{427,000} \times 100$	103.5
May	$\dfrac{460,000}{427,000} \times 100$	107.7

June	$\dfrac{433,000}{427,000} \times 100$	101.4
July	$\dfrac{447,000}{427,000} \times 100$	104.7
August	$\dfrac{470,000}{427,000} \times 100$	110.1

The index shows that the materials costs are generally rising although there is a fall back in June which has been made up for by the highest level yet in August.

9.3 Indices to measure inflation

Published indices that can be useful to the management accountant are the Consumer Price Index (CPI) and the Retail Price Index (RPI). These indices published on a monthly basis by the Government and are used as measures of general price changes and inflation.

If we have a series of cost or income figures measured over a fairly long time period then they could have been distorted by price changes over the period and may not necessarily show the correct position.

We can use the RPI to adjust all of the figures in the time series into current day prices by using the formula:

$$\text{Current price adjusted figure} = \text{Actual sales} \times \frac{\text{RPI in current year}}{\text{RPI in year of sales}}$$

 Example

Suppose that a company has recorded annual sales over the last six years as follows:

	£
20X0	735,000
20X1	764,000
20X2	791,000
20X3	811,000
20X4	833,000
20X5	856,000

The average RPI for each of those years was as follows:

	RPI
20X0	144.3
20X1	149.8
20X2	153.0
20X3	157.2
20X4	161.9
20X5	170.0

Show the sales for the last six years in terms of current year (20X5) prices and explain what this shows.

Solution

	Actual sales	RPI adjustment	Price adjusted sales
	£		£
20X0	735,000	× 170.0/144.3	865,900
20X1	764,000	× 170.0/149.8	867,000
20X2	791,000	× 170.0/153.0	878,900
20X3	811,000	× 170.0/157.2	877,000
20X4	833,000	× 170.0/161.9	874,700
20X5	856,000		856,000

Whereas the original, unadjusted figures indicated a fairly substantial increase in sales over the period, once the sales are adjusted to current day prices, a different picture appears. In fact the sales increased very gradually until 20X2 and have been in decline for the last three years.

When comparing costs or income over time the management accountant should consider the effects of either general inflation by using the RPI or more specific price changes that affect the cost or income by using a price index specifically related to that cost or income.

10 Summary

The cost accountant is mainly concerned with the proper recording and analysis of costs incurred in a business in a manner that will enable management to control current operations and plan and make decisions for the future.

Effective communication with the workforce and management is vital and will be achieved via the following:

(a)   a suitable organisational structure;

(b)   reports produced on a timely basis.

This chapter also considered internal and external information which affects forecasts.

Forecasts of future events are normally based on historical information. Information may be available from a wide variety of sources both internal and external to the business.

Time series analysis helps with the isolation of trends, although these still may not be easy to extrapolate into the future. Remember that you are using historic data which will not reflect future economic and environmental changes.

Also, you must be able to calculate the seasonal variations and be able to de-seasonalise data if required.

In this chapter we also look briefly at sampling techniques and you should be aware of the definitions of the main sampling methods. Finally, we studied index numbers. This is a simple technique but does frequently appear in examinations.

11 Test your knowledge

Workbook Activity 1

Match the data in the first column with the appropriate source in the second column (only 1 source possible) :

Data	Source
TV licence fee cost	Office for National Statistics
Cost of electricity generated by wind power	BBC Website
Inflation trends in the UK	HMRC publications
	Gross National Product
	The Environment Agency

Workbook Activity 2

Who would you contact in each of the following situations?

- You want to identify the production capacity of the firm
- You want to forecast the price of raw materials
- The draft budget has been reviewed by the Budget Committee and is ready to be submitted for final approval

Choose from :

- Trade union representative
- Managing Director
- Buyer
- Board of Directors
- Production Planning Manager

Workbook Activity 3

Regression line

A regression line has been calculated as y = 192 + 2.40x, where x is the output and y is the total cost. You are required to:

(a)   Explain this formula.

(b)   Use it to predict the total cost for (i) 500 units and (ii) 1,500 units.

Workbook Activity 4

From the following data, revise the income forecast.

Next year's income is forecast at £5,974,000. This assumes a 3% increase in selling price.

In the light of increasing competition the marketing manager has decided not to make the increase.

The forecast should be revised to _____

Select from:

- £5,626,000
- £5,800,000
- £5,974,000
- £6,153,000

Workbook Activity 5

In IST Ltd, this year sales amount to £1,325,000. Analysis of recent years show a growth trend of 2% per annum. The seasonal variation has been:

- Quarter 1   + £12,000
- Quarter 2   +£18,000
- Quarter 3   –£25,000
- Quarter 4   –£5,000

You have been asked to forecast the income for each quarter of next year:

Quarter	£
1	
2	
3	
4	
Year	

Workbook Activity 6

Price indices

A product which cost £12.50 in 20X0, cost £13.65 in 20X1. Calculate the simple price index for 20X1 based on 20X0.

Workbook Activity 7

Eastoft Feeds and Fertilisers Ltd uses a number of standard raw materials for its product range. Product F4's main raw material is 'EF1'. The average price per tonne for this material, which is subject to seasonal change, for each quarter during 2001 was as below. The material is in short supply.

2001	Q1	Q2	Q3	Q4
Average price per tonne	£40	£44	£64	£76
Seasonal variation	–£4	–£8	+£4	+£8

Complete the following calculations of the seasonally adjusted price of raw material 'EF1'. Assuming a similar pattern of price movements were to continue, you are asked to determine the likely purchase price per tonne for each of the 4 quarters of 2002.

2001	Q1	Q2	Q3	Q4
Actual price per tonne				
Seasonal variation				
Trend				
2002				
Trend (+ £8 per quarter)				
Seasonal variation				
Forecast price per tonne				

Workbook Activity 8

Garden Care is a division of Alton Products plc. The sales director of Garden Care, Hazel Brown, has noticed a distinct trend and pattern of seasonal variations for one of Garden Care's products since the product was introduced in the third quarter of 1997. She provides you with the following sales volumes for the product.

Units sold by quarter

Year	Quarter 1	Quarter 2	Quarter 3	Quarter 4
1997			142	142
1998	150	150	142	158
1999	150	166	142	174
2000	150	182*		

*Estimate

(a) Complete the following calculations :

Year	Quarter	Actual	4 quarter total	4 quarter average	Centred trend	Seasonal variation
1997	3	142				
	4	142				
1998	1	150				
	2	150				
	3	142				
	4	158				
1999	1	150				
	2	166				
	3	142				
	4	174				
2000	1	150				
	2	182				

(b)   **Complete the following analysis of seasonal variations**

	Quarter 1	Quarter 2	Quarter 3	Quarter 4	Residual
1998					
1999					
Total					
Average					
Adjustment for residual					
Seasonal variations					

(c)   Calculate the forecast demand for quarter 2:

Trend

Seasonal variation

────

Forecast

Actual (estimate)

Residual

────

(d)   Suggest **TWO** reasons why there might be a difference between the forecast figure calculated in (c) and the result given in the data.

Reason 1	
Reason 2	
Reason 3	
Reason 4	

Workbook Activity 9

Forecast for energy costs

Next year, energy costs are forecast at £2,970,000. This assumes a 4% increase in energy consumption, as well as a 4% increase in gas and electricity tariffs.

However, energy saving measures are being proposed. Instead of increasing, consumption should be reduced by 10%

The energy budget should be :

* £2,566,080
* £2,570,192
* £2,745,931
* £2,855,770

Dealing with fixed overheads

Introduction

Overhead is the general term used to describe costs which are not direct costs of production. They are also known as indirect costs and they may be indirect production costs or indirect non-production costs. When a management accountant is trying to ascertain the cost of a product or service, there are two possible approaches available for dealing with overheads.

Firstly, apportionment and allocation of all production overheads may be used to arrive at a 'full' cost per unit. This is known as absorption costing and is considered first. Remember that as well as the indirect production cost there are indirect non-production costs. These non-production costs are never included in the cost of the product, or stock or cost of sales.

Alternatively, one can use only direct costs to arrive at the cost per unit and leave indirect costs as a general overhead not related to units of output. This approach is generally known as marginal costing and will be dealt with later in the chapter.

This chapter contains the essential understanding of accounting for overheads and overhead absorption which is necessary for your further studies.

KNOWLEDGE

- Describe the internal charges made to attribute indirect costs to production (Element 1.4)

- Recognise expenses as different types of cost (Element 3.4)

SKILLS

- Correctly code, classify and allocate cost & revenue data to responsibility centres (Element 1.2)

CONTENTS

1 Allocation, apportionment and absorption of overheads

2 Activity-based costing (ABC)

1 Allocation, apportionment and absorption of overheads

1.1 Introduction

We have already identified two types of costs that make up the full production cost of a unit:

(a) Direct costs are those that can be uniquely identified with an individual cost unit (e.g. direct materials, direct labour, direct expenses).

(b) Indirect costs (overheads) are costs incurred in production but not easily 'traced' to individual units, e.g. machine power (variable), factory rent (fixed), heat and light (semi-variable).

The problem we are considering here is how to divide indirect production costs between cost units, in order to prepare a 'standard' total cost per unit for budgeting, stock valuation and pricing purposes.

The method used to divide production overheads between production units is made up of three processes: allocation, apportionment and absorption.

Step 1   Identify the indirect cost with a cost centre

This can be done in two ways depending on the nature of the cost.

(a) **Allocation**

 Definition

Where the indirect cost is borne entirely by one cost centre, the entire cost is allocated to that cost centre.

(b) **Apportionment**

 Definition

Where the indirect cost is shared by more than one cost centre, the cost is apportioned between the cost centre.

Step 2   Identify the indirect costs of the cost centre calculated in Step 1 with the cost units produced by that centre.

This is called absorption.

 Definition

Absorption is the technique of relating a cost centre's indirect costs to the units produced by the cost centre.

We shall now look at each of these in more detail.

1.2   Cost allocation

Certain cost items will be incurred entirely by one cost centre. Allocation deals with this type of cost and simply allots it to the cost centre which has incurred the cost.

Cost centre	Allocated cost
Canteen Tea bags	Spaghetti Chef's wages
Packing department	Cardboard String

1.3   Cost apportionment (primary)

More frequently, however, the benefit of an item of cost will be shared by a number of cost centres. The overhead will be split or apportioned between the relevant cost centres on an 'equitable' basis.

The rent of buildings, for example, can relate to the total floor space occupied by a number of different departments and it is usual to allot the rental charge to those departments in proportion to the floor space they occupy.

Nature of cost	Possible bases of apportionment
Rent and rates	Floor area occupied by various departments
Lighting and heating	Cubic capacity of locations or metered usage
Insurance of stocks	Value of stockholdings in various locations

Example

A general cost in a manufacturing company is factory rental. Annual rental costs are £80,000. How should this cost be apportioned between production departments and service departments?

Rental costs are usually apportioned between departments on the basis of the floor space taken up by each department. For example, suppose that three departments have floor space of 10,000 square metres, 15,000 square metres and 25,000 square metres, and annual rental costs are £80,000. If we apportion rental costs between the departments on the basis of their floor space, the apportionment would be as follows.

Annual rental	£80,000
Total floor space (10,000 + 15,000 + 25,000)	50,000 square metres
Apportionment rate (£80,000/50,000)	£1.60/square metre

	£
Apportion to department with 10,000 square metres	16,000
Apportion to department with 15,000 square metres	24,000
Apportion to department with 25,000 square metres	40,000
	———
	80,000
	———

 Example

The costs of heating and lighting might also be apportioned on the basis of floor space. Alternatively, since heating relates to volume rather than floor space, it could be argued that the costs should be apportioned on the volume of space taken up by each department. Yet another view is that electricity costs relate more to the consumption of electrical power by machines, therefore the apportionment of these costs should be on the basis of the number and power of the machines in each department.

A reasonable argument could be made for any of these bases of apportionment.

1.4 Cost apportionment (secondary)

After completing the allocation and primary apportionment stages, you should have assigned all costs to cost centres.

Some cost centres, however, will not have production units passing through them; these cost centres are called service departments (e.g. quality control department, works canteen). Before the final stage of absorption into cost units can be carried out, it is necessary to perform a further type of apportionment whereby the total costs of the service cost centres are reassigned to production cost centres. This is known as secondary apportionment. This should be done on a fair basis to reflect the benefit derived from the service centre. The following example is an illustration of primary and secondary apportionment.

Example

Overhead Analysis Sheet   Period Ending.....................

	Total	Production		Service	
		Assembly	*Finishing*	*Stores*	*Canteen*
	£	£	£	£	£
Overheads allocated directly to cost centres	133,000	49,000	36,000	27,000	21,000
Overheads to be apportioned					
Rent (Apportionment basis: ....)	76,000	26,000	24,000	15,000	11,000
Equipment depreciation (Apportionment basis: ....)	15,000	8,000	1,000	5,000	1,000
Total overhead	224,000	83,000	61,000	47,000	33,000
Apportioning of stores (Apportionment basis: ....)		31,000	16,000	(47,000)	
Apportioning of canteen (Apportionment basis: ....)		14,000	19,000		(33,000)
		128,000	96,000	–	–

1.5   Absorption

Having collected all indirect costs in the production cost centres via overhead allocation and apportionment, the cost has to be spread over the output of the production cost centre.

The allotment of accumulated overhead costs to cost units is called overhead absorption. The absorption rate is normally calculated at the start of the period and therefore based on budgeted quantities. Various methods of absorption exist and the one most fitting should be chosen.

The following are the most common methods you will encounter.

(a)   **Rate per unit**

The simple unit rate is obtained by dividing total budgeted overheads by the number of units budgeted to be produced. However, where more than one product is produced, this is an unsatisfactory basis for absorbing overheads as it will not reflect the relative demands of each product on the production departments through which they pass.

(b)   **Alternative bases of absorption**

There are a number of bases commonly used as an alternative to the simple unit rate:

- rate per direct labour hour;

- rate per machine hour;

- percentage of material cost;

- percentage of wage cost;

- percentage of total direct cost (prime cost).

It is important to appreciate, however, that whichever method or combination of methods is used, the result will only be an approximate estimate of what that product actually costs.

In practice, many businesses use a 'direct labour hour rate' or 'machine hour rate' in preference to a rate based on a percentage of direct materials cost, direct wages or prime cost, as it may be possible to associate some overheads either with labour time or with machine time.

It may be possible to analyse the total overhead apportioned to each production department into fixed and variable elements. In this case a variable overhead rate per unit and a fixed overhead rate per unit can be calculated.

The absorption rates will normally be calculated at the beginning of a period and hence be based on budgeted costs and production levels. This can lead to problems when actual costs and volumes are not the same as budgeted leading to over- or under-absorption.

 Example

For the year ended 31 December 20X4 the planned overhead for the Machining Cost Centre at Cuecraft Ltd was:

Overhead £132,000
Volume of activity 15,000 machine hours

In January 20X4 the cost centre incurred £12,000 of overhead and 1,350 machine hours were worked.

Task

Calculate the pre-determined overhead rate per machine hour and the overhead under or over-recovered in the month.

Solution

Absorption rate, based on the budget:

$$\frac{\text{Planned overhead}}{\text{Machine hours}} = \frac{£132,000}{15,000 \text{ machine hours}} = £8.80 \text{ per machine hour}$$

	£
Overhead absorbed	
1,350 machine hours at £8.80	11,880
Overhead incurred	12,000
Under-absorption	120

Here, the amount of overheads actually charged to production are £11,880, which is less than actual expenditure. We therefore have under-absorption of overhead.

Under-recovery of overheads is shown as a separate item in the costing profit and loss account. Since production has been charged with less overheads than the amount of overheads incurred, an adjustment to profit for under-absorption is downwards. In other words, under-absorption is a 'loss' item.

2 Activity-based costing (ABC)

2.1 Criticisms of absorption costs

Historically a direct labour rate for absorption of all fixed overheads was a very common method, as production tended to be highly labour-intensive. Such items as rent would be apportioned using the area involved, but the absorption rate would usually be labour hours. It was reasonable to assume that the more labour time spent on a product, the more production resources in general were being used. Thus the product should be charged with a higher share of the overheads.

However, nowadays, production is far more mechanised. This has two impacts as follows:

(a)   A higher proportion of the overheads is accounted for by machine-related costs (power, depreciation, maintenance, etc).

(b)   The amount of labour time spent upon a unit is far less representative of its final significance in the use of production resources.

To take a simple example, Product A may use 9 machine hours and 1 labour hour, whilst Product B requires 1 machine hour and 4 labour hours. The traditional approach would charge B with four times as much production overhead (including machine costs) as A, even though it takes half the time overall.

In this example, one solution would be to use machine hours as a basis. However, this still tries to relate all overhead costs, whatever their nature, to usage of machines. This would not necessarily be appropriate for, say, costs of receiving and checking materials going into the production process. This will be more likely to depend upon the number of times an order of material is received into stores for a particular product.

2.2 Activity-based costing (ABC) approach

Professors Robin Cooper and Robert Kaplan at the Harvard Business School have developed a costing system called activity-based costing (ABC) which avoids the problems experienced by traditional costing methods. If management are keen to control costs, then it is vital that they should know the activities that cause costs to arise.

(a) **Cost drivers**

Those activities that are the significant determinants of cost are known as cost-drivers. For example, if production-scheduling cost is driven by the number of production set-ups, then that number is the cost-driver for the cost of production-scheduling. The cost-drivers represent the bases for charging costs in the ABC system, with a separate cost centre established for each cost-driver.

(b) **Cost pools**

Where several costs are 'driven' by the same activity (e.g. engine oil, machine breakdown and repairs) then these costs are put into 'cost pools' and the total of the cost pool is absorbed by, say, machine hours.

2.3 Mechanics of ABC

The mechanics of operating an ABC system are similar to a traditional costing system.

The significant cost drivers need to be ascertained and a cost centre is established for each cost driver. Costs are allocated to products by dividing the cost centre costs by the number of transactions undertaken.

For example, in Plant Y a set up of a production run would be a cost driver. The cost of the engineers who do the set ups would be a cost centre. If the cost of the engineers is say £280,000 and the number of sets ups is 500, then the charging out rate is $\frac{280,000}{500}$ = £560. A product which has a number of small production runs will thus have a greater proportion of these costs relative to the quantity of the product produced, than a product with large production runs.

Other overheads will be allocated to products in a different way; which way depends upon the cost drivers which have been ascertained.

Example

Plant Y produces about one hundred products. Its largest selling product is Product A; its smallest is Product B. Relevant data is given below.

	Product A	Product B	Total products
Units produced pa	50,000	1,000	500,000
Material cost per unit	£1.00	£1.00	
Direct labour per unit	15 minutes	15 minutes	
Machine time per unit	1 hour	1 hour	
Number of set ups p.a.	24	2	500
Number of purchase orders for materials	36	6	2,800
Number of times material handled	200	15	12,000
Direct labour cost per hour			£5

Overhead costs

	£
Set up	280,000
Purchasing	145,000
Materials handling	130,000
Machines	660,000
	————
	1,215,000
	————

Total machine hours are 600,000 hours.

Traditional costing (absorbing overheads on machine hours):

Unit cost	A £	B £
Material cost	1.00	1.00
Labour cost	1.25	1.25
Overhead per machine hour		
$\frac{1,215,000}{600,000} = 2,025$	2.025	2.025
	————	————
	4.275	4.275
	————	————

The above costings imply that we are indifferent between producing Product A and Product B.

Using an ABC approach would show:

Step 1   Calculate the direct material and labour costs as for the traditional approach.

Unit cost	A	B
	£	£
Material cost	1.00	1.00
Labour cost	1.25	1.25
	2.25	2.25

Step 2   Calculate the overheads that will be charged to each product by:

(a)   Calculating the overhead cost per cost driver for each type of overhead (e.g. cost per set-up).

(b)   Charge cost to each unit by calculating the unit cost accordingly.

	A	B
	£	£

Overheads:

Set up

$$\frac{280,000}{500} = £560 \text{ per set up}$$

	A	B
$\frac{560 \times 24}{50,000}$	0.27	
$\frac{560 \times 2}{1,000}$		1.12

Purchasing:

$$\frac{145,000}{2,800} = £51.786 \text{ per purchase order}$$

	A	B
$\frac{36 \times 51,786}{50,000}$	0.04	
$\frac{6 \times 51,786}{1,000}$		0.31

Materials handling:

$$\frac{130,000}{12,000} = 10.833 \text{ per time}$$

$$\frac{200 \times 10.833}{50,000}$$ 0.04

$$\frac{15 \times 10.833}{1,000}$$ 0.16

Machines:

$$\frac{660,000}{600,000} = £1.10 \text{ per machine hour}$$ 1.10 1.10

	1.45	2.69
Add: Direct material and labour costs	2.25	2.25
	£3.70	£4.94

Commonsense would lead us to conclude that ABC is a more accurate representation of the relative real costs of the two products.

What must be considered, however, is whether the benefits of this approach outweigh the costs of implementing and applying the system.

The following example again contrasts a traditional product costing system with an ABC system and shows that an ABC system produces much more accurate product costs.

Example

Mayes plc has a single production centre and has provided the following budgeted information for the next period.

	Product A	Product B	Product C	Total
Production and sales (units)	40,000	25,000	10,000	75,000
Direct material cost	£25	£20	£18	£1,680,000
Direct labour hours	3	4	2	240,000
Machine hours	2	4	3	210,000
Number of production runs	5	10	25	40
Number of component receipts	15	25	120	160
Number of production orders	15	10	25	50

Direct labour is paid £8 per hour.

Overhead costs in the period are expected to be as follows:

	£
Set-up	140,000
Machine	900,000
Goods inwards	280,000
Packing	200,000
Engineering	180,000
	1,700,000

What are the unit costs of each product using:

(a)   the traditional approach?

(b)   the ABC method?

Solution

(a)   A traditional costing approach would cost each product as follows:

	Product A	Product B	Product C
	£	£	£
Direct materials	25.00	20.00	18.00
Direct labour (@ £8 per hour)	24.00	32.00	16.00
Overhead (@ £7.08 per hour – see below)	21.24	28.32	14.16
Total cost	70.24	80.32	48.16

Overhead recovery rate = $\dfrac{£1,700,000}{240,000}$

= £7.08 per direct labour hour

(b)   An ABC system needs to investigate the cost determinants for the indirect overheads not driven by production volume. Assume that these are as follows.

Cost	Cost driver
Set-up	Number of production runs
Goods inwards	Number of receipts
Packing	Number of production orders
Engineering	Number of production orders

The machine overhead of £900,000 is likely to be related primarily to production volume, so it will be recovered on the basis of machine hours used = $\dfrac{£900,000}{210,000}$ = £4.29 per machine hour (after rounding)

The cost per activity for each of the other cost centres is as follows.

Set-up cost $\dfrac{£140,000}{40}$ = £3,500 per set-up

Goods inwards $\dfrac{£280,000}{160}$ = £,1750 per order

Packing $\dfrac{£200,000}{50}$ = £4,000 per production order

Engineering $\dfrac{£180,000}{50}$ = £3,600 per order

An ABC approach would allocate overheads to each of the product groups as follows:

	Product A	Product B	Product C
	£	£	£
Set-up costs			
5 × £3,500	17,500		
10 × £3,500		35,000	
25 × £3,500			87,500
Machine costs (rounded down)			
(2 × 40,000) × £4.29	343,000		
(4 × 25,000) × £4.29		429,000	
(3 × 10,000) × £4.29			128,000
Goods inwards costs			
15 × £1,750	26,250		
25 × £1,750		43,750	
120 × £1,750			210,000
Packing costs			
15 × £4,000	60,000		
10 × £4,000		40,000	
25 × £4,000			100,000
Engineering costs			
15 × £3,600	54,000		
10 × £3,600		36,000	
25 × £3,600			90,000
Total overhead	500,750	583,750	615,500
Average overhead per unit			
£500,750/40,000	£12.52		
£583,750/25,000		£23.35	
£615,500/10,000			£61.55
This compares to the traditional overhead absorption of:			
	£21.24	£28.32	£14.16

It can be seen that product C is significantly under-costed under the traditional system, while products A and B are over-costed. This situation arises because the large proportion of costs driven by product C is not picked up under the traditional costing system. Since it is the cost-drivers identified in the ABC system which generate the costs in the first place, the ABC system will produce a more accurate final analysis.

3 Summary

This chapter has revised several fundamental cost accounting topics from your earlier studies, in particular the treatment of overheads including:

- allocation/apportionment/absorption;
- service departments;
- over-/under-absorption;
- activity based costing approach;
- limiting factor analysis.

4 Test your knowledge

 Workbook Activity 1

Sandsend Engineers Ltd specialise in agricultural engineering. The business is divided into three cost centres: machining, fabrication and outside contract work.

The budgeted overhead for the quarter ended 31 March 2003 shows:

Cost centre	Machining	Fabrication	Outside contracts	Total
	£	£	£	£
Allocated overhead	21,000	25,500	19,500	66,000
Apportioned overhead	15,000	16,100	9,100	40,200
	36,000	41,600	28,600	106,200
Budgeted machine hours	4,000	5,200		
Budgeted labour hours			1,950	

In early January, the company receives an order for a replacement door on a grain silo for a local farmer. The specification of costs includes:

Direct material   £3,100

Direct labour rate per hour   £7.50

Machine hours and labour hours per cost centre:

Machining   12 hours

Fabrication   8 hours

Outside contracts   6 hours

The business has a pricing policy based on full absorption costing principles. It adds 10% to production costs to cover for administration, selling and distribution. It then plans for profit based on 25% of the selling price or contract price.

Complete the following:

Using absorption costing principles, the contract price of the replacement grain silo door will be £_____ (to the nearest '£'.)

Workbook Activity 2

Roberts and Ranson are partners trading as licensed accounting technicians. They employ one other fully qualified technician and two trainees, together with a general administration assistant.

The budgeted salaries for the year comprise:

	£
Roberts	30,000
Ranson	30,000
Qualified senior	18,500
Trainee (1)	10,500
Trainee (2)	12,000
Administrator	14,500*
Total	**115,500**

*The administrator's salary is to be treated as overhead.

The budgeted overheads include:

	£
Building occupancy costs	9,100
Telephone, postage, stationery	4,700
Other overheads	11,200
Total	**25,000**

The total forecast labour hours for the year include:

	Hours
Partners	3,760
Qualified senior	1,880
Trainees (split equally)	3,760
Total	**9,400**

Clients' work is priced on full absorption costing principles. Overhead is recovered on labour hours. The labour charge-out rates for partners, the qualified senior and the trainees are based on their budgeted salaries divided by their labour hours.

The business accepts a new client, the White Rose Hotel, and the senior partner estimates, having met with the client, that the hours required on the work will be:

	Hours	
Partners	5	
Qualified senior	12	
Trainees	6	(3 hours each)
Total	**23**	

The pricing policy is based on adding an element for profit which will yield a 30% profit margin on the price charged to the client.

You are required to complete the OAR, charge-out rates and estimated fees calculation schedules below.

Overhead Absorption rate £

Building Occupancy

Telephone, postage and stationery

Other overheads

Administrator's salary

Total Overheads

Number of labour hours

Overhead absorption rate per labour hour

£

Partner's labour charge-out rate	=		per hour
Qualified senior	=		per hour
Trainee (1)	=		per hour
Trainee (2)	=		per hour

White Rose Hotel Estimated fee

£

Direct labour

Partners	=	
Qualified seniors	=	
Trainee (1)	=	
Trainee (2)		

Total Direct Labour

Overheads

Total Overhead cost

Total Cost

Thus charge to client

Workbook Activity 3

Refer again to the scenario in Activity 1, Sandsend Engineers Ltd.

The actual overhead incurred during the quarter ended 31 March 2003 was:

	£
Machining	37,800
Fabrication	42,000
Outside work	29,100
	108,900

Overhead is recovered on machine hours in machining and fabrication, and labour hours on outside work.

The actual level of activity in the quarter was:

Machining	4,250 machine hours
Fabrication	5,300 machine hours
Outside work	1,975 labour hours

Required:

(a) Calculate the overhead recovered in each cost centre for the period.

(b) Post both the actual overhead incurred and the overhead recovered to the overhead control ledger account for the period, showing the under or over recovery transferred to the profit and loss account.

 Workbook Activity 4

Blidworth Loam Ltd manufacture a single product 'Cricketloam' and supply this product to cricket clubs for grounds at professional level through to village greens.

Its cost specification includes the following budgeted details per tonne of product, together with budgeted data for the current year:

Direct labour hours	4.5
Labour rate per hour	£8.50
Direct material	1.1 tonnes per tonne of good output
Material cost	£25 per tonne
Variable production overheads (total)	£378,000
Fixed production overheads (total)	£250,000
Selling price per tonne	£132
Production volume	12,000 tonnes
Sales volume	11,500 tonnes

Complete the following:

The budgeted marginal cost will be £_____per _____.

The contribution will be £_____per _____.

Workbook Activity 5

Refer again to the scenario outlined in Blidworth Loam Ltd.

The accounting technician and the planning engineer have recently analysed the value adding processes and identified various activities, cost drivers within those activities and current volumes of production and decide to apply the ABC methodology.

Budgeted plans 2003

	Activity	Cost pool £	Cost driver volume
(1)	Process set up	260,000	200 set ups
(2)	Material procurement	74,000	50 purchase orders
(3)	Maintenance	64,000	12 maintenance plans
(4)	Material handling	120,000	2,500 material movements
(5)	Quality costs	80,000	200 inspections
(6)	Order processing	30,000	1,000 customers
Total		**£628,000**	

The company plan to produce 1,000 tonnes per month which will require the following approximate activity demand:

17 set ups   ;   4 purchase orders; 1 maintenance plan;

210 material movements;   16 inspections;   80 customers.

Complete the following:

(a)

Process Setup: The cost driver rate will be £_____ per _____.

Material Procurement: The cost driver rate will be £_____ per _____.

Maintenance: The cost driver rate will be £_____ per _____.

Material handling: The cost driver rate will be £_____ per _____.

Quality Costs: The cost driver rate will be £_____ per _____.

Order Processing: The cost driver rate will be £_____ per _____.

(b) Using ABC, complete the following to determine the amount of overhead to be recovered per tonne of product.

17	setups	x	£1,300	=	£22,100
4	Purchase orders	x	£1,480	=	£5,920
1	Maintenance plan	x	£5,333	=	£5,333
210	Material movements	x	£10,080	=	£10,080
16	Inspections	x	£6,400	=	£6,400
80	customers	x	£2,400	=	£2,400

Total cost   **£52,233**

Thus, the overhead cost per tonne of product would be: £_____ per tonne.

 ## Workbook Activity 6

MIF is a manufacturing company. Select an appropriate accounting treatment for each of the following costs :

- Re-design of the website
- Holiday pay for operatives on the production line
- Material wastage in the production process
- Cost of the IT department
- Administrative wages
- Maintenance services
- Production equipment cleaning
- Depreciation of machinery

Options available are :

- Allocate to administrative overheads
- Direct costs
- Allocate to marketing overheads
- Charge to production in a machine hour overhead rate
- Charge to production in a labour overhead rate
- Activity based charge to production cost centres

Preparing budgets

3

Introduction

Having considered the ways in which cost, revenue and other business data may be collected, processed and analysed, we now turn to the task of putting this information to use in the future planning of the business.

The planning process starts with the identification of long term corporate objectives, based upon which a strategy is designed, resource utilisation and capital expenditure planned and ultimately short-term, quantified budgets are prepared. This chapter looks at this overall process.

In all Budgeting examinations you will be required to prepare budgets. You should also be prepared to discuss the budget preparation process and to suggest improvements to budget presentation.

KNOWLEDGE

- Justify the uses of budgetary control for planning, co-ordinating, authorising and cost control (Element 2.2)

- Identify the correct budget to prepare according to organisational requirements (Element 2.3)

- Recognise the effect that capacity, production and sales constraints have on budgets (Element 2.6)

- Describe the purpose of revenue and costs forecasts and how they link to budgets (Element 3.2)

CONTENTS

1   Budget preparation

2   Functional budgets

3   Problems in exam questions

4   Practical aspects of functional budgets

5   The master budget

SKILLS

- Schedule the required production resources to meet forecasts (Element 1.4)

- Budget in accordance with the organisation's costing systems, stating any assumptions made (Element 1.5)

- Prepare accurate cash flow forecast to facilitate the achievement of organisational objectives (Element 1.6)

- Prepare draft budgets from forecast data (Element 1.7)

- Break down budgets into time periods according to organisational needs (Elements 1.8)

- Plan and agree draft budgets with all parties involved (Element 1.9)

- Calculate the effect that variations in capacity on costs, production and sales will have on budgeted costs and revenues (Element 2.1)

- Analyse critical factors affecting costs and revenues and draw clear conclusions (Element 2.3)

- Identify and evaluate options and solutions to increase profitability or reduce financial losses or exposure to risk (Element 2.4)

KAPLAN PUBLISHING

1 Budget preparation

1.1 Limiting factors

The level of activity at which a business can operate will very seldom be unlimited. Limitations may be imposed, for example, by:

- market demand for its products or services;

- the number of skilled employees available;

- the availability of material supplies;

- the space available either as a working area or for the storage of goods;

- the amount of cash or credit facilities available to finance the business.

Therefore, when a manager starts to prepare a budget he should review the elements in it and identify where limiting factors (or governing factors) exist.

They will not all be equally significant; but where one particular limitation is of major importance it may be necessary to budget for that item first and to construct the rest of the budget around it. This can happen not merely in one department but for the company as a whole, when the item concerned may be referred to as the principal budget factor or key factor.

Quite commonly, the rate of growth in sales is the principal budget factor and this would have to be forecast before any other budget plans were made.

It is essential to identify the principal budget factor and any other limiting factors at an early stage in the budgeting process so that management may consider whether:

- it is possible to overcome the limitation which they impose (e.g. by finding new markets for sales or by obtaining alternative supplies or substitute raw materials);

- the limitations imposed must be accepted and the business's budgets must be produced within those limitations.

Example

Barbecue Limited manufactures two products for which the following details are available.

	Product X		Product Y
Selling price	£38		£38
Direct materials 8 units @ £1	£8	4 units @ £1	£4
Labour 4 hours @ £2	£8	6 hours @ £2	£12
Variable overhead 4 machine hours @ £3	£12	3 machine hours @ £3	£9
Fixed overheads	£5		£7

Maximum demand for X is 2,500 units.

Maximum demand for Y is 2,000 units.

Calculate the optimum production plan for Barbecue in each of the following two situations:

(a) Labour in the next period is limited to *16,000* hours, with no limit on machine hours.

(b) Machine hours in the next period are limited to *12,000* hours, with no limit on labour hours.

Solution

We would like to produce Xs and Ys up to the point where maximum demand is reached. (There is no point producing beyond this, because customers do not want any more.) So ideally we would like to produce 2,500 X and 2,000 Y. To do this we would require the following resources.

	Labour hours	Machine hours
2,500 X	10,000	10,000
2,000 Y	12,000	6,000
	22,000	16,000

If labour is limited to 16,000 hours we will not have enough labour hours to achieve this. Similarly, if machine hours are limited to 12,000 our production will be restricted.

To tackle this problem we begin by calculating the contribution earned per unit of each product.

Contribution for each unit of X = £ (38 − 8 − 8 − 12) = £10 per unit
Contribution for each unit of Y = £ (38 − 4 − 12 − 9) = £13 per unit

(a) Labour is limited so we calculate the contribution earned per labour hour for each product.

X = £10/4 = £2.50 per labour hour

Y = £13/6 = £2.17 per labour hour

You get more contribution per labour hour for × than for Y so make as many Xs as possible.

Available hours = 16,000 2,500 Xs require 10,000 hrs

The remaining hours are all used to make as many Ys as possible.

Remaining Ys will take six hours each to make so produce 6,000/6 = 1,000 Ys.

Contribution = (2,500 × £10) + (1,000 × £13) = £38,000

(b) In this case, machine hours are the scarce resource so we calculate contribution per machine hour.

X = £10/4 = £2.50 per machine hour

Y = £13/3 = £4.33 per machine hour

Now it is better to make Ys. Making 2,000 Ys requires 2,000 × 3 = 6,000 machine hours. That leaves us a further 6,000 machine hours for making Xs.

6,000 remaining hours for X means making 6,000/4 = 1,500 Xs

Contribution = (1,500 × £10) + (2,000 × £13) = £41,000

Note that in the examination, if you are told the maximum demand for a product it is a big hint that this method should be used.

2 Functional budgets

2.1 Budgets to be produced

The budgets that a business produces will generally be a standard set of budgets that starts with the sales budget and progresses through budgets for the costs associated with those sales.

You will typically be asked to produce the following budgets for a business that manufactures the goods that it sells. Note that generally you will produce the budgets for the number of units bought and sold before translating those into revenues and costs.

(a)   The sales budget

(b)   The production budget of finished goods. This will follow from the sales budget. It will be the same as the sales budget unless there are changes in the stocks held of finished goods.

(c)   The raw materials purchases budget. This will follow from the production budget.

The raw materials purchased will in general terms be:

the number of finished goods produced × the raw material per unit, (after adjustments for changes in stocks of materials and process losses).

(d)   The labour budget, and

(e)   The overheads budget.

2.2   Sales, production, materials, labour and overheads budgets

We shall first of all look at a simple budget example.

 Example

Toys Ltd budgets to sell 10,000 play cubes at £10 per cube in the month of July 20X8.

Stocks of finished cubes were 3,000 cubes at the start of the month and were budgeted to be 4,000 cubes at the end of the month.

Each cube requires 0.5 kg of material that costs £1 per kg. Opening stocks of material were 1,000 kg at the start of the month and are budgeted to be 750 kg at the end of the month.

Each cube requires 0.25 hours of direct labour. The labour rate is £12 per hour.

Production overheads are absorbed into production at the rate of £15 per hour.

Task

Produce the budgets for sales, production, materials, labour and overheads.

Solution

Step 1 – the sales budget

Number of cubes budgeted to be sold = 10,000 cubes

Budgeted sales revenue 10,000 × £10 = £100,000

Step 2 – the production budget

The standard layout for this is as follows – always work in units (cubes) first

	cubes
Sales budget	10,000
Closing stock	4,000
	14,000
Opening stock	3,000
Production of finished goods	11,000 cubes

(**Tutorial note.** There are no costs associated with the finished goods because the company manufactures them. The cost of the goods will be found when we deal with the budgets and costs of raw materials, labour and overheads. However we have to prepare the production budget in order to be able to prepare the raw materials budget.)

Step 3 – the raw materials budget

The standard layout for this is as follows – always work in units (kg) first. In this case remember that 1 cube requires 0.5 kg of raw material.

	Kg
For production budget 11,000 × 0.5kg	5,500
Closing stock	750
	6,250
Opening stock	1,000
Purchases of raw material	5,250 kg

Budgeted purchases of raw materials = 5,250 × £1 = £5,250

Step 4 – the labour budget

To calculate the cost of labour we have to return to the production budget because the cost of labour is determined by the level of production.

Number of labour hours budgeted for month = 11,000 cubes × 0.25 hours = 2,750hrs

Cost of direct labour = 2,750hrs × £12 = £33,000

Step 5 – the overhead budget

To calculate the cost of overheads we have to return to the labour budget because the cost of the overhead is based on the number of hours worked.

Number of labour hours budgeted for month =   2,750 hrs

Cost of overhead = 2,750hrs × £15 =   £41,250

3   Problems in exam questions

3.1   The raw materials budget with losses

A question may be set where the there is a percentage loss of raw materials in the production process. In practice this may be due to such things as evaporation, faulty materials supplied or materials damaged in the process.

Consider the example above, changing the raw material details to:

Each cube requires 0.5 kg of material that costs £1 per kg. Opening stocks of material were 1,000 kg at the start of the month and are budgeted to be 750 kg at the end of the month. 5% of materials are lost during the manufacturing process.

The calculation of raw materials purchased budget would be changed as follows:

	kg
For production budget 11,000 × 0.5kg	5,500
Closing stock	750
	6,250
Opening stock	1,000
	5,250
Material required for production	5,250
Process loss 5,250 × (5/95) =	276
Purchases	5,526 kg

Budgeted cost of purchases of raw materials = 5,526 × £1 = £5,526

Note that the loss is 5/95 × the material required for production. It is not 5/100 × the material required for production.

The reason for this is that the process loses 5% of the 'gross' amount purchased. We therefore have the following percentages

Purchases	100%
Losses	5%
Material required production	95%

The losses are therefore 5/95 of what is left after the loss (5,250kg) which is what is required for production.

3.2 The production budget with losses

A question may be set where the there is a percentage loss of finished goods. In practice this may be due to such things as items rejected as inferior by quality control, items damaged in the warehouse or theft.

Consider the example above, changing the finished goods details to read:

Stocks of finished cubes were 3,000 cubes at the start of the month and were budgeted to be 4,000 cubes at the end of the month. 4% of finished goods are rejected as unsuitable.

The calculation of the production budget would be changed as follows:

	cubes
Sales budget	10,000
Closing stock	4,000
	14,000
Opening stock	3,000
	11,000
Finished goods required	11,000
Loss 11,000 × (4/96) =	458
Production required	11,458

As before, note that the loss is 4/96 × the finished goods required It is not 4/100 × the finished goods required.

The reason for this is that the business loses 4% of the 'gross' amount produced. We therefore have the following percentages

Produced	100%
Losses	4%
Finished goods required	96%

The losses are therefore 4/96 of what is left in the warehouse after the loss (11,000 units) which is what is required for sales and stock.

3.3 Calculating the sales budget and stocks of finished goods

Exam questions will frequently present information regarding sales and stocks as follows.

 Example

XYZ has 13 accounting periods of four weeks during the year. It had sales of £40,000 in accounting period 5 and budgets for sales to increase by 3% for each accounting period.

The company budgets to have closing stock at the end of an accounting period equal to two weeks sales of the following period.

Produce the budget for sales and stock for accounting periods 6, 7 and 8.

Solution

	Period 6 £	Period 7 £	Period 8 £	Period 9 £
Sales 40,000 × 1.03	41,200			
41,200 × 1.03		42,436		
42,436 × 1.03			43,709	
43,709 × 1.03				45,020
Opening Stock	20,600(W1)	21,218	21,854	
Closing stock	21,218(W2)	21,854(W3)	22,510(W4)	

Workings

1 £41,200 × 0.5 (i.e. two weeks sales of a 4 week period) = £20,600

2 £42,436 × 0.5 = £21,218

3 £43,709 × 0.5 = £21,854

4 £45,020 × 0.5 = £22,510

The example below illustrates the preparation of the functional budgets, starting with projected sales information.

 Example

The following data will be used to explain the technique of budget preparation:

Hash Ltd makes two products – PS and TG. Sales for next year are budgeted at 5,000 units of PS and 1,000 units of TG. Planned selling prices are £100 and £140 respectively.

Hash Ltd has the following opening stock and required closing stock.

	PS units	TG units
Opening stock	100	50
Projected closing stock	1,100	50

You are also given the following data about the materials required to produce PS and TG and the machining and finishing processes involved in production.

	PS	TG
Finished products:		
Kg of raw material X,. per unit of finished product	12	12
Kg of raw material Y, per unit of finished product	6	8
Direct labour hours per unit of finished product	8	12

Standard rates and prices:

Direct labour	£6.00 per hour
Raw material X	£0.72 per kg
Raw material Y	£1.56 per kg

Production overheads:

Variable	£1.54 per labour hour
Fixed	£0.54 per labour hour
	———
	£2.08 per labour hour
	———

You are required to prepare the functional budgets.

Solution

(a) **The sales budget**

The sales budget represents the plan in terms of the quantity and value of sales, for sales management. In practice this is often the most difficult budget to calculate.

What is next year's sales budget?

The sales budget would be:

	Total	PS	TG
Sales units	6,000	5,000	1,000
Sales value	£640,000	£500,000	£140,000

In practice a business would market many more than two products. Moreover, the sales budget would probably be supported by subsidiary budgets to show analysis according to:

(i) responsibility e.g. Northern area, Western area, etc.;

(ii) type of customer e.g. wholesale, retail, government, etc.

(b) The production budget

The production budget is usually expressed in quantity and represents the sales budget adjusted for opening/closing finished stocks and work in progress.

The production budget would be:

	PS units	TG units
Sales budget	5,000	1,000
Add projected closing stock	1,100	50
	6,100	1,050
Less opening stock	100	50
Production in units	6,000	1,000

The production budget needs to be translated into requirements for:

(i)   raw materials;

(ii) direct labour;

(iii) factory overheads;

(iv) closing stock levels.

(c) The raw materials and purchases budget

(Remember that Hash Ltd is going to produce 6,000 units of PS and 1,000 units of TG.)

		PS kg		TG kg
Raw material usage				
X	6,000 × 12 kg	72,000	1,000 × 12 kg	12,000
Y	6,000 × 6 kg	36,000	1,000 × 8 kg	8,000

		PS £		TG £
Budgeted purchases:				
X	72,000 × £0.72	51,840	12,000 × £0.72	8,640
Y	36,000 × £1.56	56,160	8,000 × £1.56	12,480
		108,000		21,120

(d) **The direct labour budget**

			PS		TG
Usage	6,000 × 8 hrs		48,000 hrs	1,000 × 12 hrs	12,000 hrs
Cost	48,000 × £6		£288,000	12,000 × £6	£72,000

(e) **Production overheads**

		PS		TG
Variable costs	48,000 hours × £1.54	73,920	12,000 × £1.54	18,480
Fixed costs	48,000 hours × £0.54	25,920	12,000 × £0.54	6,480
		99,840		24,960

One of the most important points illustrated by this example is how the budgets are inter-related.

It is a simple example and you should be aware that in practice budgeting can be more than simply an arithmetical exercise. The practical problems are discussed later.

3.4   The budgeted profit and loss account

The budgeted profit and loss account shows the net profit by deducting the budgeted costs from the budgeted sales revenue.

Using the example above the budgeted profit and loss account would be as follows.

	£	£
Sales	500,000	140,000
Materials	108,000	21,120
Labour	288,000	72,000
Production overheads	99,840	24,960
Production cost	495,840	118,080
add opening stock (working)	8,264	5,904
less closing stock (working)	90,904	5,904
Cost of sales	413,200	118,080
Profit	86,800	21,920

KAPLAN PUBLISHING

Working

Stock values = (production cost/units produced) × units of stock.

1   Opening stock of PS = (495,840/6,000) × 100 = £8,264
2   Closing stock of PS = (495,840/6,000) × 1,100 = £90,904
3   Opening stock of TG = (118,080/1,000) × 50 = £5,904
4   Closing stock of TG = (118,080/1,000) × 50 = £5,904

4   Practical aspects of functional budgets

4.1   Sales budgets

The sales income budget is uniquely difficult to prepare because it involves forecasting the actions of people outside the business (the potential customers).

The extent to which sales forecasting is necessary will depend on the period covered by the outstanding order book and on the consistency of the conversion rate from enquiries to orders. If there is a well-filled order book for some months ahead then less reliance will need to be placed on forecasting techniques.

Forecasts may be made in a variety of ways. The method used will depend on the nature of the business and the amount of information available, but a generalised formal procedure might be as follows:

- Review past years' sales for whatever period is appropriate to the company's business cycle.

- Analyse the time series to identify seasonal, cyclical and random fluctuations.

- Extrapolate from past years' figures, assuming no changes in products or prices. Adjust the extrapolation for proposed changes which are controllable by the company, such as price alterations, changes in marketing effort, the introduction of new products, and the discontinuance of existing products (depending on the products' life cycles).

- Adjust for market changes due to external factors, such as government controls, action of competitors or social changes affecting demand. In particular, appropriate adjustments should be made for changing price levels or seasonal trends.

- Check that the resultant quantities are compatible with the quantities that can be purchased or produced.

- Check acceptability of forecast to sectional sales managers. In addition, other personnel who might contribute towards making realistic forecasts of trends should be consulted.

- Check consistency of forecast with long-term corporate plans.

The forecasting method outlined above depends on the existence of a 'time series' of figures from which extrapolation can be made and is mainly applicable to items in continuous demand. For other types of business, the sales forecast will be based on some form of market survey or on subjective estimates by people familiar with the market concerned.

Whichever forecasting method is used, the forecast should take account of significant anticipated changes in circumstances which would affect the validity of any statistically derived calculations.

4.2 Cost budgets

Budgeting for costs, in the same way as budgeting for sales, begins with facts. What facts they are will depend on the nature of the business; but every business will employ people, and most businesses will use materials of some kind. A manufacturing business will use tools and probably machinery. Floor space will be needed, also office equipment and perhaps motor vehicles.

All these requirements will be related in some way to the output of the business – its sales and any changes in stocks or work in progress.

In practice there are a wide range of different ways to budget for costs, as follows:

- If standards for cost units are available, then there may be computer programs to identify the material and labour standards relative to a given output. It then remains for departmental managers to budget for material wastage or spoilage, labour efficiency and idle time.

 Example

The quarterly production requirements for product Omega are shown below. 4 % of production fails the quality checks and must be scrapped. How many items of Omegas must be manufactured to allow for waste?

	Month 1	Month 2	Month 3
Required units	99,000 units	108,000 units	96,000 units
Manufactured units			

KAPLAN PUBLISHING

	Month 1	Month 2	Month 3
Solution			
Required units	99,000 units	108,000 units	96,000 units
Manufactured units	$\dfrac{99,000}{96\%} =$ 103,125 UNITS	$\dfrac{108,000}{96\%} =$ 112,500 UNITS	$\dfrac{96,000}{96\%} =$ 100,000 UNITS

- In a business carrying out long-term contracts, cost units (contracts) may be identical with cost centres (each contract having its own controller).

- In some businesses it may be sufficiently accurate for the budget for direct materials cost to be an extrapolation from past total figures, without any attempt at detailed justification or analysis.

4.3 Use of standards in budgeting

Budgeting will inevitably make use of standard costs, as in the worked example above, and you should ensure you are familiar with the techniques and principles involved in their determination.

However, budgeting will generally extend beyond the simple multiplication of planned production levels by the standard usages and costs for each product for the following reasons:

- Different ranges of output levels will often lead to changes in unit variable costs (e.g. materials discounts, learning effects, etc).

- Some variable costs will not vary neatly with production and will need to be estimated for each particular activity level (e.g. wastage, idle time, production set-up costs).

- Fixed costs are independent of production levels, although they may be stepped.

- A large proportion of a business's costs will not be directly involved in the production process (e.g. administration, marketing, capital expenditure, etc).

The following sections describe the common problems encountered in budgeting for the most common cost elements: labour, materials and overheads.

4.4 Budgeting for numbers and costs of employees

When budgeting for the number and costs of people to be employed, the starting point must be to assess the work to be done by people with various skills and this is equally necessary for manual, clerical and managerial activities.

Having defined what work is to be done, the establishment of budgets for the employment of people falls into two main stages:

- planning the number of people needed;
- calculating the relevant costs.

In defining the productive workload for the budget year it will be necessary to balance the requirements of the sales budget against the productive capacity available. If there is excess capacity over the year as a whole then a decision will be needed whether to operate below full capacity or to use the excess capacity in making goods for stock or getting ahead with work in progress for the following year.

If the sales budget does not provide a steady workload month by month, then in phasing the budgets it may be decided to keep productive output constant and to balance out the short-term differences by fluctuations in work-in-progress or finished stock.

The degree of precision possible in budgeting for numbers of people employed will depend on the type of work involved and the extent to which work measurement is possible.

4.5 Budgeting for the cost of materials

Considerable effort can be involved in preparing detailed budgets of quantities and purchase prices of materials. Whether this effort is justified will depend on the significance of materials in relation to total costs, and the extent to which effective control can be exercised.

The starting point for materials budgeting is the quantity of material to be used during the budget year, whether in retail sales or in production or for indirect use.

The form of the materials usage budget will depend on the nature of the business. Where repetitive operations are carried out it will be possible, and worth the effort, to set standards for the usage of the various items of material, and these standards can be associated with the production forecast to build up the total material requirements.

The purchase prices to be applied to the usage of the various items may be obtained from stock ledger records or recent purchase invoices, subject to adjustment for forecast price changes, using index numbers as necessary.

In budgeting for indirect materials (such as small tools, machine coolants and lubricants, fuel, cleaning materials and office stationery) the common practice is to budget merely for a total cost extrapolated from past experience. It will be important for control purposes, however, that the budget working papers contain as much detail as possible about anticipated usage, even though the individual items may not be evaluated separately.

4.6 Budgeting for overheads

The nature of overheads will depend on the type of business, but common categories are as follows:

(a) Premises charges

(b) Costs of plant, motor vehicles and other fixed assets

(c) Communication expenses

(d) Travelling and entertaining

(e) Insurances

(f) Discretionary costs

(g) Financial policy costs

(h) Random costs

4.7 Calculating budget and actual overheads

Earlier in the chapter we saw how budgeted overhead absorption rates (OARs) were calculated. The guidance notes to Budgeting state that examinations might require you to use overhead absorption rates to deduce budgeted and actual activity levels.

4.8 Budgeted activity level

If we know the overhead absorption rate and the budgeted fixed overhead then the budgeted activity level can be found.

$$OAR = \frac{\text{Budgeted fixed overhead}}{\text{Budgeted activity level}}$$

Therefore:

$$\text{Budgeted activity level} = \frac{\text{Budgeted fixed overhead}}{OAR}$$

Example

A business has an overhead absorption rate of £2 per unit produced. The budgeted fixed overhead was £400,000. What was the budgeted activity level?

Solution

$$\text{Budgeted activity level} \quad = \quad \frac{\text{Budgeted fixed overhead}}{\text{OAR}}$$

$$= \quad \frac{£400,000}{£2}$$

$$= \quad 200,000 \text{ units}$$

4.9 Actual activity level

When overheads are absorbed, this is done on the basis of the actual production level using the budgeted overhead absorption rate. Any under or over absorption is due to the difference between the overhead absorbed and the overhead actually incurred.

Under/over absorption = Overhead absorbed – overhead incurred

 Example

You are given the following information:

Budgeted fixed overhead	£250,000
Actual fixed overhead	£280,000
Budgeted activity level	100,000 units
Under absorption	£5,000

What was the actual activity level for the period?

Solution

$$\text{OAR} \quad = \quad \frac{£250,000}{100,000}$$

$$= \quad £2.50 \text{ per unit}$$

$$\text{Overhead absorbed} \quad = \quad £280,000 - £5,000$$

$$= \quad £275,000$$

Actual activity level	=	$\dfrac{\text{Fixed overhead absorbed}}{\text{OAR}}$
	=	$\dfrac{£275,000}{£2.50}$
	=	110,000 units

4.10   Permanent budget record

For every type of revenue or cost it is highly desirable that a permanent budget record be prepared, giving the detailed calculations from which the budgeted amount has been derived. In particular, the data relevant to projecting forecasts of income and expenditure must be identified. This will not only impose a discipline on the budget preparation but will also:

- facilitate the eventual explanation of any differences between budgeted and actual results;

- provide a starting point for budget revisions or for the preparation of budgets in future years.

The important features of such a record are as follows:

- details of the budget calculation;

- comparison with the actual figures for the previous year;

- basis of variability, noting how the amount is related to such factors as levels of output or numbers of people employed.

4.11   Capital expenditure budget

All short-term operating budgets are in effect abstracts from a continuously developing long-term plan. This, however, is particularly true of the capital expenditure budget because the major items included in it will not be completed within the bounds of any one budget year.

The main purpose of the capital expenditure budget, therefore, is to provide a forecast of the amount of cash likely to be needed for investment projects during the year ahead. It also indicates what items of plant, equipment, vehicles and so on will be needed for the purpose of implementing the profit and loss (or operating) budget; and therefore it must be submitted for approval at an early stage in the budgeting timetable.

Any capital expenditure budget would include the following:

- a brief descriptive title for the project;

- the total required expenditure;

- an analysis of the costs over various time periods;

- where appropriate, expenditure to date on the project;

- estimates of future benefits from the project;

- investment appraisal calculations including details of assumptions made.

- intangible benefits from the expenditure.

5 The master budget

5.1 Introduction

The master budget for approval by the board will take the form of a budgeted profit and loss account, a forecast balance sheet as at the year-end and a cash budget. These will be supported by such summaries of the various functional budgets as may be required, and by calculations of the key ratios which indicate conformity with the objectives for the year.

Cash budgets will be assessed in Budgeting, so you should be aware of their existence.

5.2 The forecast balance sheet

In arriving at the forecast balance sheet, it will be necessary to take account of the following:

- The capital expenditure budget.

- Changes in stock levels and work in progress (as calculated in connection with the budgeting of material and labour costs). If work in progress and finished stocks are valued on a TAC basis, then it will be necessary to calculate overhead recovery rates.

- Changes in debtor balances. Subject to any special delays in collection, the closing debtor balances will be calculated by applying the company's normal credit terms to the phased budget of sales.

- Changes in creditor balances. In theory, the closing creditors will be calculated by applying a normal credit period to the phased budgets of material purchases, subcontracted work and any other relevant items. In practice, it may be necessary to review the budgeted cash flow before finalising a decision on the credit to be taken.

- Changes in the cash balance. Initially, the closing cash balance may be taken as the balancing figure on the balance sheet, but at some stage this should be validated by building up a cash budget itemised from the other budgets. This is discussed in the following paragraph.

5.3 The cash budget

The purposes of the cash budget are as follows:

- To ensure that the various items of income and expenditure budgeted departmentally, and subject to the normal credit policy of the business, will result in cash flows which enable the company to pay its way at all times; in other words, to ensure that there is a practical plan.

- Where the cash flow over the year as a whole is satisfactory but there are intermediate periods of difficulty in financing operations, to give a basis from which the timing of particular items can be re-planned.

- Where cash proves inadequate to finance the plan as originally envisaged, to give the financial controller an opportunity to seek sources of additional capital. (If the budget cannot be financed as it stands, then a revised budget will have to be prepared.)

- Like any other budget, to provide a basis for control during the forth-coming year.

5.4 Proforma receipts and payments cash budget

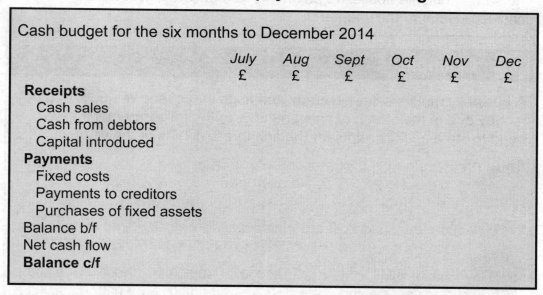

Cash budget for the six months to December 2014

	July £	Aug £	Sept £	Oct £	Nov £	Dec £
Receipts						
Cash sales						
Cash from debtors						
Capital introduced						
Payments						
Fixed costs						
Payments to creditors						
Purchases of fixed assets						
Balance b/f						
Net cash flow						
Balance c/f						

Each cash budget has to be amended to reflect the particular circumstances of the business.

For example, businesses with only cash sales will not need the line for cash from debtors. Also, other sources of income may arise, such as proceeds from the sale of fixed assets.

There are many sorts of cash payments; possibly cash purchases as well as credit purchases, wages and salaries to employees or the drawings of a proprietor, and each must be detailed line by line under the payments heading.

The crucial point to remember is that all cash inflows and all cash outflows over the budget period must be considered. As you work through the following examples and questions, you will see examples of different receipts and payments but note how the basic proforma above is used to find the net cash balance.

In the exam, you will be given a proforma cash budget which will help you to make sure that you have included all relevant figures.

5.5 Lagged receipts and payments

Sales are often made on credit and customers do not pay until subsequent periods. The credit terms offered to customers will be decided by the managers and a general pattern of receipts from these customers can therefore be established. The cash budget needs to show the actual cash expected to be received from debtors in the period rather than the actual sales made to debtors in the period.

The same principle applies to payments to creditors which will be considered later in the chapter.

Example

A business makes sales on credit and finds that it receives 50% of the money due in the month of sale and 50% in the following month. We need to state cash receipts for the first three months of the year.

Solution

	Dec £	Jan £	Feb £	Mar £
Sales	10,000	12,000	14,000	16,000
The cash receipts will be:				
50% in month of sale	5,000	6,000	7,000	8,000
50% in subsequent month	–	5,000	6,000	7,000
Giving:				
Total cash receipts	5,000	11,000	13,000	15,000

The above example shows how payments from debtors for a particular month are not the same as sales to debtors for that month, so in a simulation do not fall into the trap of simply using the credit sales figures.

5.6 Sales on credit and discounts

In some businesses a cash or settlement discount is offered to customers for payment within a certain time period. This means that although the cash is received sooner, a lower amount is received than was invoiced. This must be taken into account when preparing the cash budget.

 Example

A business offers a 3% discount for payment received from credit customers in the month of sale. The business has found that 40% of customers take advantage of this by paying in the month of sale, 50% of customers pay in the month after the sale and 10% of customers pay two months after the month of sale.

Credit sales for the business are as follows:

	Actual			Budgeted	
	February £	March £	April £	May £	June £
Credit sales	20,000	22,000	24,000	18,000	21,000

What are the cash receipts from debtors for the three months ending 30 June?

Solution

Cash inflow

		April £	May £	June £
February sales	– 20,000 × 10%	2,000		
March sales	– 22,000 × 50%	11,000		
	22,000 × 10%		2,200	
April sales	– 24,000 × 40% × 97%	9,312		
	24,000 × 50%		12,000	
	24,000 × 10%			2,400
May sales	– 18,000 × 40% × 97%		6,984	
	18,000 × 50%			9,000
June sales	– 21,000 × 40% × 97%			8,148
Cash inflow		22,312	21,184	19,548

Note that the cash received in the month of sale is 97% of the amount invoiced as these customers have taken advantage of the settlement discount.

5.7 Sales quantities and prices

In the examples so far you have been given the monetary amount of the sales in each month in order to calculate the receipts from debtors. However, you may be given information about the sales quantity in units each month and the selling price per unit. From this, the total monetary amount of the sales for the month can be calculated.

5.8 Payments to creditors

The determination of the cash payments that are to be made to creditors each month can be a little more complicated than the calculation of the receipts from debtors as the information can be expressed in a variety of different ways. The simplest form in which you might come across payments to creditors' information is similar to that for receipts from debtors – you will be told the amount of credit purchases and the payment pattern to creditors.

 Example

A business estimates that its credit purchases for February and March will be £14,000 but will increase by 10% each month thereafter. Its payment pattern to creditors is that 60% are paid in the month following the purchases and the remaining 40% two months after the purchase.

What are the payments to creditors for the three months of April, May and June?

Solution

	February £	March £	April £	May £	June £
Purchases (increasing by 10% each month)	14,000	14,000	15,400	16,940	18,634
Payments to creditors					
– February purchases 14,000 × 40%			5,600		
– March purchases 14,000 × 60%			8,400		
14,000 × 40%				5,600	
– April purchases 15,400 × 60%				9,240	
15,400 × 40%					6,160
– May purchases 16,940 × 60%					10,164
Cash payments			14,000	14,840	16,324

6 Summary

The budget must be prepared in a logical and orderly manner, ensuring co-ordination and co-operation between departments and different levels of management. Final proposals must be fully understood and accepted by all involved via a clear set of instructions and detailed discussions where necessary.

You should be prepared to discuss the types of budgets that may be required for a particular business and how they might be prepared, probably with numerical illustrations.

7 Test your knowledge

 Workbook Activity 1

Your organisation (AAT CA D94)

Your organisation is about to commence work on the preparation of the forthcoming year's annual budget.

As assistant management accountant, you have been asked to assist budget-holders and to respond to any queries which they may raise in the course of submitting their budget proposals.

The following notes are extracts taken from your organisation's budget manual.

'The key or principal budget factor in our organisation's budgetary process is sales volume ... The need for co-ordination in the budgetary process is paramount ...'.

The marketing manager is a budget holder and she has approached you with a number of queries concerning the above extract.

Required:

Prepare a memo for the marketing manager which provides brief answers to the following queries:

(a) What is meant by the term *key factor* and why is the determination of this factor so important in the budgetary process?

(b) How can co-ordination be achieved?

 Workbook Activity 2

You are employed as the assistant management accountant at Wimpole Ltd where one of your duties is the preparation of budgets every four weeks. You report to Ann Jones, the senior management accountant.

Wimpole Ltd makes several products, two of which are the Alpha and the Beta. Budget data for the two products for the four weeks ending 1 February 2002 is shown below.

Production and sales data	Alpha	Beta
Budgeted sales volume	2,000 units	3,000 units
Opening finished stocks	300 units	297 units
Closing finished stocks	500 units	595 units
Material per unit	10.00 metres	12.00 metres
Labour per unit	1.150 hours	1.380 hours

Note: Production takes place evenly over the four weeks.

Material data	
Cost of material per metre	£17.00
Opening material stock	8,750 metres
Closing material stock	15,530 metres
Wastage rate of material	3% of material issued to production

Labour data

46 employees work a guaranteed 35-hour week. The guaranteed wage for each employee is £210.00 per week.

Any overtime necessary is paid at a rate of £8.00 per hour.

Since collecting the original budget data, you have discovered that:

- The maximum amount of material available from the supplier for the four weeks ending 1 February 2002 will be 61,580 metres. The wastage is material left over after lengths have been cut to make Alphas and Betas but before any labour cost has been incurred. The wastage has no scrap value.

- Betas are sold to a large furniture retailer under a long-term contract that cannot be broken. The budgeted sales volume of 3,000 Betas for the four weeks ending 1 February 2002 must be provided under the contract.

- It is not possible to reduce the level of any of the opening or closing stocks.

Required:

Prepare the following information for Ann Jones for the four weeks ended 1 February 2002:

(a) The production budget in units for Alpha and Beta assuming there was no shortage of materials.

(b)   A statement taking into account the shortage of material and showing the:

(i)   Metres of material available for production before any wastage.

(ii)   Metres of material required for Beta production (including any wastage).

(iii) Metres of material available for Alpha production. (iv) Number of Alphas to be produced. (v) Labour hours to be worked.

(vi)   Cost of labour budget.

(c)   The revised budgeted sales volumes for Alpha and Beta.

Data

Ann Jones is preparing the budgeted operating statement for a third product, the Delta, using a computer spreadsheet. Although she has entered selling price and cost data, these are uncertain and may be changed before the budget is agreed.

She asks you to complete the spreadsheet for the Delta using formulae that will allow a revised budgeted operating profit to be calculated automatically if price, cost and volume data change.

Required:

Using the template provided below, enter formulae for:

(a)   Turnover

(b)   Total variable cost

(c)   Contribution

(d)   Fixed costs

(e)   Operating profit

in cells B6 to B10 of the spreadsheet.

	A	B
1	Selling price per unit	£140
2	Variable cost per unit	£70
3	Fixed costs per 4-week period	£40,000
4	Volume per period	1,000
5	4 weeks ending	1 February 2002
6	Turnover	
7	Total variable cost	
8	Contribution	
9	Fixed costs	
10	Operating profit	

Workbook Activity 3

You are a management accountant employed by Aspen Ltd and you report to Adrian Jones, the managing director. One of your responsibilities is the production of budgets. Aspen Ltd only has one customer, Advanced Industries plc, for whom it makes the Omega, a specialist product. Advanced Industries demands that Aspen keeps a minimum closing stock of Omegas in case there is an error in the forecast requirements. There is no work-in-progress at any time.

- Both companies divide the year into four-week periods. Each week consists of five days and each day comprises eight hours.

- Advanced Industries plc has recently informed Aspen Ltd of its Omega requirements for the five periods ending Friday 25 May 2001. The details are reproduced below.

Forecast demand for Omegas					
Four weeks ending:	2 February Period 1	2 March Period 2	30 March Period 3	27 April Period 4	25 May Period 5
Number of Omegas required	5,700	5,700	6,840	6,460	6,080
Closing stock of Omegas					
Closing stocks are to equal 3 days of the next period's demand for Omegas.					

The production director gives you the following information:

- The actual opening stocks for period 1, the four weeks ending 2 February, will be 1,330 Omegas.

- Each Omega requires 6 litres of material.

- The material is currently supplied under a long-term contract at a cost of £8.00 per litre and is made exclusively for Aspen by Contrax plc.

- Contrax only has sufficient production capacity to make a maximum of 34,000 litres in any four-week period. Aspen normally purchases the material in the same four-week period it is used.

- Should Aspen require more than 34,000 litres in a four-week period, Contrax would be willing to supply additional material in the preceding period, providing it had spare capacity.

- There is a readily available alternative source for the material but the cost is £12.00 per litre.

- Before buying from the alternative source, any shortage of material in a period should be overcome, where possible, by first purchasing extra material from Contrax in the immediately preceding period.

- There are 78 production employees who are paid a guaranteed basic wage of £160 per 40-hour week.

- Each Omega should take 2 labour hours to make but, due to temporary technical difficulties, the workforce is only able to operate at 95% efficiency in periods 1 to 4.

- Any overtime incurred is payable at a rate of £6.00 per hour.

Required:

Adrian Jones asks you to prepare the following budgets for each of the periods 1 to 4:

(a) The production budget in Omegas using the stock levels given in the data.

(b) The material purchases budget in litres.

(c) The cost of the material purchases.

(d) The labour budget in hours including any overtime hours.

(e) The cost of the labour budget including the cost of any overtime.

Data

On receiving your budgets, Adrian Jones, the managing director, tells you that:

- He is concerned about the cost of the planned overtime and the extra cost of purchasing materials from the alternative supplier.

- The minimum demand in any four week period is forecast to be 5,700 Omegas.

- It is not possible to reduce costs by Advanced Industries plc improving its current method of forecasting.

However, he believes that some immediate and longer-term cost savings are possible.

Required:

Write a memo to Adrian Jones. In your memo you should:

(a) Use the budget information prepared above to identify ONE immediate possible cost saving proposal other than renegotiating the conditions imposed by Advanced Industries plc.

(b) Calculate the value of the cost savings in the proposal identified in part (a).

(c) Use the forecast minimum demand for Omegas to show whether or not:

   (i) the need to obtain material supplies from the alternative source is a short-term problem, and

   (ii) the need for overtime payments is also a short-term problem.

(d) Suggest TWO cost savings which may be possible in the longer term.

 Workbook Activity 4

You are employed as a management accountant in the head office of Alton Products plc. One of your tasks involves helping to prepare quarterly budgets for the divisional companies of Alton Products. Each quarter consists of 12 five-day weeks for both production and sales purposes.

One division, Safety Care, makes two chemicals, Delta and Omega. These are sold in standard boxes. Both products use the same material and labour but in different proportions. You have been provided with the following information relating to the two products for quarter 3, the 12 weeks ending 29 September 2000.

	Delta	Omega
Budgeted sales		
Quarter 3: 12 weeks to 29 September 2000	3,000 boxes	2,400 boxes
Quarter 4: 12 weeks to 22 December 2000	3,300 boxes	2,640 boxes
Finished stocks for quarter 3		
Opening stock	630 boxes	502 boxes
Closing stock (days sales in quarter 4)	6 days	8 days
Production inputs		
Material per box	12 kilograms	15 kilograms
Labour per box	3 hours	6 hours
Material stocks and costs for quarter 3		
Opening stock (kilograms)	13,560	
Closing stock (kilograms)	21,340	
Budgeted purchase price per kilogram	£7.00	

Labour costs for quarter 3

52 production employees work a 36 hour week and are each paid £180 per week. Any overtime is payable at £7.50 per hour.

Faulty production

10% of production is found to be faulty on completion. Faulty production has to be scrapped and has no scrap value.

Required:

The production director of Safety Care asks you to prepare the following for quarter 3:

(a) The number of boxes of *Delta* and *Omega* planned to be in closing stock.

(b) The number of labour hours available for production before incurring overtime.

(c) The production budget for *Deltas* and *Omegas* required to meet the budgeted sales.

(d) The material purchases budget in kilograms and cost.

(e) The labour budget in hours and cost.

Workbook Activity 5

You have recently been promoted to the post of management accountant with Northern Products Ltd, a company formed four years ago. The company has always used budgets to help plan its production of two products, the Exe and the Wye. Both products use the same material and labour but in different proportions.

You have been asked to prepare the budget for quarter 1, the 12 weeks ending 24 March 2000. In previous budgets the closing stocks of both raw materials and finished products were the same as opening stocks. You questioned whether or not this was the most efficient policy for the company.

As a result, you have carried out an investigation into the stock levels required to meet the maximum likely sales demand for finished goods and production demand for raw materials. You conclude that closing stocks of finished goods should be expressed in terms of days sales for the next quarter and closing stocks of raw materials in terms of days production for the next quarter.

Your findings are included in the data below which also shows data provided by the sales and production directors of Northern Products Ltd.

Product data

		Exe	Wye
•	Budgeted sales in units, quarter 1	930 units	1,320 units
•	Budgeted sales in units, quarter 2	930 units	1,320 units
•	Budgeted material per unit (litres)	6 litres	9 litres
•	Budgeted labour hours per unit	12 hours	7 hours
•	Opening units of finished stock	172 units	257 units
•	Closing units of finished stocks (days sales next quarter)	8 days	9 days
•	Failure rate of finished production*	2%	3%
•	Finance and other costs of keeping a unit in stock per quarter	£4.00	£5.00

* Failed products are only discovered on completion of production and have no residual value.

Other accounting data

•	Weeks in accounting period	12 weeks
•	Days per week for production and sales	5 days
•	Hours per week	35 hours
•	Number of employees	46 employees
•	Budgeted labour rate per hour	£6.00
•	Overtime premium for hours worked in excess of 35 hours per week	30%
•	Budgeted cost of material per litre	£15.00
•	Opening raw material stocks (litres)	1,878 litres
•	Closing raw material stocks (days production next quarter)	5 days
•	Financing and other costs of keeping a litre of raw material in stock per quarter	£1.00

Required:

(a) Calculate the following information for *quarter 1,* the 12 weeks ending 24 March 2000:

    (i) The number of production days.

    (ii) The closing finished stock for Exe and Wye in units.

    (iii) The labour hours available before overtime has to be paid.

(b) Prepare the following budgets for quarter 1, the 12 weeks ending 24 March 2000:

    (i) The production budget in units for Exe and Wye including any faulty production.

    (ii) The material purchases budget in litres and value.

    (iii) The production labour budget in hours and value including any overtime payments.

(c) Calculate the savings arising from the change in the required stock levels for the 12 weeks ending 24 March 2000.

 Workbook Activity 6

Wilmslow Ltd makes two products, the Alpha and the Beta. Both products use the same material and labour but in different amounts. The company divides its year into four quarters, each of 12 weeks. Each week consists of five days and each day comprises seven hours.

You are employed as the management accountant to Wilmslow Ltd and you originally prepared a budget for quarter 3, the 12 weeks to 17 September 1999. The basic data for that budget is reproduced below.

Original budgetary data: quarter 3
12 weeks to 17 September 1999

Product	Alpha	Beta
Estimated demand	1,800 units	2,100 units
Material per unit	8 kilograms	12 kilograms
Labour per unit	3 hours	6 hours

Since the budget was prepared, three developments have taken place:

1   The company has begun to use linear regression and seasonal variations to forecast sales demand. Because of this, the estimated demand for quarter 3 has been revised to 2,000 Alphas and 2,400 Betas.

2   As a result of the revised sales forecasting, you have developed more precise estimates of sales and closing stock levels:

- The sales volume of both the Alpha and Beta in quarter 4 (the 12 weeks ending 10 December 1999) will be 20% more than in the revised budget for quarter 3 as a result of seasonal variations.

- The closing stock of finished Alphas at the end of quarter 3 should represent five days' sales for quarter 4.

- The closing stock of finished Betas at the end of quarter 3 should represent 10 days' sales for quarter 4.

- Production in quarter 4 of both Alpha and Beta is planned to be 20% more than in the revised budget for quarter 3. The closing stock of materials at the end of quarter 3 should be sufficient for 20 days production in quarter 4.

3   New equipment has been installed. The workforce is not familiar with the equipment. Because of this, for quarter 3, they will only be working at 80% of the efficiency assumed in the original budgetary data.

Other data from your original budget which has not changed is reproduced below:

- 50 production employees work a 35-hour week and are each paid £210 per week.

- Overtime is paid for at £9 per hour.

- The cost of material is £10 per kilogram.

- Opening stocks at the beginning of quarter 3 are as follows:
  - Finished Alphas   500 units
  - Finished Betas   600 units
  - Material   12,000 kilograms

- There will not be any work in progress at any time.

Required:

The production director of Wilmslow Ltd wants to schedule production for quarter 3 (the 12 weeks ending 17 September 1999) and asks you to use the revised information to prepare the following:

(a)   The revised production budget for Alphas and Betas.

(b)   The material purchases budget in kilograms.

(c)   A statement showing the cost of the material purchases.

(d)   The labour budget in hours.

(e)   A statement showing the cost of labour.

 Workbook Activity 7

Tipton Ltd makes two types of container for the chemical industry, the Exe and the Wye. Both containers use the same type of material and labour but in different amounts. You are the Management Accountant and you are responsible for preparing the production and resource budgets for both products. The company operates a five-day week for both production and sales and prepares production and resource budgets every 20 working days.

You are given the following information relating to period 1, the 20 working days ending 30 January 2004.

Forecast sales volumes	Exe	Wye
Period 1: 20 days to 30 January 2004	8,820 units	5,800 units
Period 2: percentage increase over period 1	20%	30%

Finished stocks

- At the beginning of period 1, there will be 4,410 Exes and 2,320 Wyes in finished stock.

- The finished stock of Exes at the end of period 1 must be equal to ten working days sales of Exes in period 2.

- The finished stock of Wyes at the end of period 1 must be equal to eight working days sales of Wyes in period 2.

Materials

- Each Exe requires 5 square metres and each Wye requires 7 square metres of materials.

- The cost of material is £2.00 per square metre. There has been no change in the price of materials for several months. 2% of material issued to production is lost through wastage.

- At the beginning of period 1, the opening material stock will be 16,950 square metres.

- At the end of period 1, the closing material stock will be 18,000 square metres.

Labour

- Tipton produces six Exes per labour hour and four Wyes per labour hour.

- The company employs 22 production employees who work a 35-hour, five-day week.

- The labour rate per hour is £8.00 and any overtime is at a premium of 50% per hour.

- Any overtime premium is charged to the production overhead account and not directly to production.

Production overheads

- Overheads are charged to production at the rate of £12.00 per labour hour.

Required:

Prepare the following information for period 1, the 20 working days ending 30 January 2004:

(a)   production budgets in units for the Exe and the Wye;

(b)   material purchase budget in square metres;

(c)   cost of materials purchases budget;

(d)   budgeted labour hours to be worked, including any overtime;

(e)   cost of labour budget;

(f)   cost of production budgets for the Exe and the Wye.

Data

Susan Fellows is the Production Director of Tipton Ltd. She tells you that there will not be sufficient factory capacity in period 2 to meet the likely demand for the Exe and the Wye. One way of overcoming the capacity constraint in period 2 is to increase production of Exe in period 1 as Exe requires less material and labour than Wye. She tells you that:

- the surplus capacity of the factory in period 1 is equivalent to 88 labour hours and the production employees would be willing to work these extra hours;

- Tipton can obtain up to 2,000 square metres of extra material for period 1.

Required:

Write a memo to Susan Fellows. In your memo you should:

(a) identify whether it is the material or labour constraints that limit extra Exe production;

(b) prepare a revised production budget in units after allowing for the increased production of Exes;

(c) briefly identify TWO other short-term ways of overcoming the capacity constraint in period 2.

 Workbook Activity 8

The following data and estimates are available for ABC Ltd for June, July and August:

	June	July	August
Sales	£45,000	£50,000	£60,000
Wages	£12,000	£13,000	£14,500
Overheads	£8,500	£9,500	£9,000

The following information is available regarding direct materials:

	June	July	August	September
Opening stock	£5,000	£3,500	£6,000	£4,000
Material usage	£8,000	£9,000	£10,000	
Closing stock	£3,500	£6,000	£4,000	

Notes:

(1) 10% of sales are for cash, the balance is received the following month.

The amount to be received in June for May's sales is £29,500.

(2) Wages are paid in the month they are incurred.

(3) Overheads include £1,500 per month for depreciation. Overheads are settled the month following. £6,500 is to be paid in June for May's overheads.

(4) Purchases of direct materials are paid for in the month purchased.

(5) The opening cash balance in June is £11,750.

(6) A tax bill of £25,000 is to be paid in July.

Required:

(a) Calculate the amount of direct material purchases in EACH of the months of June, July and August.

(b) Prepare cash budgets for June, July and August.

 Workbook Activity 9

XYZ Ltd has the following forecast sales at list price for the nine months to 29 February 20X2:

June	£40,000	September	£48,000	December	£44,000
July	£44,000	October	£40,000	January	£42,000
August	£50,000	November	£45,000	February	£50,000

- 60% of the company's sales are on credit, payable in the month after sale. Cash sales attract a 5% discount off list price.

- Purchases amount to 40% of selling price, and these are paid for two months after delivery.

- Stock is maintained at a level equal to 50% of the following month's sales, except that in November stock is to be increased by £2,000 (at cost prices) to ensure that XYZ Ltd has a safety stock during the period when its major supplier shuts down. This safety stock will be released in March.

- Wages comprise a fixed sum of £2,000 per month plus a variable element equal to 10% of sales; these are payable in the month they are incurred.

- Fixed costs amount to £7,500 per month, payable one month in arrears, of which £1,500 is depreciation.

- XYZ Ltd has capital expenditure/receipts scheduled as follows:

Acquisitions:

	£
September	15,000
November	10,000
February	4,000

Disposal:

October	8,000

- Corporation tax, payable in November, amounts to £44,000.

- The bank balance on 1 September 20X1 is expected to be £5,000.

Task

Prepare a cash flow forecast for XYZ Ltd for EACH of the six months from September 20X1 to February 20X2, using a row and column format.

Workbook Activity 10

Prepare a cash forecast for May from the following budget data

Budget data	March £	April £	May £	June £	Cash forecast	May £
Invoiced sales	2,500	3,000	2,800	4,000	Opening Cash balance	(500)
Purchases	900	1,300	1,250	1,200	Customer receipts	
Wages	500	510	520	480		
Other overheads	600	660	620	630	**Payments**	
Capital expenditure	–	1,200	–	–	For purchases	
					For wages	
Average terms					For overheads	
					For capital expenditure	

Half of customers take 1 month to pay. Half take 2 months.

Purchases paid for after 2 months

Wages paid in the current month

Other overheads paid after one month

Capital expenditure paid in the current month

Total	
Closing cash balance	

Workbook Activity 11

You are required to complete the working schedules and Operating Budget below. In the Exam, the shaded cells will be completed for you.

Working schedules

Materials

	Kg	£
Opening stock	2,100	2,000
Purchases	15,500	27,125
Sub-total	17,600	29,125
Used		
Closing stock	1,200	

Closing stock to be valued at budgeted purchase price

Labour

	Hours	£
Basic time at £12 per hour		
Overtime		
Total		

It takes 4 minutes to make each item
8 staff work 200 basic hours each

Overtime is paid at time and a half (50% above basic rate)

Overhead

	Hours	£
Variable at £1.50 per hour		
Fixed		3,500
Total		

Variable overhead recovered on total labour hours

Operating budgets

		Units	£
Sales revenue at	£2.50 each	29,000	
Opening stock of finished goods		4,000	7000
Cost of production		30,000	
Materials			
Labour			
Overhead			
Total			
Closing stock of finished goods *valued at budgeted production cost per unit*		5000	
Cost of goods sold			
Gross Profit			

Overheads

	£
Administration	2,780
Marketing	2,500
Total	5,280
Operating profit	

Budgetary control – flexing budgets 4

Introduction

This chapter is, first of all, concerned with the classification of costs by behaviour. Much of the information here has been met in previous units so should be considered to be revision of relevant areas.

Some costs change when activity levels change, whilst others do not. The ability to isolate cost elements by behaviour is essential to management who are concerned with predicting future costs as part of the planning and decision making processes. It will also be necessary to enable a marginal costing approach to be taken, as covered in the next chapter.

In order to be able to compare actual figures to budgeted figures to give a meaningful analysis, a flexible or flexed budget must be prepared. This will lead to budget variances and the broad principles are similar to those already studied in the chapters on variance analysis.

A further important aspect of budgeting that appears in examinations is the effect of the budgeting process and the final budget on the motivation of managers and employees.

KNOWLEDGE	CONTENTS
• Justify the uses of budgetary control for planning, co-ordinating, authorising and cost control (Element 2.2)	1 Cost centres
	2 Cost classification
	3 Cost behaviour
• Explain the relationship between budgetary control, product lifecycles, and forecasts and planning (Element 2.4)	4 Cost estimation
	5 The high/low method
	6 Flexing budgets
• Recognise expenses as different types of cost (Element 3.4)	7 Flexible budgets

SKILLS

- Calculate the effect that variations in capacity on costs, production and sales will have on budgeted costs and revenues. (Element 2.1)
- Prepare an accurately flexed budget (Element 2.2)
- Check and reconcile budget figures on an ongoing basis (Element 3.2)

- Inform management of any significant issues arising from budgetary control (Element 3.6)

1 Cost centres

Definition

A cost centre is a location, function or item(s) of equipment in respect of which costs may be accumulated and related to cost units for control purposes.

A cost centre therefore is used as an initial collection point for costs; once the total cost of operating the cost centre for a period has been ascertained, it can be related to the cost units that have passed through the cost centre.

The location, function or item of equipment referred to in the definition can be directly related to production, to a service department or to a business.

1.1 Examples of cost centres

Production	Assembly line
	Packing machine
Service department	Stores
	Canteen
	Quality control
Service	Tax department (accountants)
	Ward (hospital)
	Faculty (college)

1.2 Responsibility for cost centres

Control can only be exercised by people, and for every cost somebody must be responsible; so whether a cost centre is impersonal or personal there must always be a manager in whose sphere of responsibility that cost centre is included.

1.3 Profit centres

 Definition

A profit centre is a location, function or item(s) of equipment in respect of which costs and revenues may be ascertained for the purposes of control of the resulting profit.

Thus, while the paint shop in a factory might be treated as a cost centre (to monitor the costs incurred there), a large company might treat its French operations as a profit centre (since they generate both costs and revenues).

2 Cost classification

2.1 Types of cost classification

Costs can be classified (collected into logical groups) in many ways. The particular classification selected will depend upon the purpose for which the resulting analysed data will be used.

Purpose	Classification
Cost control	By nature – materials, labour, overheads, etc.
Cost accounts	By relationship to cost units – direct/ indirect costs, etc.
Budgeting, contribution analysis	By behaviour – fixed/variable costs.
Decision-making	Relevant and non-relevant costs.
Responsibility accounting	Controllable and uncontrollable costs.

You will come across these classifications in more detail as you work through this study text. At this stage, we will revise the basic classification terms used in cost accounting.

2.2 Direct and indirect costs

For cost accounting purposes, the costs of the business will be classified in quite a different way from the analysis required by a financial accountant for the profit and loss account in published accounts.

The basic classification of costs in cost accounting may be illustrated as follows.

Example

	£	£
Direct costs		
Direct materials		250,000
Direct labour		120,000
Direct expenses		10,000
		———
Prime cost (= total of direct costs)		380,000
Indirect production costs		25,000
		———
Production cost		405,000
Indirect non-production costs		
Administration overhead	20,000	
Selling and distribution overhead	25,000	
	———	
		45,000
		———
Total cost		450,000
		———

2.3 Direct costs

Definition

Direct costs are costs which can be related directly to one cost unit. Direct costs comprise direct materials, direct labour and direct expenses.

For example, considering a cost unit of a chair, direct costs will include the cost of wood and screws used (direct material cost) and the cost of manufacturing labour hours per chair (direct labour cost).

In a service context, the direct costs relating to, say, a student enrolled at a college would include the costs of books provided, individual tuition and marking costs.

2.4 Indirect costs

 Definition

Indirect costs cannot be identified directly with a cost unit and are often referred to as *overheads.*

For stock valuation purposes a distinction needs to be made between overheads incurred in the production process (factory costs, e.g. factory rent and rates, power etc) and non-production costs.

Non-production costs are indirect costs involved in converting finished goods into revenue, comprising:

(a)   administrative overhead costs (e.g. executive salaries and office costs); and

(b)   marketing, selling and distribution overhead costs.

Non-production costs are not included in stock valuation since they are not costs of making a product, but costs of selling it. Stock on hand at the end of a period is valued at total production cost only, including production overheads (in a total absorption costing system).We shall return to this point in the next chapter.

Considering the cost unit of a chair, the salaries of the sales representatives who promote and sell the chairs to retail outlets would be a selling overhead.

Indirect costs associated with a college would include premises running costs, lecturers' salaries and administrative staff costs.

Overhead costs can always be identified with cost centres; and because cost centres are the responsibility of particular functional managers one will find overheads classified according to the main functional divisions of the business.

3 Cost behaviour

3.1 The nature of costs

We mentioned earlier the need for cost classification by behaviour for budgeting purposes. In order to make predictions of future cost levels, we must determine the basis of the charge.

As an example, consider the cost of direct materials expected next month. The charge would depend on the amount used and the cost per unit. The amount used would depend, in turn, on the production anticipated for the period.

In order to derive this cost therefore we must make an estimate such as the following:

(a)	Production levels	10,000 units
(b)	Usage of materials per unit:	
	Material A	2 kg
	Material B	1 kg
	Material C	0.2 kg
(c)	Costs of materials:	
	Material A	30 pence per kg
	Material B	25 pence per kg
	Material C	50 pence per kg

Estimate of next month's material cost

		£
Material A	20,000 kg @ 30p/kg	6,000
Material B	10,000 kg @ 25p/kg	2,500
Material C	2,000 kg @ 50p/kg	1,000
		———
Total estimated material cost		9,500
		———

3.2 Variable costs

What have we done? We have set up a simple mathematical model which will, for any level of production, usage and cost of materials, enable the total level of cost in a future period to be predicted. The direct materials example was perhaps the easiest to use and, in practice, we may wish to deal with other variables which affect the cost such as wastage rates thus producing a slightly more complex model.

Direct labour costs may tend to vary due to changes in productivity and other factors in addition to the more obvious variables such as grade and rate of payment. A certain amount of estimation will still be required; if payment is on a production related basis we would expect a cost which, like materials, will vary in line with the volume of production.

At this stage, therefore, we have come to the rule-of-thumb guide that direct material, labour and expenses will probably vary roughly in line with anticipated production levels or the level of activity. We call such costs **variable** costs.

3.3 Fixed costs

This will not be the case with all costs. If we take the cost of rent and rates, for example, the charge is not determined on the basis of the intensity of usage of the premises but rather on the basis of time. Costs that are unaffected by the volume of production are called **fixed costs**. Rent and rates are an example. Labour paid on a time basis would also fall under this heading. How then can we predict the cost of such expenses for next month? Well, there is no difficulty in doing this as all we have to do is consult our rental agreement and the rates notice and we can forecast with complete certainty what these costs will be for the month.

3.4 Classification of costs by behaviour

The above example illustrates the need for cost behaviour classification. For cost prediction purposes, we must make a distinction between costs which vary with production or activity levels (variable costs) and those which do not (fixed costs). There also exists a type of cost which moves in sympathy with production levels but contains an element which does not, such as an electricity charge which contains a minimum standing charge plus an element which relates to the usage of the period. Such a cost would be described as semi-variable or mixed.

 Definition

Variable costs are those that vary (usually assumed in direct proportion) with changes in level of activity of the cost centre to which they relate (e.g. output volume), for example the raw material used in a product. It should be noted that the variable cost per unit may not remain constant over a wide range. It may be possible, for example, to obtain discounts for large purchases of material, reducing the cost per unit.

Fixed costs are those that accrue with the passage of time and are not affected by changes in activity level; they are therefore also known as period costs, for example rent of premises.

Stepped costs are fixed over a range of output and then suddenly increase in one big jump, for example a staffing level of up to 20 people may only require one supervisor but, if the staff level is more than 20, an extra supervisor will be needed.

Semi-variable (mixed) costs contain both a fixed and a variable element. When output is nil, the fixed element is incurred, but they also increase, like variable costs, as output increases. An example is telephone charges where there is a fixed rental to which is added the charge for calls made. These are also sometimes known as semi-fixed costs.

3.5 Graphical illustrations

Various cost behaviour patterns are illustrated in the graphs below.

(a) **Variable cost:** direct materials, the purchase price per unit being constant

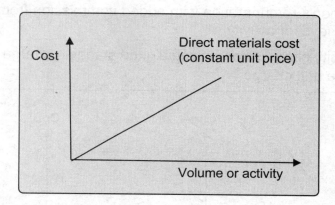

(b) **Fixed cost:** rent of factory payable under a long-term lease

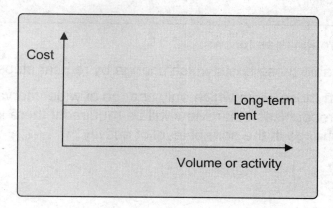

(c) **Stepped costs**

    (i)   Canteen cost where additional assistants are required as increases in activity result in larger numbers of factory personnel

    (ii)   Rent of premises, additional accommodation eventually being required

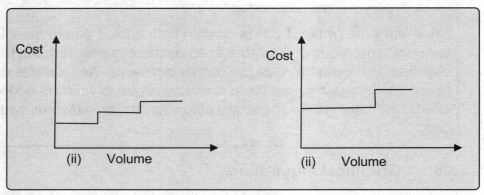

(d) **Semi-variable costs**

    (i)   Direct materials cost (trade discount at higher levels of activity)

    (ii)   Salesmen's remuneration with added commission from a certain level of activity

    (iii) Electricity charges comprising a fixed standing charge and variable unit charge

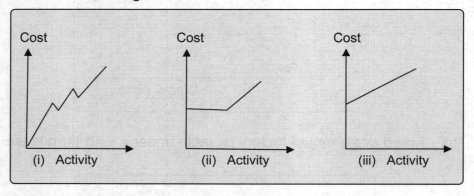

The common approach is as follows:

(a)   Treat as variable those costs which change by regular steps.

(b)   Treat as fixed those costs which only change at wide intervals of activity; this recognises that review will be required if there is a permanent change in the normal level of activity.

4 Cost estimation

4.1 Introduction

As we have seen, some costs may have both fixed and variable elements. These will need to be identified for budgeting purposes.

If it is not easy to do this directly (as it is in the case of the telephone cost, where the bill clearly shows the fixed charge and rate per unit), then an analysis of past cost and volume data will need to be carried out. 7.2 Methods of cost estimation It is assumed that there is a linear relationship, i.e.:

Total cost = Fixed cost + (Variable cost per unit × Units produced)

and that the total fixed cost and the variable cost per unit are constant at all levels of production unless told otherwise.

Possible techniques include the high/low method and linear regression.

5 The high/low method

5.1 Introduction

This is a simple method of estimating future costs from past results. It takes the costs for the highest and lowest activity levels, and assumes that a linear relationship covers the range in between.

 Example

Widgets are produced by a process that incurs both fixed and variable costs.

Total costs have been recorded for the process for each of the last six months as follows.

Month	Output (units)	Total cost £
1	4,500	33,750
2	3,500	30,500
3	5,100	34,130
4	6,200	38,600
5	5,700	38,000
6	4,100	31,900

(a) What is the estimated fixed cost element and estimated variable cost per unit?

(b) What would be the estimated total cost at the budgeted activity level for month 7 of 6,000 units?

Solution

Select the months with the highest and lowest output levels as follows.

	Output (units)	Total cost £
Lowest output	3,500	30,500
Highest output	6,200	38,600
Increase	2,700	8,100

For an increase of 2,700 units, cost has increased by £8,100. If we assume that the fixed cost element remains constant, this cost increase must represent a change in variable costs only.

Assuming a straight-line relationship, then the variable cost per unit =

$$\frac{£8,100}{2,700} = £3 \text{ per unit}$$

Note that the factor determining which values to choose is the total cost at the highest output level and the total cost at the lowest output level. These are not necessarily the highest and lowest costs. The high/low observations are always based on the independent variable (in this case, output).

We can now substitute back into either of the two output levels to obtain the fixed cost.

At the 3,500 units level:

	£
Total cost	30,500
Variable cost (3,500 × £3)	(10,500)
Fixed costs	20,000

As a check on the accuracy of the calculations, at the 6,200 units level:

	£
Total costs	38,600
Variable cost (6,200 × £3)	(18,600)
Fixed costs	20,000

(a) Therefore the estimated fixed cost element is £20,000 and the estimated variable cost is £3 per unit.

(b) At an output level of 6,000 units the total estimated cost would be:

	£
Variable cost (6,000 × £3)	18,000
Fixed cost	20,000
Total cost	38,000

5.2 Advantages of high-low method

- Simple to operate.

- Easy to understand.

5.3 Disadvantages of high-low method

The problem with the high-low method is that it could give a completely inaccurate result. This is because we are only considering two sets of data, and ignoring all of the others.

It is possible that the points we have chosen are completely unrepresentative of the rest of the data. This is a distinct possibility since we have chosen the two points at the extreme ends of the activity range.

At these levels it is more likely that operating conditions will be atypical compared with more normal output. One way around this problem is to choose the 'next to highest' and 'next to lowest' figures, but this destroys some of the simplicity of the model.

6 Flexing budgets

6.1 Variable and fixed costs

In connection with expense budgeting, the budget working sheets should include some indication of the 'basis of variability' of each item of cost.

The most common general bases of variability of costs are in line with sales or the volume of productive output. In some systems of budgetary control, therefore, costs are divided between those which tend to vary with the output or sales achieved, and those which tend to remain fixed regardless of sales or the volume of output over an expected range of volumes.

6.2 Flexed budgets

This distinction having been established then, for variable costs, it is possible to establish in any period an allowable level of cost appropriate to the output actually achieved. This new level is known as the budget allowance for that volume of output. This is also known as a flexed budget. The total variance from the original budget figure will then be divided into two parts:

- The difference between the original budget and the budget allowance, assumed to arise from the nature of the business. This is sometimes referred to as an 'activity variance' and may be excluded from sectional control reports.

- The difference between the budget allowance and the actual cost incurred. This, by definition, should not have occurred and might be thought of as the 'controllable variance' of the manager concerned.

A system incorporating budget allowances is referred to as flexible budgetary control.

This idea has been seized on by writers of textbooks and setters of examination questions and converted into the concept of 'flexible budgets'; in other words, at the beginning of the year there should be a schedule showing what the various cost allowances would be at various levels of output. With spreadsheet packages being used to assist budgeting, it is now becoming more common in practice.

Example

You are the budget officer of Majestic Limited, which produces a single product. The following forecasts have been prepared from the best information available for the production costs to be incurred at the highest and lowest production levels likely to be encountered in any particular period.

	Production level	
	10,000 *units*	20,000 *units*
	£	£
Direct materials	2,000	4,000
Direct labour	15,000	30,000
Warehouse rental	8,000	13,000
Machine maintenance	2,400	3,000
Factory rent, rates, etc	4,000	4,000
Factory power	4,500	6,300

Machine maintenance is under contract with the machine supplier. The period cost is based upon the production level and is charged at £15 per 100 units, with a minimum charge payable of £2,400 per period.

Warehouse rent is fixed per warehouse per period. One warehouse is sufficient to cope with the storage demands up to 12,500 units. Should production exceed this level, a further warehouse will need to be rented for the period, at an additional cost of £5,000. This will give sufficient space to cover the highest production level.

All other variable costs and the variable part of semi-variable costs follow constant linear patterns.

Required:

Prepare a set of flexible budgets which show the budget allowance for the period for the following activity levels: 10,000 units; 12,500 units; 15,000 units; 17,500 units; 20,000 units.

Solution

The following steps illustrate a good approach to such a question. You may like to try preparing your own answer as we go through before looking at our solution at the end.

1   **Draw up a proforma statement**

    This will have the cost headings listed down the left-hand side and columns headed up with each production level; in this case, five columns will be needed. It is also a good idea to have an additional column next to the cost headings in which to insert references to workings (e.g. 'Note 2' etc).

    The statement should also have a heading.

2   **Insert known figures**

    You have already been given the costs for the lowest and highest production levels, so put these in.

3   **Deal with the particular costs you have further information about (in this case, machine maintenance and warehouse rental)**

    Machine maintenance

    This cost will be fixed up to a certain production level (to cover the minimum charge) and will then rise linearly (at £15 per 100 units or £0.15 per unit).

The level up to which the minimum charge is applicable is £2,400/£0.15 = 16,000 units. So the charge for the 12,500 and 15,000 unit levels will also be £2,400.

For 17,500 units the charge will be 17,500 × £0.15 = £2,625 and for 20,000 units it will reach 20,000 × £0.15 = £3,000 (as given).

These can now be inserted in your statement.

Warehouse rental

This is an example of a 'stepped' fixed cost. It will remain at £8,000 for all levels up to (and including) 12,500 units, and will rise to £13,000 for all levels above this.

These can now be inserted in your statement.

4   Deal with remaining costs

These will be strictly fixed, strictly variable or semi-variable.

Strictly fixed costs

These will be obvious – here, factory rent and rates must be fixed within the range, as the costs for the lowest and highest production levels are the same.

Insert this fixed cost across all levels on your statement.

Strictly variable costs

Usually direct materials and direct labour costs will be strictly variable. You can see here that, as the production level doubles, so does the cost. Use either level to determine the cost per unit.

Direct materials: £2,000/10,000   =   £0.20 per unit

Direct labour: £15,000/10,000   =   £1.50 per unit

Use these to calculate the appropriate cost for the other levels and insert them on the statement.

Semi-variable costs

These costs will not be the same for the two extreme levels, but they will not increase proportionately from one to the other either. If you are not sure, calculate a cost per unit at the two levels; these will not be the same, as they would be if the cost were strictly variable.

In this example, the power cost is semi-variable. It can be split between the fixed and variable elements by the 'high-low' method which we saw in Chapter 2.

	Production level (units)	Cost £
Highest	20,000	6,300
Lowest	10,000	4,500
Change	+10,000	+1,800

Variable cost = £1,800/10,000 = £0.18 per unit

Using the lowest level to determine the fixed cost element:

	£
Total cost	4,500
Less: Variable element (10,000 × £0.18)	(1,800)
Fixed element	2,700

So for each level, the total power cost can be calculated as follows.

£2,700 + £0.18 × Production level

For example, the cost for 15,000 units will be as follows.

£2,700 + £0.18 × 15,000 = £5,400

The remaining costs can be calculated in this way and the statement completed, as below.

	Production level				
	10,000 units £	12,500 units £	15,000 units £	17,500 units £	20,000 units £
Direct materials	2,000	2,500	3,000	3,500	4,000
Direct labour	15,000	18,750	22,500	26,250	30,000
Warehouse rental	8,000	8,000	13,000	13,000	13,000
Machine maintenance	2,400	2,400	2,400	2,625	3,000
Factory rent, rates	4,000	4,000	4,000	4,000	4,000
Factory power	4,500	4,950	5,400	5,850	6,300
Total	35,900	40,600	50,300	55,225	60,300

6.3 Budgetary control statement

A typical continuation to the above example would be the requirement to produce a budgetary control statement (or budget report) given some actual data for the period.

Example

In period 3 Majestic Limited produced 17,500 units and incurred the following costs.

	£
Direct materials	3,200
Direct labour	29,750
Warehouse rental	13,000
Machine maintenance	3,150
Factory rent, rates, etc	3,800
Factory power	4,720

Produce a budgetary control statement to compare these actual costs with the flexed costs that would be budgeted for.

Solution

The budgetary control statement will compare the actual costs with the relevant budget allowances from the flexible budget to highlight variances.

In this case, the relevant flexed budget is that for 17,500 units.

We have also included the original budget (for 20,000 units). This is good practice, as it is probable that a lot of managers who see the budgetary control statement will have had access to the original budget. If they don't see those figures on the statement, they will think they were given the wrong information before, or else they will think they are being given the wrong information now!

	20,000 units original budget (£)	17,500 units flexed budget (£)	17,500 units actual (£)	Flexed to actual variance (£)
Direct materials	4,000	3,500	3,200	300 F
Direct labour	30,000	26,250	29,750	3,500 A
Warehouse rental	13,000	13,000	13,000	–
Machine maintenance	3,000	2,625	3,150	525 A
Factory rent, rates, etc	4,000	4,000	3,800	200 F
Factory power	6,300	5,850	4,720	1,130 F
	60,300	55,225	57,620	2,395 A

You may then be asked to comment on the variances, suggesting any further investigations or action that might be required.

Note that if the actual costs for output of 17,500 units were compared to the original budget of 20,000 units of output, the resulting variances would be meaningless.

7 Flexible budgets

A system incorporating budget allowances is referred to as flexible budgetary control.

This idea has been seized on by writers of textbooks and setters of examination questions and converted into the concept of 'flexible budgets'; in other words, at the beginning of the year there should be a schedule showing what the various cost allowances would be at various levels of output. With spreadsheet packages being used to assist budgeting, it is now becoming more common in practice.

Example

You are the budget officer of Majestic Limited, which produces a single product. The following forecasts have been prepared from the best information available for the production costs to be incurred at the highest and lowest production levels likely to be encountered in any particular period.

	Production level	
	10,000 *units*	20,000 *units*
	£	£
Direct materials	2,000	4,000
Direct labour	15,000	30,000
Warehouse rental	8,000	13,000
Machine maintenance	2,400	3,000
Factory rent, rates, etc	4,000	4,000
Factory power	4,500	6,300

Machine maintenance is under contract with the machine supplier. The period cost is based upon the production level and is charged at £15 per 100 units, with a minimum charge payable of £2,400 per period.

Warehouse rent is fixed per warehouse per period. One warehouse is sufficient to cope with the storage demands up to 12,500 units. Should production exceed this level, a further warehouse will need to be rented for the period, at an additional cost of £5,000. This will give sufficient space to cover the highest production level.

All other variable costs and the variable part of semi-variable costs follow constant linear patterns.

Required:

Prepare a set of flexible budgets which show the budget allowance for the period for the following activity levels: 10,000 units;12,500 units;15,000 units; 17,500 units; 20,000 units.

Solution

The following steps illustrate a good approach to such a question. You may like to try preparing your own answer as we go through before looking at our solution at the end.

1   **Draw up a proforma statement**

This will have the cost headings listed down the left-hand side and columns headed up with each production level; in this case, five columns will be needed. It is also a good idea to have an additional column next to the cost headings in which to insert references to workings (e.g. 'Note 2' etc).

The statement should also have a heading.

2 Insert known figures

You have already been given the costs for the lowest and highest production levels, so put these in.

3 Deal with the particular costs you have further information about (in this case, machine maintenance and warehouse rental)

Machine maintenance

This cost will be fixed up to a certain production level (to cover the minimum charge) and will then rise linearly (at £15 per 100 units or £0.15 per unit).

The level up to which the minimum charge is applicable is £2,400/£0.15 = 16,000 units. So the charge for the 12,500 and 15,000 unit levels will also be £2,400.

For 17,500 units the charge will be 17,500 × £0.15 = £2,625 and for 20,000 units it will reach 20,000 × £0.15 = £3,000 (as given).

These can now be inserted in your statement.

Warehouse rental

This is an example of a 'stepped' fixed cost. It will remain at £8,000 for all levels up to (and including) 12,500 units, and will rise to £13,000 for all levels above this.

These can now be inserted in your statement.

4 Deal with remaining costs

These will be strictly fixed, strictly variable or semi-variable.

Strictly fixed costs

These will be obvious – here, factory rent and rates must be fixed within the range, as the costs for the lowest and highest production levels are the same.

Insert this fixed cost across all levels on your statement.

Strictly variable costs

Usually direct materials and direct labour costs will be strictly variable. You can see here that, as the production level doubles, so does the cost. Use either level to determine the cost per unit.

Direct materials: £2,000/10,000　　=　　£0.20 per unit

Direct labour: £15,000/10,000　　=　　£1.50 per unit

Use these to calculate the appropriate cost for the other levels and insert them on the statement.

Semi-variable costs

These costs will not be the same for the two extreme levels, but they will not increase proportionately from one to the other either. If you are not sure, calculate a cost per unit at the two levels; these will not be the same, as they would be if the cost were strictly variable.

In this example, the power cost is semi-variable. It can be split between the fixed and variable elements by the 'high-low' method which we saw in a previous chapter.

	Production level (units)	Cost £
Highest	20,000	6,300
Lowest	10,000	4,500
Change	+10,000	+1,800

Variable cost = £1,800/10,000 = £0.18 per unit

Using the lowest level to determine the fixed cost element:

	£
Total cost	4,500
Less: Variable element (10,000 × £0.18)	(1,800)
Fixed element	2,700

So for each level, the total power cost can be calculated as follows.

£2,700 + £0.18 × Production level

For example, the cost for 15,000 units will be as follows.

£2,700 + £0.18 × 15,000 = £5,400

The remaining costs can be calculated in this way and the statement completed, as below.

	Production level				
	10,000 units	12,500 units	15,000 units	17,500 units	20,000 units
	£	£	£	£	£
Direct materials	2,000	2,500	3,000	3,500	4,000
Direct labour	15,000	18,750	22,500	26,250	30,000
Warehouse rental	8,000	8,000	13,000	13,000	13,000
Machine maintenance	2,400	2,400	2,400	2,625	3,000
Factory rent, rates	4,000	4,000	4,000	4,000	4,000
Factory power	4,500	4,950	5,400	5,850	6,300
Total	35,900	40,600	50,300	55,225	60,300

8 Summary

Much of cost accounting is about gathering information about current costs and making predictions about future costs. Some costs, direct costs, can be allocated directly to a cost unit whereas other costs, indirect costs or overheads, are allocated initially to a cost centre.

Costs can also be usefully classified according to their behaviour. This is particularly useful when budgeting costs for future periods or for making decisions about activity levels. Costs can be classified as variable, fixed, stepped or semi-variable.

For semi-variable costs the fixed element and the variable element will need to be identified for forecasting purposes. This can be done using the high/low method.

9 Test your knowledge

 Workbook Activity 1

You have recently been appointed as the management accountant of Parkside Manufacturing Ltd. Parkside Manufacturing makes a single product, the Delta. The previous management accountant has already prepared an analysis of budgeted and actual results for the year to 30 November 2000. These are reproduced below.

Parkside Manufacturing Ltd
Operating statement for year ended 30 November 2000

Volume (number of Deltas)	Budget 100,000		Actual 125,000		Variance
	£000	£000	£000	£000	£000
Turnover		2,000		2,250	250 (F)
Material	600		800		200 (A)
Light, heat and power	200		265		65 (A)
Production labour	120		156		36 (A)
Rent, rates and depreciation	140		175		35 (A)
Administrative expenses	110		110		Nil
		1,170		1,506	
Profit		830		744	86 (A)

Key: (F) = favourable
(A) = adverse

Judith Green, the production director, tells you that the following assumptions were made when the budget was originally prepared:

- Material is entirely a variable cost.

- Light, heat and power is a semi-variable cost. The fixed element included in the budgeted figure was £40,000.

- Production labour is a stepped cost. Each production employee can make up to 10,000 Deltas. Each production employee was budgeted to receive a basic wage of £12,000 per year with no overtime and no bonuses.

- There are no part-time employees.

- Rent, rates and depreciation, and administrative expenses are fixed costs.

Required:

(a) In preparation for the next Board meeting of Parkside Manufacturing Ltd, calculate the:

   (i) budgeted cost of material per Delta;

   (ii) budgeted variable cost per Delta of light, heat and power; (iii) number of production employees assumed in the budget.

(b) Prepare a statement which compares the actual results of Parkside Manufacturing with the flexed budget and identify any variances.

Data

On receiving your flexible budget and variances, Judith Green tells you that:

- She does not understand why there is a need for the two types of budget, the one prepared by the previous management accountant and the flexed budget prepared by yourself.

- She does not know if it is necessary to investigate all variances.

- She is concerned that the original budgeted sales volume was so different from the actual sales volume and is considering the use of linear regression to improve sales forecasting of Deltas.

Required:

Judith Green asks you to write a brief report in preparation for the Board meeting. In your report you should:

(a) Briefly explain the different purposes of the two types of budget and explain which one should be used to compare with the actual results.

(b) Suggest THREE general factors that need to be taken into account in deciding whether or not to investigate variances.

(c) Briefly explain THREE limitations to the use of linear regression in sales forecasting.

Workbook Activity 2

Visiguard Ltd is a division of Alton Products plc. It makes a single product, the Raider. Just over a year ago, the chief executive of Alton Products, Mike Green, was concerned to find that Visiguard was budgeting to make only £20,000 profit in the year to 31 May 2000. As a result, he imposed his own budget on the division. His revised budget assumed:

- increased sales volume of the Raider;

- increased selling prices; and

- that suppliers would agree to reduce the cost of the material used in the Raider by 10%.

The only other changes to the original budget arose solely as a result of the increased volume in the revised budget.

The original budget and the revised budget imposed by Mike Green are reproduced below, together with the actual results for the year to 31 May 2000.

Visiguard Limited
Budgeted and actual operating statements for one year ended
31 May 2000

	Original budget	Revised budget	Actual results
	£	£	£
Sales and production volume	10,000	11,000	11,600
	£	£	£
Turnover	1,400,000	1,760,000	1,844,400
Variable materials	400,000	396,000	440,800
Production and administrative labour	580,000	630,000	677,600
Light, heat and power	160,000	164,000	136,400
Fixed overheads	240,000	240,000	259,600
Budgeted profit	20,000	330,000	330,000

Required:

Using the information provided in the two budgets, calculate the following:

(a)   The unit selling price of the Raider in the revised budget.

(b)   The material cost per Raider in the revised budget.

(c)   The variable cost of production and administrative labour per Raider.

(d)   The fixed cost of production and administrative labour.

(e)   The variable cost of light, heat and power per Raider.

(f)   The fixed cost of light, heat and power.

Data

On receiving the actual results for the year, Mike Green states that they prove that his revised budget motivated managers to produce better results.

Required:

Write a memo to Mike Green. Your memo should:

(a)   Use the information calculated before to prepare a flexed budget statement for Visiguard including any variances.

(b)   Identify TWO situations where an imposed budget might be preferable to one prepared with the participation of managers.

(c)   Briefly discuss whether or not his requirement that material costs be reduced would have motivated the managers of Visiguard.

(d)   Identify TWO ways in which profit could have increased without additional effort by the managers of Visiguard.

Workbook Activity 3

Rivermede Ltd makes a single product called the Fasta. Last year, Steven Jones, the managing director of Rivermede Ltd, attended a course on budgetary control. As a result, he agreed to revise the way budgets were prepared in the company. Rather than imposing targets for managers, he encouraged participation by senior managers in the preparation of budgets.

An initial budget was prepared but Mike Fisher, the sales director, felt that the budgeted sales volume was set too high. He explained that setting too high a budgeted sales volume would mean his sales staff would be demotivated because they would not be able to achieve that sales volume. Steven Jones agreed to use the revised sales volume suggested by Mike Fisher.

Both the initial and revised budgets are reproduced below complete with the actual results for the year ended 31 May 1999.

Rivermede Ltd – Budgeted and actual costs for the year ended 31 May 1999

	Original budget	Revised budget	Actual results	Variances from revised budget
Fasta production and sales (units)	24,000	20,000	22,000	2,000 (F)
	£	£	£	£
Variable costs				
Material	216,000	180,000	206,800	26,800 (A)
Labour	288,000	240,000	255,200	15,200 (A)
Semi-variable costs				
Heat, light and power	31,000	27,000	33,400	6,400 (A)
Fixed costs				
Rent, rates and depreciation	40,000	40,000	38,000	2,000 (F)
	575,000	487,000	533,400	46,400 (A)

Assumptions in the two budgets

1 No change in input prices.

2 No change in the quantity of variable inputs per Fasta.

As the management accountant at Rivermede Ltd, one of your tasks is to check that invoices have been properly coded. On checking the actual invoices for heat, light and power for the year to 31 May 1999, you find that one invoice for £7,520 had been incorrectly coded. The invoice should have been coded to materials.

Required:

(a) Using the information in the original and revised budgets, identify:

- the variable cost of material and labour per Fasta;

- the fixed and unit variable cost within heat, light and power.

(b) Prepare a flexed budget, including variances, for Rivermede Ltd after correcting for the miscoding of the invoice.

Data

On receiving your flexed budget statement, Steven Jones states that the total adverse variance is much less than the £46,400 shown in the original statement. He also draws your attention to the actual sales volume being greater than in the revised budget. He believes these results show that a participative approach to budgeting is better for the company and wants to discuss this belief at the next board meeting. Before doing so, Steven Jones asks for your comments.

Required:

Write a memo to Steven Jones. Your memo should:

(a) *Briefly* explain why the flexed budgeting variances differ from those in the original statement given.

(b) Give TWO reasons why a favourable cost variance may have arisen other than through the introduction of participative budgeting.

(c) Give TWO reasons why the actual sales volume compared with the revised budget's sales volume may not be a measure of improved motivation following the introduction of participative budgeting.

Workbook Activity 4

You are an accounting technician employed by Telford plc. Telford has a subsidiary, Shifnal Ltd that makes one product, the Omega. Barry Jones, the Finance Director of Telford, has asked you to prepare a statement analysing the performance of Shifnal Ltd. He gives you a copy of the company's latest operating statement and tells you the assumptions made about costs when preparing the statement.

Shifnal Ltd: operating statement – 12 months ended 30 November 2003

	Budget	Actual
Number of Omegas produced and sold	120,000	95,000
	£000	£000
Turnover	4,800	3,990
Variable expenses		
Material A	480	456
Material B	840	665
Material C	360	266
Semi-variable expenses		
Light, heat and power	290	249
Water	212	182
Stepped expenses		
Labour	200	168
Maintenance	60	54
Fixed expenses		
Rent and rates	360	355
Distribution expenses	600	620
Administrative expenses	300	280
Operating profit	1,098	695

Assumptions made

- Budgeted semi-variable expenses

  - The variable cost of light, heat and power was £2.00 per Omega.

  - The fixed cost of water was £20,000 per year.

- Budgeted stepped expenses

  - For every £5,000 spent on labour, Shifnal could produce up to 3,000 Omegas.

  - For every £10,000 spent on maintenance, Shifnal could produce up to 20,000 Omegas.

- The budgeted selling price per Omega was the same throughout the year.

- There were no stocks of any kind.

Required:

(a) Calculate the budgeted selling price per Omega.

(b) Calculate the budgeted variable cost per Omega of:

(c) (i) material A;

    (ii) material B;

    (iii) material C.

(c) Calculate the:

    (i) budgeted fixed cost of light, heat and power;

    (ii) budgeted variable cost of water per Omega.

(d) Prepare a statement showing Shifnal's actual results, the flexible budget and any variances.

Investigating and reporting variances 5

Introduction

In this chapter we shall start by revising the variances we calculated in the previous chapter. We shall then concentrate on the ways in which management uses these variances. This will include investigating the causes of the variances, seeking ways to control the variances and ways in which the variances can be reported.

KNOWLEDGE

- Explain the significance of budget variances (Element 2.5)

- Explain the principles of standard costing (Element 3.1)

SKILLS

- Check and reconcile budget figures on an ongoing basis (Element 3.2)

- Review and revise the validity of budgets in the light of any significant anticipated change (Element 3.3)

- Identify variances between budget and actual income / expenditure (Element 3.4)

- Analyse the variances and explain the impact that this will have on the organisation (Element 3.5)

- Inform management of any significant issues arising from budgetary control (Element 3.6)

- Present any recommendations with a clear rationale to appropriate people (Element 3.7)

CONTENTS

1   Reconciling budgeted and actual performance

2   Measuring the significance of variances

3   Investigation of variances

4   Responsibility accounting and the interdependence of variances

5   Exchange rates and price variances

1 Reconciling budgeted and actual performance

1.1 Introduction

We have seen that standard costs are developed in advance of the period under review. During the course of that period, actual costs are compared with standard costs. Any variances are isolated for investigation as to their cause, enabling corrective action to be taken as soon as possible.

Management will wish to see a clear and succinct summary of the results for the period and in particular will want any unusual or unexpected items to be brought to their attention (exception reporting). In general, this will take the form of a reconciliation between budgeted and actual profits which highlights the variances between them. To be useful as a management tool, the reconciliation should be part of an overall report to management.

 Example

You have already covered in the previous chapter the calculation of basic cost variances.

The following budgeted and actual data for TJB Limited for 20X1 will be used to revise the principles and computations, and lead on to reporting these variances.

TJB Limited – Budgeted profit for the year ending 31 December 20X1

Produce and sell   10,000 units

		Produce and sell 10,000 units	
		£	£
Budgeted sales units	10,000		100,000
Production cost	£/unit		
Direct materials – 10,000 tons @ £1 per ton (1 ton per unit)	1.00	10,000	
Direct labour – 20,000 hours @ 50p per hour (2 hours per unit)	1.00	10,000	
Fixed production overhead – 20,000 hours @ 75p per hour	1.50	15,000	
Total budgeted production cost	3.50	35,000	
Budgeted profit for the period			65,000

During the year to 31 December 20X1, the following actual results were obtained.

TJB Limited – Actual profit for the year ending 31 December 20X1

Production and sales 8,000 units

	£	£
Sales		96,000
Production cost		
Direct materials – 7,750 tons purchased and used (£1.0968 per ton)	8,500	
Direct labour – 16,500 hours paid (£0.4545 per hour)	7,500	
Fixed production overhead incurred	15,500	
Total actual production cost		31,500
Total profit		64,500

The purpose of a cost analysis is to reconcile the budgeted costs of £35,000 to the actual costs of £31,500.

Such a reconciliation is a budgetary control statement or budgetary control report.

Solution

Cost variances

	Flexed budget cost of producing 8,000 units £	Actual cost of producing 8,000 units £	Difference (variance) £	
Direct materials	8,000	8,500	500	A
Direct labour	8,000	7,500	500	F
Fixed production overhead	12,000	15,500	3,500	A
Total	28,000	31,500	3,500	A

All these total variances can be analysed into at least two further types of variance:

(a) a price variance;

(b) a usage or utilisation variance, which in some cases can be broken down further.

Total direct material cost variance

		£
(a)	The actual amount of material used at the actual price	8,500
(b)	The standard amount of material that should have been used for the actual production at the standard price – 8,000 tons × £1	8,000
	Total variance	500 A

To analyse this further we need first to get the actual amount of material used at the standard price: the direct materials price variance.

Direct materials price variance

	Tons	£
Actual materials purchased, at actual price	7,750	8,500
Actual materials purchased, at standard price per ton (£1)	7,750	7,750
Materials price variance	–	750 A

We next need to compare this with the standard materials that should have been used for that level of production: the direct materials usage variance.

Direct materials usage variance

	Tons	£
Actual materials used at standard price	7,750	7,750
Standard materials allowed for production achieved at standard price	8,000	8,000
Materials usage variance (@ £1 per ton)	250	250 F

Total direct material cost variance = £750 A + £250 F
= £500 A

Total direct labour cost variance

		£
(a)	The actual hours paid at the actual rate per hour	7,500
(b)	The standard time allowed to produce the output, priced at the standard rate per hour (16,000 × £0.50)	8,000
	Total variance	500 F

The total variance can be analysed into rate and efficiency variances as with materials.

Labour rate variance

	Hours	£
Actual hours paid at actual rate per hour	16,500	7,500
Actual hours paid at standard rate per hour (50p/hour)	16,500	8,250
Direct labour rate variance	–	750 F

Total labour efficiency variance

	Hours	£
Actual hours paid at standard rate per hour	16,500	8,250
Standard hours allowed for production achieved at standard rate per hour (50p)	16,000	8,000
Direct labour usage variance		250 A

Total direct labour cost variance = £750 F + £250 A
= £500 F

Total fixed overhead cost variance

	£
Actual fixed overhead cost	15,500
Standard cost absorbed into actual production (8,000 × £1.50 per unit)	12,000
Total fixed overhead cost variance	3,500 A

This is then analysed into price (expenditure) and volume variances. The volume variance is then sub-analysed into usage (efficiency) and capacity variances.

Fixed overhead price variance

	£	
Actual fixed overhead cost	15,500	
Budgeted fixed overhead cost	15,000	
Fixed overhead price variance	500	A

This variance is also known as the fixed overhead expenditure variance.

Fixed overhead volume variance

This is the under-absorption (at standard rates) due to the lower actual production level than that budgeted.

	Units	£	
Actual production	8,000		
Budgeted production	10,000		
Fixed overhead volume variance (in units)	2,000		
Valued at standard absorption rate (£1.50 per unit)		3,000	A

The variance is adverse because we have under-absorbed fixed overhead by 2,000 units' worth. We thus require an extra charge to the cost account to compensate for this under-absorption.

The £3,000 adverse volume variance can be analysed further.

Fixed overhead efficiency variance

	Hours		
Actual hours worked for actual production	16,500		
Standard hours allowed for actual production achieved	16,000		
Efficiency variance @ £0.75 per hour	500	= £375	A

Fixed overhead capacity variance

		Hours	
Actual hours worked		16,500	
Budgeted hours for the period		20,000	
		——————	
Capacity variance @ £0.75 per hour		3,500 = £2,625	A
		——————	

The two variances add up to the volume variance (£375 + £2,625 = £3,000 adverse), and shows that the principal reason for our under-production was a failure to devote sufficient hours to production (3,500 hours short).

Having computed all the variances, we can now reconcile budgeted costs with actual costs.

		Adverse	Favourable	
		£	£	£
Total budgeted cost				28,000
Cost variances				
Materials	Price	750		
	Usage		250	
Labour	Rate		750	
	Efficiency	250		
Fixed overheads	Expenditure	500		
	Usage	375		
	Capacity	2,625		
		——————	——————	
Total/net cost variances		4,500	1,000	3,500
				——————
Total actual cost				31,500
				——————

1.2 Marginal costing

The previous example of TJB Limited was based upon total absorption costing as the fixed production overhead was absorbed into the standard cost of the product. Under marginal costing the fixed overhead is charged to the profit and loss account as a period cost and is not absorbed into the cost of the product.

For the purpose of variances this means that the only fixed overhead variance that exists is the fixed overhead price or expenditure variance. There is no volume variance.

1.3   Materials price variance and price changes

In some examination tasks you may be given information about specific price indices that have affected the materials prices during the period. In these circumstances it is then possible to split the materials price variance into that element that relates to the price increase and any other cause of the variance.

 Example

The standard material cost for a business' single product is 4 kg at a price of £12.00 per kg. The standard price was set when the index for this material price stood at 120. During August, 10,000 units of the product were made using 42,000 kgs at a total cost of £525,000. The August price index for this material is 122.

What is the total materials price variance, the element relating to the price increase and the element relating to other causes?

Solution

Total materials price variance

		£
Standard cost of actual materials	42,000 × £12.00	504,000
Actual cost		525,000
		———
		21,000 Adverse
		———

This adverse variance of £21,000 can then be split into the element relating to the price increase and the element relating to other factors:

Variance relating to price increase

		£
Standard cost of actual materials	42,000 × £12.00	504,000
Adjusted price for actual materials	42,000 × (£12.00 × 122/120)	512,400
		———
		8,400 Adverse
		———

Variance relating to other factors

		£
Adjusted price for actual materials	42,000 × (£12.00 × 122/120)	512,400
Actual cost		525,000
		———
		12,600 Adverse
		———

2 Measuring the significance of variances

2.1 Introduction

As we have seen, the key tool for management control within a standard costing system is some form of variance analysis report or budgetary control statement. The aim is to prepare a report to management on a routine basis in which variances are clearly identified and can be acted upon as appropriate.

In exercising control, it is generally impracticable to review every variance in detail at each accounting period and attention will usually be concentrated on those variances which have the greatest impact on the achievement of the budget plan.

2.2 Identifying significant variances

One method of identifying significant variances is to express each variance as a percentage of the related budget allowance or standard value. Those showing the highest percentage deviation would then be given the most urgent attention.

This method, however, could result in lack of attention to variances which, although representing a small percentage of the standard value, nevertheless involve significant sums of money. Both percentages and absolute values should be looked at in deciding where the priorities for control actually lie.

In practice, management will review the variance report presented to them and decide which variances should be investigated on the basis of whether the costs of investigation are outweighed by the benefits.

Management will often request a more detailed analysis and explanation of specific variances to be produced as the decision as to whether or not a variance merits investigation may need more information than is provided in the original variance report.

2.3 Fluctuating variances – looking at trends

The variances of a particular period may not be representative of a general trend. Items like stationery costs can fluctuate widely from month to month, dependent on the amount of stationery that has been invoiced.

Sometimes, the accountant will make estimated adjustments to either the budget or the actual figures in an attempt to give a better picture of the underlying trend but this is not a completely satisfactory way of dealing with the matter.

The simplest way of getting the month's figures into context is to show also the accumulated cost for the year to date. High cost and low cost periods will then be revealed but will balance out in the cumulative figures.

A development of the above idea is also to report each period the manager's latest forecast compared with the annual budget. It will then be possible to see whether variances from budget currently being reported are likely to continue to accumulate during the remainder of the year, or whether they will be offset by later opposite variances.

Although this technique of forecasting is dependent on managers' subjective assessments, it is a good way of ensuring that the correct control action gets taken on the current figures.

 Example

You might like to spend a few minutes considering what the report below tells you about the business.

Profit and loss account – Seven periods cumulative to … 20…

	Budget £000	Actual £000	Variances for (A) £000	Budget £000	Actual £000	Variances for (A) £000	Budget £000	Latest forecast £000
Sales	500	600	100	3,500	3,420	(80)	6,000	6,200
Direct cost of sales	280	322	(42)	1,960	1,951	9	3,500	3,850
Factory overhead	58	69	(11)	420	400	20	700	750
Administration and selling costs	122	123	(1)	840	800	40	1,320	1,147
Total costs	460	514	(54)	3,220	3,151	69	5,520	5,747
Operating profit	40	86	46	280	269	(11)	480	453
Profit: Sales %	8	14.3	–	8	7.9	–	8	7.3

Solution

(a) Sales, which had obviously been below budget for the first six periods of the year, are significantly in excess of budget for period 7 (reducing the cumulative shortfall to £80,000), and are now expected to exceed the budget for the year as a whole.

(b) Direct costs are naturally higher when sales are higher. The percentage of direct costs to sales value is not consistent, however, as the following calculations show:

	Budget	Actual
Period 7	56.0%	53.7%
Cumulative to date	56.0%	57.0%
Forecast for whole year	58.3%	62.1%

For the seven periods as a whole, direct costs have been in excess of the budgeted percentage and even though the budget for the twelve months provides for an increase in that percentage the forecast actual increase is still higher. Period 7 in isolation shows an anomalous result, perhaps due to some peculiarity in sales mix.

(c) The variance on factory overhead, which is favourable over the seven periods as a whole, has become adverse in period 7 and is forecast as adverse for the year as a whole (though not at the rate experienced in period 7).Failure to budget adequately for inflationary increases is one possibility.

(d) Administration and selling costs have a cumulative favourable variance to date of £40,000 against a budget of £840,000, i.e. 4.8%. By the end of the year a favourable variance of £173,000 (13.1% on budget) is expected. It would appear that considerable economies are planned, and have already commenced. The fact that period 7 above shows a small adverse variance is not significant. Such results can emerge in administration costs, which can be influenced by random occurrences like a large purchase of stationery or a major visit overseas by the managing director.

2.4 Comparing against forecasts

Some large organisations in the UK have taken the idea of comparing against forecasts a step further. Many companies employ the following comparisons.

	Comparison	Information
1	Budget v actual	What progress have we made towards achieving objectives?
2	Budget v forecast	Will we continue to progress towards achievement of objectives?
3	Budget v revised forecast	Will suggested corrective actions lead us back to achievement of objectives?
4	Latest forecast v previous	Why are the forecasts different and are circumstances getting better or worse?
5	Actual v past forecast	Why were forecasts incorrect and can they be improved?

It may not be necessary to perform each of these control comparisons every month or quarter. The actual versus past forecast may only be necessary annually or less frequently.

It must be remembered that managers will need to be motivated to produce these forecasts and use them. They must be educated to recognise why and how they can use them to enable them to do a better job and not feel that they are just another means for higher level management to check on them and apply pressure.

Finally, this year's results are sometimes compared with those for the corresponding period last year. In some cases this may be helpful in establishing a trend, but it must never be forgotten that the budget is this year's plan, and it is against that plan that performance must be controlled.

3 Investigation of variances

3.1 Introduction

Variance analysis, if properly carried out, can be a useful cost-controlling and cost-saving tool. However, the traditional variance analysis seen so far is only a step towards the final goal of controlling and saving costs.

3.2 Generalised reasons for variances

The causes of variances can be classified under four headings:

- Planning errors
- Measurement errors
- Random factors
- Operational causes

Planning errors lead to the setting of inappropriate standards or budgets. This may be due to carelessness on the part of the standard setter (not taking account of known changes in the production process or expected price rises, for example) or due to unexpected external changes (a market shortage of a resource leading to increased price. These need to be isolated from hindsight information and a revision of the standard considered for future budgets.

Measurement errors include errors caused by inaccurate completion of timesheets or job cards, inaccurate measurement of quantities issued from stores, etc. The rectification of such errors or errors caused by random factors will probably not give rise to any cost savings (though this is a generalisation).

Random factors are by definition uncontrollable, although they need careful monitoring to ensure that they are not, in fact, one of the other types of variance.

3.3 Operational causes of variances

Examples of some specific reasons for individual variances are shown below.

Variance		Possible causes
Materials:	Price	Bulk discounts
		Different suppliers/ Different Materials
		Unexpected delivery costs
		Different buying procedures
	Usage	Different quality material
		Theft, obsolescence, deterioration
		Different quality of staff
		Different mix of material
		Different batch sizes and trim loss
Variance		**Possible causes**
Labour:	Rate	Different class of labour
		Excessive overtime
		Productivity bonuses
		National wage negotiations
		Union action
	Efficiency	Different levels of skill
		Different working conditions
		The learning effect
		Lack of supervision
		Works to rule
		Machine breakdowns
		Lack of material
		Lack of orders
		Strikes (if paid)
		Too long over coffee breaks
Overhead:	Price	Change in nature of overhead
		Unforeseen price changes
	Volume	Excessive idle time
		Increase in workforce

It will nearly always be useful to consult staff working in operational departments to resolve any queries in the data as they will have 'local' knowledge of the day-to-day operations.

Example

An adverse materials usage variance of £50,000 arose in a month as follows:

Standard cost per kg	£10
Actual cost per kg	£12
Units produced	2,000
Standard quantity per unit	25 kg
Actual quantity used	55,000 kg

	£
Standard cost of actual usage (55,000 kg × £10)	550,000
Standard cost of standard usage (2,000 × 25 kg × £10)	500,000
	————
Adverse usage variance	50,000
	————

On further investigation, the following is ascertained.

1 The actual quantity used was based on estimated stock figures. A stocktake showed that 53,000 kg were in fact used.

2 3,000 kg is the best estimate for what might politely be called the monthly 'shrinkage' but, in less polite circles, theft.

3 2,000 kg of stock were damaged by hoodlums who broke into the stores through some of the shaky panelling.

4 The supervisor feels that existing machinery is outmoded and more efficient machinery could save 1,000 kg a month.

Additional considerations

1 A security guard would cost £9,000 a year to employ and would stop 20% of all theft. Resultant dissatisfaction amongst works staff might cost £20,000 per annum.

2 Given the easy access to stores, vandals might be expected to break in every other month; £10,000 would make the stores vandal-proof.

3 New machinery would cost £720,000.

Analyse the usage variance in the light of this information and comment on your results.

Solution

The original £50,000 usage variance could be analysed as follows:

		Adverse/(favourable) *variance* *£*
(a)	Bad measurement (53,000 – 55,000) × £10	20,000
(b)	Theft (3,000 × £10)	30,000
(c)	Damage (2,000 × £10)	20,000
(d)	Obsolete machinery (1,000 × £10)	10,000
(e)	Other operational factors (balance)	(30,000)
		50,000

In each case, the variances should be studied and compared with the cost of rectification.

(a) **Bad measurement** – Assuming no costly decisions were made, or are likely to be made in the future, such as over-stocking, the component is of no future consequence.

(b) **Theft** – Annual cost due to theft is 12 × £30,000 or £360,000; 20% of this saved would amount to £72,000 at a cost of £9,000 + £20,000, thus the security guard is worth employing.

(c) **Damage** – Annual cost due to vandalism is 6 × £20,000 or £120,000; this would presumably be avoided by spending £10,000 now; again worthwhile.

(d) **Obsolete machinery** – Annual cost of using old machines is 12 × £10,000 or £120,000; the cost of making this saving (the saving would increase as purchase prices increased or if production increased) is £720,000; the decision over this investment would require further consideration such as discounted cash flow analysis.

(e) **Other factors** – We now see a favourable usage variance once all known factors above have been accounted for. This may need further investigation, particularly if it affects the quality of goods produced.

3.4 Fixed overhead variances

These are worth a special note, due to the particular nature of the fixed overhead volume variance.

We have seen that the volume variance is a product of the TAC system, and represents the adjustment for over-/under-absorption of fixed costs due to actual production being higher or lower than budgeted. Unlike the other variances, it does not actually represent a cost saving or overspend.

If this is the case, is it worth spending any time on the investigation of fixed overhead volume variances? Does it really matter if overheads are under-/over-absorbed, since it will all be adjusted for in the end?

The problem with having an inappropriate absorption rate is that decisions may have been taken on a unit cost that is too high or too low – for example, in setting the price of a product. If this is too high, sales may have been unnecessarily lost; if it is too low, profit margins may have been significantly eroded.

To minimise such effects of over-/under-absorption, regular reviews should be conducted of expenditure and activity levels arising throughout the period. The absorption rate can then be adjusted if it is felt necessary to reflect more recent estimates of expenditure and activity levels.

3.5 The cost of variance analysis

The provision of any information involves the costs of collecting the basic data, processing it, and reporting the results. Variance analysis is no exception and, as with other forms of management information, the benefits to which it gives rise must be commensurate with the costs incurred.

(a) Variance analysis allows 'management by exception' and it is presumably for this purpose that a standard costing system has been introduced.

(b) When variances are known to exist, failure to make adequate investigations, even on a random basis, will weaken the control system and thus the motivation of managers.

(c) The amount of analysis required can sometimes be reduced by defining levels of significance below which detailed investigation is not required.

(d) The costs of clerical work can be over-estimated. In most working days there will be some spare capacity that can be utilised without extra cost.

What has to be considered, therefore, is the amount of detail that can be incorporated usefully in variance analysis. This will fall into two categories:

(a) **Including more detailed codings** in source documents indicating causes and responsibilities. Such coding is likely to involve people outside the accounts department, who may be unwilling to give time to the task. How useful the analysis will be, will depend on whether or not it is practicable to identify causes and responsibilities at the time the document is initiated.

(b) **Investigations and re-analysis of variances after the event**. This can involve the time of quite senior people, but the process of investigation may well be more useful from the point of view of the management of the business than any quantity of formal variance calculations.

4 Responsibility accounting and the interdependence of variances

4.1 Introduction

It is part of any system aimed at improving the performance of a business or any part of the business, that actions shall be traced to the person responsible. This may give the impression of 'laying the blame', but it is equally possible to award praise (and remunerate accordingly).

We have seen that responsibility accounting is a system which recognises various decision centres within a business and traces costs (and possibly revenues) to the individual managers who are primarily responsible for making decisions about the items in question.

Example

An opportunity arises for a buying department to obtain a consignment of a particular material at an exceptionally low price. The purchase is made; a favourable price variance is recorded and the buying department is duly praised.

Subsequently, when products are being manufactured using this type of material, significant adverse material usage variances and labour efficiency variances are recorded, and are initially regarded as the responsibility of the department where the work is done.

Is it fair to blame the adverse variances on the operational departments?

Solution

Investigations may reveal a number of relevant facts, for example:

- The 'cheap' material was of poor quality, and in consequence much of it was wasted in the process of machining. The resultant material usage and labour efficiency variances should presumably be regarded as the responsibility of the buying department, to offset the favourable price variance.

- Due to an employee leaving it had been necessary to use an operator who was not familiar with the job. At least part of the excess usage of materials could be attributed to this cause; but whether it should be regarded as the responsibility of the operating department or of the personnel department (for failing to recruit a replacement) is still open to question. If the employee who left had been highly paid, his removal might cause a favourable wage rate variance in the period under review – an offset to the adverse efficiency variance.

- The tools used had been badly worn, thus causing excessive time on the job. It would be necessary to consider whether this condition was attributable to the operating department (failing to sharpen tools or to requisition replacements) or to the tools store-keeper or to the buying department (for failing to buy on time or for buying poor quality items again).

The important points to bear in mind are as follows:

- Different types of variance can be inter-linked by a common cause.

- In many cases, the responsibility for variances cannot be identified merely by reference to the cost centre where the variance has been reported. Responsibility may be shared by several managers or may lie completely outside the cost centre in which the variance has arisen.

5 Exchange rates and price variances

5.1 Introduction

Material price variances are sometimes caused by movements of the exchange rate of a currency when the materials are imported from an overseas country.

The following table illustrates the effect on the Sterling price in the UK of good which is imported from the United States if the exchange rate of the pound and dollar changes:

Price of good in US	Exchange rate	Price of good in UK
$1	£1 = $1.50	£ $\frac{1}{1.50}$ = £0.67
$1	£1 = $2.00	£ $\frac{1}{2.00}$ = £0.50

The price of the good in the US does not change, but as the exchange rate changes, the UK price also changes.

Thus, when £1 = $1.50, the imported good costs £0.67. But when the pound strengthens against the dollar (so that you now buy $2 rather than $1.50 for every pound), the imported good becomes cheaper – it now only costs £0.50.

The dollar price of course remains the same. However, because £1 buys more dollars, UK importers get more for their money so that the UK price in pounds falls.

5.2 Price variances

How does this affect price variances?

The first thing to note is that it doesn't affect the total variance – that can still be calculated as before. However, a changing exchange rate does affect the way we can analyse and explain a price variance.

Consider the following example.

 Example

D Ltd buys 2,000 kg of material for £2,000 in March 20X5. The standard cost of the material was set at £1.05 per kg when the standards were set in May 20X4. The material is imported from the US. The exchange rate has changed from £1 = $1.50 in May 20X4 to £1 = $1.65 in March 20X5.

(a) **Calculating the price variance using the traditional method.**

Amount that should have been paid for 2,000 kg	=	£2,100
= 2,000 × £1.05		
Amount actually paid	=	£2,000
		____
Price variance		£100 (F)
		____

(b) **Calculating the price variance taking account of the changed exchange rate.**

The person responsible for purchasing the materials may feel pleased if they are given credit for the £100 favourable variance.

However, things may not be as they seem.

Hence, we shall separate out the effect of the exchange rates. We do this by altering the standard cost in line with the exchange rate and calculating two price variances.

(i) a price variance caused by the exchange rate (sometimes referred to as a 'planning variance' because a factor outside the company control has caused the original standard to be wrong);

(ii) a price variance caused by the way the company actually bought the materials (sometimes called an 'operating variance' because it is caused by the normal operations of the company).

The relevant prices and variances can be set out as follows:

Original standard cost = 2,000 kg × £1.05   =   £2,100

£191 (F) (Planning)

Exchange rate adjusted= 2,000 kg × $\left[£1.05 \times \dfrac{1.50}{1.65}\right]$ =   £1,909

£91 (A) (Operating)

Actual cost = 2,000 × £1.00   =   £2,000
Total variance   £100 (F)

The total variance is still £100 (F) but this is due to a movement in the exchange rate. The company's operations have resulted in an unfavourable price variance of £91.

6   Summary

In this chapter we have examined ways of measuring the significance of variances and the way in which management might introduce controls based on the variance reports provided to them. The investigation of variances is a part of this process and it is important that you understand the causes of variances and their typical remedies.

We then considered briefly responsibility accounting and the possible interaction of variances. This is a very important area in the context of management appraisal. As we have seen, purchasing of cheap materials may cause a knock-on effect into the working of those materials thereby giving the impression that the workforce (and by implication the managers of the workforce) are inefficient. This will not be the case as the problems are caused by poor purchasing of materials rather than inefficient labour.

Finally, we examined very briefly how spreadsheets can be used to simplify report preparation.

7 Test your knowledge

 Workbook Activity 1

Excelsior Manufacturing Company

Excelsior Manufacturing Company produces a single product on an assembly line. As budget officer you have prepared the following production budgets from the best information available, to represent the extremes of high and low volume of production likely to be encountered by the company over a three month period.

	Production of 4,000 units £	Production of 8,000 units £
Direct materials	80,000	160,000
Indirect materials	12,000	20,000
Direct labour	50,000	100,000
Power	18,000	24,000
Repairs	20,000	30,000
Supervision	20,000	36,000
Rent, insurance and rates	9,000	9,000

Supervision is a 'step function'. One supervisor is employed for all production levels up to and including 5,000 units. For higher levels of production, an assistant supervisor (£16,000) is also required. For power, a minimum charge is payable on all production up to and including 6,000 units. For production above this level, there is an additional variable charge based on the power consumed.

Other variable and semi-variable costs are incurred evenly over the production range.

Required:

(a) Prepare a set of flexible budgets for presentation to the production manager to cover the following levels of production over a period of three months:

   (i)   4,000 units

   (ii)   5,000 units

   (iii) 6,000 units

(iv) 7,000 units

(v) 8,000 units

(b) During the three months July to September (covering most of the summer holiday period) 5,000 units were produced. Costs incurred during the three-month period were as follows:

	£
Direct materials	110,000
Indirect materials	14,000
Direct labour	70,000
Power	18,000
Repairs	30,000
Supervision	20,000
Rent, insurance and rates	8,000

Note that **price variances** have been eliminated from the figures for direct and indirect materials and **rate variances** have been eliminated from the labour and supervision costs.

Required:

You are preparing a budget report for presentation to the production manager. For each variance suggest any further investigations which might be required and any action which might be taken by the production manager.

 Workbook Activity 2

WH Limited (AAT CA D94)

WH Limited uses a standard costing system which produces monthly control statements to manufacture product M, a perishable, high quality raw material which is carefully weighed by direct employees. Some wastage and quality control rejects occur at this stage. The employees then compress the material to change its shape and create product M.

All direct employees are paid a basic hourly rate appropriate to their individual skill level and a bonus scheme is in operation. Bonuses are paid according to the daily rate of output achieved by each individual.

A standard allowance for all of the above operational factors is included in the standard cost of product M. Standard cost data for one unit of product M is as follows:

		Standard cost £ per unit
Direct material X:	4.5 kg × £4.90 per kg	22.05
Direct labour:	10.3 hours × £3.50 per hour	36.05
Standard direct cost		58.10

The production manager has approached you for further explanations concerning the standard costing control system. He is particularly interested in understanding how the standard price is set per kg of material used.

Task

As assistant accountant for WH Limited, you are asked to write a memo to the production manager which explains the following:

(a) the meaning of each of the direct cost variances calculated for product M;

(b) two possible causes of each of the variances which you have calculated for product M for November;

(c) two examples of interdependence which may be present in the variances which you have calculated for product M for November. Explain clearly why the variances may be interdependent, so that the manager can better understand the meaning of the finance director's statement.

 Workbook Activity 3

Revamp Furniture Limited

Revamp Furniture Limited manufacture a lounge chair by subjecting plasticised metal to a moulding process, thereby producing the chair in one piece.

(a) From the information provided below, you are required to analyse the cost variances and prepare a reconciliation of budgeted with actual cost incorporating the result of your analysis.

Standard/budget data

Unit variable costs:	
Direct material	6 lb at 50p per lb.
Direct labour	2 hours at 160p per hour
Budgeted fixed overhead for the year (240 working days)	£30,000
Budgeted production/sales for the year	60,000 chairs
Actual data for period 1	
Number of working days	20
Production/sales	5,200 chairs

Direct material received and used:

Delivery No 1	12,000 lb	Cost	£5,880
Delivery No 2	14,000 lb	Cost	£6,790
Delivery No 3	6,000 lb	Cost	£3,060
Direct labour hours worked	10,080	Cost	£17,540
Fixed overhead			£2,550

(b)　'Cost variances are often found, upon investigation of causes, to be interdependent.'

Briefly explain this statement using as illustrations:

(i)　material price and usage variances;

(ii)　labour rate and efficiency variances;

taken from your answer to (a) above and comment briefly on any possible interdependence between material cost variances and labour cost variances.

Performance indicators

Introduction

Cost variances, covered earlier, give one type of performance indicator – how individual operational managers perform against pre-set budget and standard cost targets. Here we continue this theme, but look at measures for productivity, efficiency etc; ratios that assist in assessment of resource utilisation; and overall profitability measures that may be applied to operating divisions and the business as a whole. We also look at the particular performance evaluation aspects of service industries, in particular the measurement of quality of service. The objective will always be to highlight activities, processes, products and business units that need some attention in order to enhance their value to the business.

KNOWLEDGE

- Explain the relationship between budgetary control, product lifecycles, and forecasts and planning (Element 2.4)

SKILLS

- Identify and evaluate options and solutions to increase profitability or reduce financial losses or exposure to risk (Element 2.4)
- Set clear targets and performance indicators to enable budgets to be monitored (Element 3.1)
- Present any recommendations with a clear rationale to the appropriate people (Element 3.7)

CONTENTS

1 Types of performance indicator

2 Ratio analysis

3 Profitability

4 Liquidity

5 Manufacturing industries

6 Service departments

7 Service sectors

8 Total quality management (TQM)

9 The balanced scorecard

10 Cost reduction and value enhancement

1 Types of performance indicator

1.1 Introduction

Performance indicators may be categorised as quantitative or qualitative.

1.2 Quantitative performance indicators

Quantitative measures are expressed in numerical terms which include the following:

(a) variances;

(b) profit, sales, costs, etc;

(c) ratios and percentages;

(d) indices.

1.3 Qualitative performance indicators

Qualitative indicators are far more subjective and cannot be expressed as an objective, numerical measure. Examples relevant to business and managerial performance would include the following:

(a) level of customer satisfaction: expressed as a subjective level 'very satisfied' … to …'not at all satisfied';

(b) staff performance grades: 'excellent', 'average', 'poor', etc;

(c) company performance: 'steady', 'volatile results', 'disappointing', etc.

1.4 Efficiency and effectiveness

Performance indicators can be used to measure the efficiency and effectiveness of organisations.

🔍 Definition

Efficiency can be defined as the relationship between inputs and outputs achieved. The fewer the inputs used by an organisation to achieve any given output, the more efficient is that organisation. In commercial organisations, efficiency is usually measured in terms of profitability, often in relation to assets employed.

Effectiveness is the degree to which an objective or target is met.

---

2 Ratio analysis

2.1 Introduction

Ratio analysis is one of the main tools utilised in appraising the performance of a company, the main advantage being that the magnitude of the individual figures is eliminated allowing the appraiser to concentrate on relative movements.

Ratio analysis is generally utilised in two ways as follows:

(a) comparison of performance year to year;

(b) comparison with other companies.

The techniques covered here occur in many branches of accountancy and it is important that you can calculate and interpret appropriate ratios.

2.2 Types of ratios

The main types of ratio used are:

(a) profitability ratios;

(b) liquidity ratios;

(c) gearing ratios;

(d) investment ratios.

Of these, profitability and liquidity ratios are of the greatest significance to the management accountant and it is those we shall examine in more detail.

Example

In order to illustrate the most common ratios, let's look at some calculations based on the summarised accounts of Knotty plc. The information from Knotty plc's financial statements will be used in the following sections.

Profit and loss account for the year ended 31 July 20X9

	Notes	20X9		20X8	
	£000	£000	£000	£000	£000
Turnover		37,589			30,209
Cost of sales		(28,380)			(22,808)
Gross profit			9,209		7,401
Distribution costs	(3,755)		(3,098)		
Administrative expenses	(2,291)		(2,030)		
		(6,046)		(5,128)	
		3,163		2,273	
Other operating income		108		0,279	
Operating profit		3,271		2,552	
Interest receivable		7		28	
		3,278		2,580	
Interest payable		(442)		(471)	
Profit on ordinary activities before taxation		2,836		2,109	
Tax on profit on ordinary activities		(1,038)		(650)	
Profit on ordinary activities after taxation		1,798		1,459	
Preference dividend		(6)		(6)	
		1,792		1,453	
Ordinary dividends		(606)		(441)	
Retained profit for the year		1,186		1,012	

Balance sheet as at 31 July 20X9

	Notes	20X9 £000	20X9 £000	20X8 £000	20X8 £000
Fixed assets					
Tangible assets			8,687		5,669
Investments			15		15
			8,702		5,684
Current assets					
Stocks		8,486		6,519	
Debtors	1	8,836		6,261	
Cash at bank and in hand		479		250	
		17,801		13,030	
Creditors: amounts falling due within one year					
Bank loans and overdrafts		(929)		(511)	
Other amounts falling due within one year		(9,178)		(6,645)	
		(10,107)		(7,156)	
Net current assets			7,694		5,874
Total assets less current liabilities			16,396		11,558
Creditors: amounts falling due after more than one year					
Debentures			(2,840)		(2,853)
Net assets			13,556		8,705

Capital and reserves		
Called up share capital		
Ordinary shares of 20p each	2	
	2,003	1,762
4.2% cumulative preference shares of £1 each	150	150
	2,153	1,912
Share premium account	123	123
Other reserves	2,576	–
Profit and loss account	8,704	6,670
	13,556	8,705

Notes

1 Debtors at 31 July 20X9 include trade debtors of £8,233,000 (20X8 £5,735,000).

2 The number of ordinary shares in issue at 31 July 20X9 was 10,014,514 (20X8 8,808,214).

3 Profitability

3.1 Return on capital employed (ROCE)

Return on capital employed (ROCE) expresses profit as a percentage of the assets in use (the capital employed in the business) and can be further subdivided into profit margin and asset turnover (use of assets):

Profit margin × Asset turnover = Return on capital employed (ROCE)

$$\frac{\text{Profit}}{\text{Turnover}} \times \frac{\text{Turnover}}{\text{Assets}} = \frac{\text{Profit}}{\text{Assets}}$$

The equation helps to demonstrate how management can influence the rate of return on capital employed:

(a) By increasing profit margins:

    (i) increase sales prices;

    (ii) reduce costs.

(b)   By increasing asset turnover (use of assets):

   (i)   increase sales;

   (ii)   reduce assets (capital employed).

3.2   Year-end or average capital employed

Ideally, the profits for the year ended 31 July 20X9 should be related to the assets in use throughout the year (the average capital employed). In practice, the ratio is usually computed using the assets at the year-end (the year-end capital employed). Using year-end figures of capital employed can distort trends and inter-company comparison; if new investment has been undertaken near to the year-end and financed (for example) by the issue of new shares, the capital employed will have risen by the total finance raised, whereas the profits will only have a month or two of the new investment's contribution.

A range of different acceptable measures of the assets in use is available; the matter of principle should be that the profit figure which is related to the capital employed should include all types of return on those assets.

Solution

For Knotty plc, a suitable calculation would be as follows.

	20X9 £000	20X8 £000
Capital and reserves	13,556	8,705
Add: Debentures	2,840	2,853
Year-end capital employed	16,396	11,558

	20X9 £000	20X8 £000
Operating profit	3,271	2,552
Interest receivable	7	28
Profit before interest payable and tax	3,278	2,580

So the return on capital employed is calculated as:

$$\frac{\text{Profit before interest and tax}}{\text{Capital and reserves and long - term debt}} \times 100\%$$

20X9 $\quad \dfrac{3,278}{16,396} \times 100 = 20.0\%$

20X8 $\quad \dfrac{2,580}{11,558} \times 100 = 22.3\%$

The capital employed figure includes the long-term debt, the debentures. Therefore, the profit used must be that available to these providers of capital, the profit before interest payable.

The rate of return on year-end capital employed has fallen in 20X9 compared with 20X8, and might indicate less effective management. To comment further, we need to sub-analyse the ratio into profit margin and asset turnover.

3.3 Profit margin

If the profitability ratios are to interlock perfectly, the profit margin will be calculated expressing the same profit before interest payable and tax as a percentage of turnover:

$$\frac{\text{Profit before interest and tax}}{\text{Turnover}} \times 100\%$$

A small problem with the approach in this example is that the profit includes interest receivable which is not represented in turnover; however, as the amount is small, this can be ignored.

In order that the profit can be related more fairly to turnover, profit margin is sometimes calculated using operating profit.

Solution

For Knotty plc: 20X9 $\dfrac{3,278}{37,589} \times 100 = 8.7\%$

20X8 $\dfrac{2,580}{30,209} \times 100 = 8.5\%$

Profit margins have improved slightly over the last year, possibly due to better cost control.

Sectors which have traditionally generated relatively high margins include publishing, electronics manufacturing, distillers and brewers, whereas food retailing and motor vehicle distribution are examples of low margin businesses.

Low margins within a sector may arise from a policy designed to increase market share by cutting selling prices, or may be due to high development costs associated with new products, both of which may be positive factors for the future. However, low margins are often associated with inefficiency and poor quality management.

Conversely, high margins relative to competitors, or improving margins, are usually taken as indicators of efficiency and good management. High margins achieved by dominating a particular market may, however, attract competitors into that market and imply lower margins in the longer term.

3.4 Asset turnover

Another aspect of efficient management is to 'make the assets work'. This may involve disposing of those 'underperforming' assets which cannot be made to generate sales, as well as developing and marketing the company's products or services.

Solution

Once again, the simplest method of computing the ratio is to relate turnover to the same figure of year-end capital employed used in calculating return on capital employed:

$$\text{Asset turnover} = \frac{\text{Turnover}}{\text{Capital employed}}$$

20X9 $\dfrac{37,589}{16,396} = 2.3$ times   20X8 $\dfrac{38209}{11,558} = 2.6$ times

---

However, as with profit margins, certain assets represented by capital employed have no turnover implications. One method of avoiding this illogicality is to exclude long and short-term investments from capital employed. For companies with substantial investments this will make a considerable difference.

Asset turnover will tend to be lower in capital-intensive manufacturing industries, which carry substantial tangible fixed assets, stocks and trade debtors, than in service industries where the principal resource is people rather than plant and machinery, and where stocks are low.

There are often trade-offs between asset turnover and profit margins in different sectors. For example, food retailers have relatively low profit margins compared to electronic equipment manufacturers, but asset turnover is higher. Typical numbers might be:

	Profit margin %	×	Asset turnover	=	ROCE %
Food retailer	3.7	×	6.7	=	24.8
Electronic equipment manufacturer	10.3	×	2.3	=	23.7

3.5 Gross profit margin

The profit margin given above used a profit figure that included non-productive overheads and sundry items of income. The gross profit margin looks at the profitability of the pure trading activities of the business:

$$\frac{\text{Gross profit}}{\text{Turnover}} \times 100\%$$

Solution

For Knotty plc: $20X9 \quad \frac{9,209}{37,589} \times 100 = 24.5\%$

$$20X8 \quad \frac{7,401}{30,209} \times 100 = 24.5\%$$

The company has maintained its gross profit margin; thus the slight rise in net profit margin must be due to overhead costs being better controlled.

4 Liquidity

4.1 Current ratio and quick ratio

When analysing a company's balance sheet without access to management information, it is customary to calculate two ratios as indicators of the company's ability to pay its way:

$$\text{Current ratio} = \frac{\text{Current assets}}{\text{Creditors due within one year}}$$

$$\text{Quick ratio (or acid test ratio)} = \frac{\text{Current assets less stocks}}{\text{Creditors due within one year}}$$

Solution

For Knotty plc:

		20X9	20X8
(a)	Current ratio	$\dfrac{17{,}801}{10{,}107} = 1.76$	$\dfrac{13{,}030}{7{,}156} = 1.82$
(a)	Quick ratio	$\dfrac{9{,}315}{10{,}107} = 0.92$	$\dfrac{6{,}511}{7{,}156} = 0.91$

4.2 Cash and funds flow analysis

Although current and quick ratios are used to measure liquidity, they are limited insofar as they concentrate on only one area of the balance sheet. If the company needs adequate cash to meet its obligations, there are sources other than the sale of stocks and the collection of amounts owed by debtors.

Analysis of cash flows is a more comprehensive method of assessing liquidity, although significant variations in the liquidity ratios may indicate important changes.

4.3 Other working capital ratios

A more detailed analysis of the movement in the elements of working capital can be made with the help of the following ratios.

4.4 Stock holding period (stock days)

Stock holding periods can be compared if they relate costs of sales as a measure of activity to stocks which are usually included at cost:

$$\frac{\text{Stocks}}{\text{Cost of sales}} \times 365\%$$

Solution

20X9 $\dfrac{8{,}486}{28{,}380} \times 365 = 109$ days

20X8 $\dfrac{6{,}519}{22{,}808} \times 365 = 104\%$

There has been a slight increase in the holding period, indicating stock is taking longer to sell. A review of stocks may be necessary to determine whether levels of obsolete or damaged stocks are increasing. There may be a deliberate policy to increase stocks.

4.5 Average debtors collection period (debtor days)

This calculation is always made using turnover since trade debtors includes the profit element:

$$\frac{\text{Trade debtors}}{\text{Turnover}} \times 365 \text{ days}$$

Solution

20X9 $\dfrac{8,233}{37,589} \times 365 = 80$ days

20X8 $\dfrac{4,735}{30,209} \times 365 = 69$ days

The company is taking approximately 11 days longer, on average, to collect its debts.

As the year-end figures may be unrepresentative (due perhaps to seasonality of sales), an average debtors figure for the year might be used if this were available.

4.6 Average creditors payment period (creditor days)

A similar calculation can be made to determine the creditors payment (settlement) period:

$$\frac{\text{Trade creditors}}{\text{Purchases or cost of sales}} \times 365 \text{ days}$$

Purchases should normally be used for this ratio but if it is not available from the information then cost of sales can be used as a substitute.

Example

Work through the following example to ensure that you understand how to calculate and interpret basic ratios.

The outline balance sheets of the Nantred Trading Co Limited were as shown below.

Balance sheets as at 30 September

	20X6		20X5	
	£	£	£	£
Fixed assets (at written-down values)				
Premises	98,000		40,000	
Plant and equipment	162,000		65,000	
		260,000		105,000
Current assets				
Stock	95,300		31,200	
Trade debtors	30,700		19,700	
Bank and cash	26,500		15,600	
	152,500		66,500	
Current liabilities				
Trade creditors	55,800		23,900	
Corporation tax	13,100		11,400	
Proposed dividends	17,000		17,000	
	85,900		52,300	
Working capital		66,600		14,200
Net assets employed		326,600		119,200
Financed by				
Ordinary share capital	200,000		100,000	
Reserves	26,600		19,200	
Shareholders' funds		226,600		119,200
7% debentures		100,000		–
		326,600		119,200

The only other information available is that:

- turnover for the years ended 30 September 20X5 and 20X6 was £202,900 and £490,700 respectively;

- profit before tax and interest (operating profit) for the years to 30 September 20X5 and 20X6 was £21,500 and £44,500 respectively.

(a) Calculate, for each of the two years, two suitable ratios to highlight the liquidity and two suitable ratios to highlight the profitability of the company.

(b) Comment on the situation revealed by the figures you have calculated in your answer to (a) above.

Solution

(a)

		20X6	20X5
(i)	$\dfrac{\text{Current assets}}{\text{Current liabilities}}$	$\dfrac{152,500}{85,900} = 1.78{:}1$	$\dfrac{66,500}{52,300} = 1.27{:}1$
(ii)	$\dfrac{\text{Quick assets}}{\text{Current liabilities}}$	$\dfrac{57,200}{85,900} = 0.67{:}1$	$\dfrac{35,300}{52,300} = 0.67{:}1$
(iii)	$\dfrac{\text{Profit before tax and interest}}{\text{Capital (net assets) employed}}$	$\dfrac{44,500}{326,600} \times 100 = 13.6\%$	$\dfrac{21,500}{119,200} \times 100 = 18.0\%$
(iv)	$\dfrac{\text{Profit before tax and interest}}{\text{Sales}}$	$\dfrac{44,500}{490,700} \times 100 = 9.1\%$	$\dfrac{21,500}{202,900} \times 100 = 10.6\%$

(b) The situation revealed by the ratios calculated in (a) above may be summarised as follows.

Liquidity ratios (i) and (ii)

The current ratio indicates a substantial surplus of current assets over current liabilities and this has improved over the year. The liquid assets (debtors and bank) to current liabilities ratio shows no change and based on past experience does not signify any liquidity difficulties.

Profitability ratios (iii) and (iv)

The overall return on capital employed has decreased by a substantial amount. This may be because full benefit has not yet been received from the additional investment of £100,000 from the debentures issued during the year. The level of net profit per £ of sales has also decreased and this may be due to the same reasons. Fortunately the overall return is high enough to mean that the 7% paid to the debenture holders is still easily achieved and the surplus return will improve returns to the ordinary shareholders, compensating them for the risk they have undertaken in introducing gearing (the debentures) into the organisation.

4.7 Comparing entities using performance indicators

Comparing an entity with a similar one may come up as a very practical task in an examination. The likely situation is where you have two firms in competition with each other, and one of them sets itself a performance indicator as a target to help it achieve a competitive advantage. The other firm must try to match or better that target.

4.8 What if? analysis

'What if? analysis' or 'scenario planning' is a technique used to test the effect on a set of figures of altering one of the variables that produced those figures. Flexible budgeting is a form of what if? analysis – what if we produce 20,000 units rather than 15,000, say?

 Example

Theta division makes only one product, the Devon. In the year to 30 June 20X5, its results were as follows:

	£
Sales	500,000
Debtors at 30 June 20X5	105,000
Cash at 30 June 20X5	20,000

The main competitor in the Devon market is Gamma Co, which sells Devons at a 15% higher price than Theta. It has been estimated that Theta could also charge a higher price without reducing sales volume. Gamma's results for the same period as Theta are as follows:

	£
Sales	700,000
Debtors	72,500
Cash	10,000

What would be the effect on the cash balance of Theta achieving Gamma's success?

Solution

The requirement in this example can be read as – what if Theta raised its prices and implemented credit controls to achieve Gamma's levels of sales and debtors?

	Theta	*Gamma*
Debtor days	$\dfrac{£105,000}{£500,000} \times 365 = 77$	$\dfrac{£72,500}{£700,000} \times 365 = 38$

Theta's revised figures

	£	£
Existing cash		20,000
Sales increase (£500,000 × 1.15) – £500,000		75,000
Change in debtors: Revised debtors (£500,000 × 1.15)		
$\times \dfrac{38}{365}$	59,863	
Existing debtors	105,000	
		45,137
Revised cash balance		140,137

Therefore Theta division would increase its cash balance by £120,137 by raising its prices and reducing its debt collection period.

5 Manufacturing industries

5.1 Introduction

The performance of a manufacturing business and its constituent activities will commonly be measured in quantitative terms, mainly monetary. However, we shall also consider relevant non-monetary and qualitative factors that can be useful.

5.2 Productivity

This is a measure of the efficiency of resource usage and expresses the rate of output in relation to resource used, often in non-financial terms.

Examples include the following:

(a)   units produced per labour or machine hour;

(b)   productive hours to total hours paid;

(c)   actual output to full capacity output;

(d)   sales units per salesperson;

(e)   value added, in total or per employee.

Productivity is closely linked with both efficiency and resource utilisation (which is considered later).

5.3   Labour activity, capacity and efficiency ratios

Three control ratios are often used to measure productivity, as follows:

Activity ratio: $\dfrac{\text{Actual output measured in standard hours}}{\text{Budgeted production hours}}$

Capacity ratio: $\dfrac{\text{Actual hours worked}}{\text{Budgeted hours}}$

Efficiency ratio: $\dfrac{\text{Actual output measured in standard hours}}{\text{Actual production in hours}}$

Example

	Budget	Actual
Output (units)	10,000	9,000
Hours worked	200	190

Calculate:

(a)   the activity ratio;

(b)   the capacity ratio;

(c)   the efficiency ratio.

Solution

(a)   Output per standard hour $= \dfrac{10,000}{200} = 50$ units

Actual output in standard hours $= \dfrac{9,000}{50} = 180$

Activity ratio: $\dfrac{180}{200} = 90\%$

In other words, the production level was only 90% of the budgeted level.

(b) Capacity ratio: $\dfrac{190}{200} = 95\%$

Only 95% of budgeted hours were actually worked and used to produce units.

(c) Efficiency ratio: $\dfrac{180}{190} = 94.74\%$

According to the budget, 50 units should have been produced in an hour and therefore in the 190 hours that were actually worked, 9,500 units should have been produced. Only 94.74% of that quantity (9,000) were actually produced.

Note that the three ratios are related to each other:

Efficiency ratio	×	Capacity ratio	=	Activity ratio
94.74%	×	95%	=	90%

5.4 Value added

> ### 🔍 Definition
>
> Value added is the pool of wealth created, out of which a business provides for:
>
> - payment of wages, salaries and other employee benefits;
> - reward for providers of capital, in the form of interest and dividends;
> - payment of government taxation;
> - maintenance and expansion of assets.
>
> It is also defined as:
>
> - the value of turnover less the cost of bought in materials and services.

Example

Value added statement

Horn Ltd

	£m
Turnover	1.35
Bought in materials and services	0.55
	———
Value added	0.80
	———
Applied as:	
To pay employee wages and other benefits	0.28
Providers of capital dividends	0.13
Government taxation	0.04
Maintenance and expansion of assets	
Depreciation	0.15
	———
Retained profit	0.20
	———

Number of employees = 20

- Value added per '£' of employee costs

$$\frac{£0.80}{£0.28} = 2.86$$

- Value added per employee

$$\frac{£0.80}{20} = £0.04m \text{ or } £40,000$$

- Value added per '£' of employee costs and depreciation

$$\frac{£0.80}{£0.43m} = 1.86$$

or, in a highly mechanised process, related to use of machinery:

- production per machine hour;
- production per machine.

5.5 Unit costs

Unit costs are the actual average cost of production of each unit of product in the period. Management will attempt to drive down unit costs over time.

5.6 Resource utilisation

This is a measure of the extent to which resources were used in relation to maximum capacity. Examples of utilisation and related measures for different resources include the following:

Machines   –   utilisation (hours used : potential hours)
           –   down time (machine down hours : total hours)

Materials   –   wastage (normal/abnormal loss percentage)
           –   stock turnover (linked to levels of slow-moving stocks)

Labour   –   utilisation (productive : total hours)
           –   absenteeism, lateness
           –   mix variances (where different grades are used)
           –   idle time (non-productive hours : total hours)
           –   labour turnover (leavers replaced : total employed)

5.7 Quality of service

For a manufacturing business, this can be categorised into quality of service to customers and quality of service from service departments. The latter is covered in the section on the service departments.

Quality of service to customers is essentially a subjective, qualitative measure, although some quantitative measures can be used in connection with it – for example, ratios such as customer returns to total sales and customer complaints per units sold. Speed of service can be measured in retail outlets or numbers waiting per checkout in a supermarket.

The main source of measure of customer satisfaction will generally be through some sort of questionnaire. This is all considered in more detail later in this chapter.

5.8 Other non-monetary measures

Quality is a particular area in which such indicators are required; two others that have recently been identified as important attributes of world-class manufacturing are innovation and flexibility.

5.9 Innovation

Innovation is concerned with the business's ability to beat their competitors in developing new products, improvements to existing ones or additional customer services.

Measurement of innovation must concentrate on its effectiveness as well as its existence – counting the number of new products developed is of little help without knowing the extent to which they have been accepted by the market. Possible measures include the following:

(a)   research and development expenditure related to new sales (in value and timing, i.e. payback);

(b)   viable new products to existing products;

(c)   percentage of total profits relating to new products/ improvements.

5.10   Flexibility

Flexibility is concerned with the business's ability to respond to customers' needs, in terms of speed of delivery of existing products, speed of reaction to changes in demand patterns and ability to respond to particular customer requests or specifications.

In a manufacturing context, it is often the case that flexibility is connected with the amounts of products using common parts. If demand for one type of product falls, it is easier to switch stock and processing to another if there is a common base between them.

6   Service departments

6.1   Introduction

Many of the measures discussed above will be relevant in the assessment of the performance of service departments within a business. Unless an internal charge-out system operates (for example, the charging of user departments per hour of computer department time spent on their work),the emphasis will be on costs rather than profits.

6.2   Types of performance indicator

As well as the normal cost variances (with activity levels based on the departments' own cost unit, e.g. maintenance hours, meals served, data processing hours), other cost ratios will be appropriate, for example:

(a)   meal cost per employee per period (canteen);

(b)   running costs per van-mile (deliveries);

(c)   cost per call-out (maintenance department).

Example

Consider a transport/distribution department. What type of cost performance indicators might be appropriate?

Solution

(a) **Standing costs** (ascertained as a rate per day), including:

  (i)   Road tax

  (ii) Insurance

  (iii) Garage and administration costs

  (iv) Drivers' wages

  (v)   Depreciation

(b) **Running costs** (ascertained as a rate per ton/mile), including:

  (i)   Fuel and lubricants

  (ii) Tyres

  (iii) Repairs

  (iv) Maintenance

Standing costs will be incurred for vehicles owned whether or not they are in use and are in the nature of stepped fixed costs. Fixed because, for each vehicle, they do not vary in amount and 'stepped' because for each additional vehicle required, costs, on a graph, will rise by a further step and remain fixed for a further range of activity until another vehicle is required.

In addition to these, there will be depot administration and establishment costs to be absorbed. These should be ascertained in total and related to the activity of the depot. Statistical information such as mileage run, loaded and empty, and tonnages carried should also be collected so that a reasonable method of absorption may be derived.

The analysis of expenditure between fixed and variable costs (standing and running costs) gives potential for the use of marginal costing and the consequent improvements in management information.

With such information available, management will be better equipped to deal with:

(a) control over costs for each vehicle or group of similar vehicles;

(b) pricing;

(c) choice of most economic vehicle for specific tasks;

(d) acceptability of contracts;

(e) vehicle purchase and replacement decisions;

(f) many other day-to-day decisions.

7 Service sectors

7.1 Introduction

Service organisations include the following:

(a) **Professional services**, such as firms of accountants, architects, surveyors, solicitors, whose main assets will be their employees and who provide individual, personalised services to their customers.

(b) **Mass services**, such as transport, which are highly capital asset based and provide a standard range of services to a wide range of customers.

(c) **Public sector services**, such as health, education and local authorities.

7.2 Types of performance indicators

Service sector measures can be considered under very similar headings as those for manufacturing organisations, although there will be a different emphasis on their relative importance.

The main difference between the two types of organisation is the nature of their output.

Output from manufacturing businesses comprises tangible, clearly identifiable products, usually of a standard design and quality which can be rejected by a customer if not required or unsuitable, and produced in advance of demand and stored until needed.

Think about a service provided to you – can it be said to have any of these characteristics? This leads to a different approach needed for performance measurement where costs per product or units per hour are of little relevance or meaning. However, in earlier chapters, we have seen that cost units do not have to be in terms of products and that measures may be activity rather than product based.

So, using similar headings as before, particular areas to be considered about the performance indicators of service organisations are productivity, unit costs, resource utilisation, profitability and quality of service.

In examinations the tasks will ask for performance indicators which are tailored to the scenario set. Make sure that you read the scenario information carefully and actually calculate the indicators that are asked for.

7.3 Productivity

Productivity can be difficult to measure, because services rarely have a standard unit of output. For example, it would be meaningless to measure a conveyancing solicitor's productivity on the basis of 'property purchase completions per month', as each will have a different degree of complexity and value to the business. Similarly, it would be inappropriate to assess a bus line on the basis of 'journeys per day', as the contribution to the company's profits would depend upon the number of people carried at each stage of the journey and how many buses were operating on the line.

Meaningful measures of productivity or efficiency for a service depend upon a clearly defined measure of activity and resources.

So, for example, the measure of activity for the bus line might be 'passenger miles' and of the resource might be 'driver hours'.

Professional firms, such as accountants and solicitors, will generally use 'chargeable hours' as a measure of activity and employees' productivity will be judged by 'chargeable hours per employee'.

7.4 Unit costs

Again, the difficulty here is in defining an appropriate unit for the activity being measured. Once this has been established, appropriate costs need to be attributed to it. So the cost of a professional chargeable hour would mainly consist of employee costs (salaries, NICs, benefits, etc.) but will also include a recovery of general overheads.

The cost of a 'passenger mile' for a transport company will include driver costs, vehicle running costs and overheads.

7.5   Resource utilisation

Resource utilisation is the extent to which available resources are used for productive service. Examples of suitable measures for various types of service businesses are illustrated by the following ratios:

Professional   Chargeable hours : Total hours available

Transport   Passenger miles : Total train miles available

Hotel   Rooms occupied : Rooms available

Car hire   Car-days hired : Car-days available

7.6   Profitability

Clearly, for the service business overall, the usual measures can apply – ROCE, profit margins, etc. Unit profitability measures will again depend upon the clear definition of the cost unit or unit of activity. The profit can then be determined by comparison of the cost per unit (as discussed above) with the income generated (e.g. the charge-out rate for a professional chargeable hour or the average fare per mile on a bus/train route).

 Activity 4

Transport company (AAT J94)

A transport company is reviewing the way in which it reports vehicle operating costs to the company management. In particular, it is interested in the use of performance ratios which will help to assess the efficiency and effectiveness of the use of its vehicles.

Information on the following items is available for each vehicle for the period as follows:

Costs

Variable costs

Fuel	Tyres
Oil	Other parts
Hydraulic fluid	Repairs and maintenance

Fixed costs

Road fund licence	Cleaning
Insurance	Depreciation
Drivers' wages	

Activity measures

Miles driven	Number of days available for use
Tonnes carried	Number of days vehicle actually used
Journeys made	

Required

You are asked to indicate six suitable performance ratios which could be used to monitor the effectiveness and efficiency of the usage of each vehicle.

Three of your ratios should relate to the efficient control of costs and three should relate to the effective usage of vehicles.

7.7 Quality of service

This has arguably more significance in the service sector than in the manufacturing sector. Customers will make their buying decisions in the service sector on the basis of how well they expect the service to be provided.

The factors contributing to quality of service will vary according to the nature of the business. As an illustration, consider the service provided to trainee accountancy students by a private college. Possible factors that would influence a potential student in their choice of college and the ways in which these might be measured are as follows:

Factor	Possible measures
Technical expertise	Pass rates
Communication	Clarity of lectures, study material and administrative information
Access	Staff/student ratios Availability of tutorial help outside lecture hours Ease of finding department/member of staff required Location of college
Friendliness	Approachability of staff
Flexibility	Ability to tailor service to individual student's needs
Facilities	Availability and standard of canteen, library, phones, etc

Aesthetics	Appearance of college
	Staff presentation
Comfort	Roominess of classrooms
	Heating/air-conditioning
	Comfort of seats, size of desks

You can no doubt think of some more factors and different ways in which those given could be measured. For example, it is perhaps a little glib to use pass rates as a measure of the college's technical expertise, as these are also likely to be significantly influenced by the abilities and commitment of the students themselves.

7.8   Quantitative and qualitative performance indicators

Having identified what needs to be measured, how can this be achieved? Some are a matter of fact or record – like pass rates or the existence of facilities; most of the rest are qualitative judgement and would need to be measured by the use of examination forms completed by students.

An overall measure of the quality of service provided by the college could be the trend in the number of students enrolling for courses, although again this can be affected by other factors, such as the location of the college and students, the policy of the students' employers and the size of the market for trainee accountants.

8   Total quality management (TQM)

 Definition

Total quality management (TQM) can be defined as 'a continuous improvement in quality, efficiency and effectiveness'.

- It aims towards an environment of zero defects at a minimum cost – the principle of 'get it right first time'.

- It requires an awareness by all personnel of the quality requirements with supplying the customer with products of the agreed design specification.

- It aims towards the elimination of waste where waste is defined as anything other than the minimum essential amount of equipment, materials, space and workers' time.

- It must embrace all aspects of operations from pre-production to postproduction stages in the business cycle.

Total quality management will, therefore, seek method changes which will help in achieving such objectives. Examples include the use of Just-in-time (JIT) production procedures whereby each component or product is produced or purchased only when needed by production or by a customer, rather than for stock.

8.1 Quality circles

An important element of TQM is that every employee is involved and anyone with an idea about how to improve quality should be heard. This is done by forming groups of employees known as quality circles. These groups normally consist of about 10 employees of differing levels of seniority and with different skills who meet regularly to discuss quality problems and put forward ideas.

8.2 The cost of quality

Traditionally failure rates, scrap and reworking were subsumed within the costs of production while other aspects of poor quality were accounted for in either production or marketing overheads. TQM does not accept the cost of poor quality as inevitable and requires that the cost of quality is highlighted in management reports. This enables alternative approaches (such as built-in quality at the design stage) to be developed.

Quality-related costs are the expenditure incurred in defect prevention and appraisal activities and the losses due to internal and external failure of a product or service through failure to meet agreed specifications.

8.3 Types of quality-related costs

Quality-related costs may be classified as follows:

(a) **Failure costs** are the costs required to evaluate, dispose of, and either correct or replace a defective or deficient product.

    (i)   Internal failure costs are costs discovered before the product is delivered to the customer. Examples include the following:

- Rework costs
- Net cost of scrap
- Disposal of defective products
- Downtime due to quality problems

(ii)   External failure costs are costs discovered after the product is delivered to customers.

Examples include the following:

- Complaint investigation and processing
- Warranty claims
- Cost of lost sales
- Product recalls

(b) **Appraisal costs** are costs of monitoring and inspecting products in terms of specified standards before the products are released to the customer. Examples include the following:

- Measurement equipment
- Inspection and tests
- Product quality audits
- Process control monitoring
- Test equipment expense

(c) **Prevention costs** include investments in machinery, technology and education programs designed to reduce the number of defective products during production. Examples include the following:

- Customer surveys
- Research of customer needs
- Field trials
- Quality education and training programmes
- Supplier reviews
- Investment in improved production equipment
- Quality engineering
- Quality circles

Example

Carlton Limited make and sell a single product.

The following information affects its costs and revenues.

1   5% of incoming material from suppliers is scrapped owing to poor receipt and storage organisation.

2   4% of material X input to the machine process is wasted owing to processing problems.

3   Inspection of storage of material X costs 10 pence per square metre purchased.

4   Inspection during the production cycle, calibration checks on inspection equipment and other checks cost £25,000 per period.

5   Production quantity is increased to allow for the downgrading of 12.5% of product units at the final inspection stage. Downgraded units are sold as 'second quality' units at a discount of 30% on the standard selling price.

6   Production quantity is increased to allow for returns from customers which are replaced free of charge. Returns are due to specification failure and account for 5% of units initially delivered to customers. Replacement units incur a delivery cost of £8 per unit. 80% of the returns from customers are rectified using 0.2 hours of machine running time per unit and are re-sold as 'third quality' products at a discount of 50% on the standard selling price. The remaining returned units are sold as scrap for £5 per unit.

7   Product liability and other claims by customers are estimated at 3% of sales revenue from standard product sales.

8   Machine idle time is 20% of gross machine hours used (i.e. running hours = 80% of gross hours).

9   Sundry costs of administration, selling and distribution total £60,000 per period.

10   Carlton Limited is aware of the problem of excess costs and currently spends £20,000 per period on training staff in efforts to prevent a number of such problems from occurring.

Give examples of internal and external failure costs, appraisal costs and prevention costs borne by Carlton Limited.

Solution

Internal failure costs. The machine processing losses, downgrading of products, and materials which are scrapped due to poor receipt and storage.

External failure costs. Product liability claims and the costs of making free replacements, including delivery costs.

Appraisal costs. Inspection during the production process, inspection of materials in storage and calibration checks.

Prevention costs. Training costs.

9 The balanced scorecard

9.1 Introduction

The balanced scorecard approach to performance indicators recognises that historically too much emphasis has been placed on financial ratios in assessing an entity's performance. A successful business will only succeed in the long-term if it keeps its customers happy as well as by making profits. The approach therefore combines financial measures with operational, organisational innovation and customer service measures. All of these perspectives must be managed by managers if the business is to prosper in the long-term.

The balanced scorecard becomes the manager's instrument panel for managing the complexity of the organisation within a dynamic external environment.

9.2 Four perspectives of the balanced scorecard

The table below is an example of a balanced scorecard performance management system which demonstrates the role of critical success factors (CSFs) and key performance indicators (KPIs) in this process.

The balanced scorecard

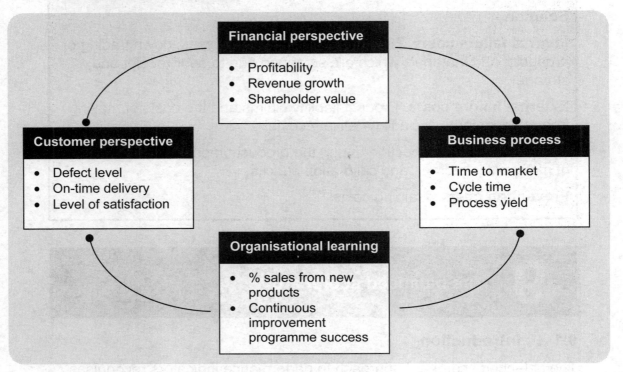

9.3   Key performance indicators

Typical key performance indicators for the balanced scorecard approach are illustrated below.

	Financial aspect	*Customer aspect*	*Business process aspect*	*Organisational learning aspect*
Strategic objective	Shareholder satisfaction	Customer satisfaction	Manufacturing excellence	New product innovation
Critical success factor	Grow shareholder wealth	Achieve preferred supplier status	State-of-the-art process plant	Successful new product development
Key performance indicators	ROCE	Number of new customers	Cycle times Unit cost % yield	% of sales represented by new products

10 Cost reduction and value enhancement

10.1 Introduction

There are few organisations which would not benefit from real efforts to keep costs to a minimum. Businesses will make more money that way, assuming quality is not compromised.

Not-for-profit organisations will make their funds go further in providing necessary services, and will be better able to meet the requirements for 'good stewardship' normally imposed on them.

> ### 🔍 Definitions
>
> **Cost reduction** is a process which leads to the achievement of real and permanent reductions in the unit costs of goods manufactured or services rendered without impairing their suitability for the use intended.
>
> **Cost control**, on the other hand, aims simply to achieve the target costs originally accepted.

Note that cost reduction is aiming to reduce unit costs, i.e. the cost per item of output. It would be possible for a cost reduction programme to increase the total costs incurred, as long as the output volume rose even more, so that the unit cost was reduced.

10.2 Implementing a cost reduction programme

Once an organisation has adopted an objective of reducing costs, the following conditions need to apply if it is to be successful.

- A clear purpose – say, to reduce labour costs by 20%, or materials by 15%.

- A good reason – economic survival, say, or the ability in the future to compete with competitors with a lower cost base.

- Commitment and involvement by senior managers.

- Excellent and positive communication with workforce and, if possible, consultation.

- Gradual introduction.

10.3 Application of cost reduction techniques

Virtually all areas of businesses and not-for-profit organisations are open to the use of cost reduction techniques, including product design, production, purchasing, marketing, distribution, finance and personnel.

Two important cost reduction techniques are target costing and value engineering.

(a) **Target costing**

Target costing starts by subtracting a desired profit margin from the market price at which an item could be sold; this gives the target cost. It is then up to the designers to plan how the product can be manufactured for that cost. If the product is currently planned to cost more than the target cost, then the plan must be modified.

(b) **Value engineering**

Value engineering is a philosophy of designing products which meet customer needs at the lowest cost while assuring the required standard of quality and reliability. The idea is to understand what it is that customers want from your products, and save costs by eliminating items that add no value in customers' eyes. For example, a manufacturer of computer components may decide that its customers place no value on a paper instruction manual or on fancy packaging, and will decide to sell its products with no manual and in a plain cardboard box.

10.4 Value enhancement

The 'flip side' of cost reduction is value enhancement namely, getting the best value from the resources that are used in the organisation. Use of the performance indicators that we have seen in this chapter will provide useful comparative measures to assess value enhancement before and after an active 'value-for-money' programme.

It should be emphasised that cost reduction and value enhancement are not just the responsibility of the accounts department of a business. All the functional specialists (designers, marketing, engineering, quality control, etc) must pool their knowledge and work side-by-side to achieve the required objectives.

10.5 Benchmarking

One way of closely monitoring one's own business is to compare the results in your business with those of closely related businesses. **Benchmarking** is the establishment of targets and comparators, through whose use relative levels of performance (particularly areas of under-performance) can be identified. By the adoption of identified best practices it is hoped that performance can be improved.

One common example is internal benchmarking, where a company is split up into business divisions, all operating in more or less the same industry, and performance indicators are calculated and compared for each division. Perhaps it is then found that one division has debtors of four months sales, while all the other divisions have debtors of less than two months sales. The division with abnormally high debtors should be able to improve its liquidity by tightening up its credit control procedures.

11 Summary

As you have seen, there are numerous possible performance indicators and their relevance will depend upon the type of organisation and the aspect of performance being assessed.

The most important ratios for you to be able to compute (and interpret) are as follows:

Profitability:
Return on capital employed (ROCE)
Gross and net profit margins

Liquidity:
Current ratio
Quick (acid test) ratio
Stock turnover
Debtors' collection period
Creditors' payment (settlement) period

Remember that a ratio on its own is not particularly useful information; it needs to be compared, internally or externally. This gives rise to problems of comparability, which you should be able to discuss.

Many of the ideas covered in earlier chapters will have relevance here (e.g. variance analysis and the use of indices).

Make sure you are quite clear about the necessary attributes of a cost unit (or unit of activity) in order for it to provide a useful basis for measurement. This is particularly important for service activities. Try to think of services you have had experience of yourself and how the various aspects may be measured.

There will rarely be a unique right or wrong answer, so do not be afraid to use your imagination!

12 Test your knowledge

 Workbook Activity 1

Barwin

As a trainee accountant, you have recently been transferred to the marketing department of Barwin, a company making sports caps, which are sold to a wide variety of wholesalers, retailers and sports clubs. Customers are categorised by the size of the account, measured in terms of annual turnover. There are a few large customers, which have a turnover greater than $2,000,000, mainly high street fashion chains.

At the other end of the scale, small customers have an annual turnover of less than $5,000. These mainly comprise of individual sports clubs and societies that tend to place orders for caps with their own club motif sewn on to the cap – the minimum order is $300. Medium-sized customers lie in the range of $5,001 to $200,000. The significance of categorising customers by the size of their account is to allow the application of different gross profit margins for sales quotations – large 10%, medium 20%, small 30%.

The sales manager is presently on holiday. His assistant, Alex Smart, has been asked to brief the sales manager on his return on the performance of the sales representatives. The sales manager is particularly keen to see which of Barwin's two regions has the better performance. He wants to give a bonus to the better team, according to Alex's recommendation. Alex has compiled the following information from the last period's account but is unsure what to do next.

Table 1	North Region	South Region
Orders taken and delivered	$	$
Large	2,000,000	4,000,000
Medium	1,200,000	2,300,000
Small	1,700,000	1,000,000
Total turnover	$4,900,000	$7,300,000

	North Region	South Region
Table 2		
Orders as a percentage of the company turnover	40.2%	59.8%
New business as a percentage of total orders	32.0%	15.5%
Cancelled orders as a percentage of total orders	9.0%	3.0%
Order value taken per km travelled	$13.61	$34.76

Table 3	North Region	South Region
Sales representatives		
– number of sales people	12	9
– total salaries of sales people	$180,000	$171,000
– fixed expenses (car leasing, telephones, etc)	$72,000	$54,000
– total km travelled*	360,000	210,000
Sales manager's salary	$32,000	$34,000

* variable cost per km = $0.10

Required:

(a)   Calculate the financial performance of the sales team in both of the two areas based on the gross profit less sales expenses. Show your results to the near $000.

(b)   On the basis of the information supplied and the expenses and profit calculated in part (a), calculate at least FOUR suitable performance ratios that will help Alex to compare the two areas. Show your results in a table.

Note: Such measures should be in addition to the performance measures already in Table 2.

(c)   Write some brief notes to assist Alex in understanding the performance of the two areas.

Workbook Activity 2

Hotel departments

A company owns and manages hotels. Each hotel has a general manager with responsibility for investment decisions.

Sub-managers are responsible for departments within the hotel. The departments and responsibilities in each hotel are:

- Accommodation (responsible for bedrooms and for the letting of rooms for meetings);

- Catering (responsible for all food and beverages);

- Household (responsible for maintenance, cleaning and laundry);

- Administration (responsible for accounting, marketing and recruitment and training).

The following information is provided for the Catering Department of one hotel for a period:

- 2,140 meals were served in the restaurant at an average price of $12.60.

- Further revenue of $4,620 was generated from the provision of food for meetings and room service.

- Sales of beverages were $18,610.

- Direct costs incurred were:
  Food/beverages $16,188
  Staff $11,784
  Other $2,640

- Target profit margin (net of direct costs) is 40%.

In addition to the direct costs incurred, the department is apportioned:

- 10% of the general occupancy costs of the hotel (e.g. rent, rates, heating, lighting). The general occupancy costs of the hotel totalled $47,320 in the period.

- 20% of the costs of the Household and Administration Departments which totalled $64,970 in the period.

Required:

(a)   Determine the net profit of the above Catering Department in the period and assess the department's profit performance.

(b)   Identify the type of responsibility centre that may be appropriate for each of the following:

   (i)   Catering Department;

   (ii)   Administration Department;

   (iii) Hotel.

(c)   Suggest two measures (one financial and one non-financial) that may be used to assess performance in each of the following:

   (i)   Accommodation Department;

   (ii)   Household Department.

(d)   Outline difficulties that may be encountered in applying performance measures effectively in the hotel group.

Workbook Activity 3

(a)   Nicholson sells mobile telephones. It supplies its customers with telephone handsets and wireless telephone connections. Customers pay an annual fee plus a monthly charge based on calls made.

The company has recently employed a consultant to install a balanced scorecard system of performance measurement and to benchmark the results against those of Nicholson's competitors. Unfortunately the consultant was called away before the work was finished. You have been asked to complete the work. The following data is available:

Nicholson – Operating data for the year ended 30 November 2007

Sales revenue	$480 million
Sales attributable to new products	$8 million
Average capital employed	$192 million
Profit before interest and tax	$48 million
Average number of customers	1,960,000
Number of telephones returned for repair	10,000
Number of bill queries	12,000
Number of customer complaints	21,600
Number of customers lost	117,600
Average number of bill queries unresolved at the end of each day	118
Average number of telephones unrepaired at the end of each day	804

Required:

Calculate the following ratios and other statistics for Nicholson for the year ended 30 November 2007.

(i)   Return on capital employed;

(ii)   Return on sales (net profit percentage);

(iii)   Asset turnover;

(iv)   Annual number of complaints per thousand customers;

(v)   Percentage of customers lost per annum;

(vi)   Average time to resolve billing queries;

(vii)   Average wait for a telephone repair;

(viii) Percentage of sales attributable to new products.

(b) The following information is for the mobile phone industry for the year ended 30 November 2007.

Industry average statistics – Mobile Telephones

Annual number of complaints per 1,000 customers	5
Percentage of customers lost per annum	3%
Average time to resolve billing queries	1.4 days
Average wait for a telephone repair	2 days
Percentage of sales attributable to new products	20%
Return on capital employed	15%
Return on sales (net profit percentage)	5%
Asset turnover	3 times

Required:

Using the industry average information and your answer to part (a), discuss the performance of Nicholson in the year ending 30 November 2007 under the four balanced scorecard headings of:

(i)   financial success;

(ii) customer satisfaction;

(iii) process efficiency; and

(iv) organisational learning and growth.

Note: State any assumptions that you make.

Budgeting – other considerations

7

Introduction

KNOWLEDGE

- Explain the behavioural aspects of budgeting (Element 2.1)

SKILLS

- Present any recommendations with a clear rationale to appropriate people (Element 3.7)

CONTENTS

1   Zero-based budgeting (ZBB)

2   Rolling budgets

3   Use of computer models in budgeting and forecasting

4   Budgets and control and motivation

5   Participation in budget setting.

1 Zero-based budgeting (ZBB)

1.1 Introduction

Zero-based budgeting is a method of budgeting that requires each cost element to be specifically justified, as though the activities to which the budget relates were being undertaken for the first time. Without approval, the budget allowance is zero.

ZBB requires the budget for every part of an organisation to be built up from 'scratch' or, in the more usual terminology, 'from base'.

The technique forces managers to consider and justify all the costs of an operation, in the light of the level of service provided and the costs of providing that service.

A range of possible output levels may be considered which should, in principle, include the 'zero-option' – although this may often not be feasible or desirable.

The costs of providing each level of service will be assessed against the level of service provided and the most appropriate chosen.

You will probably see that ZBB is as much a decision-making model (at which level should we operate) as a pure budgeting system.

1.2 The technique of zero-based budgeting

The first requirement in a ZBB process is the development of a *decision package.* This has been defined by its first proponent Peter A Pyhrr of *Texas Instruments* as:

'A document that identifies and describes a specific activity in such a manner that senior management can:

(a)   evaluate it and rank it against other activities competing for limited resources

(b)   decide whether to approve or disapprove it.'

Decision packages are developed by managers for their particular areas of responsibility. They will contain information such as:

- the function of the department

- a performance measure for the department

- costs and benefits of operating a department at a range of different levels of funding

- consequences of not operating at those levels.

The second requirement is the ranking of the decision packages, using cost/benefit analysis.

The result is a list of ranked projects or activities which senior management can use to evaluate needs and priorities in approving budgets. The resources available to the organisation for the forthcoming budget period are then allocated accordingly.

This in practice may be a formidable task, particularly in the light of the complex interrelationships that exist within an organisation, and probably no organisation can afford to take the time to examine every activity in the necessary depth every year.

A review cycle covering each activity once every three or four years may be more practical.

1.3 Advantages and limitations of zero-based budgeting

Despite considerable practical problems associated with applying ZBB throughout the organisation, it has some important benefits, particularly when compared with the alternative 'incremental' approach:

(a) it helps to create an organisational environment where change is accepted

(b) it helps management to focus on company objectives and goals

(c) it concentrates the attention of management on the future rather than on the past

(d) it helps to identify inefficient and obsolete operations within the organisation

(e) it provides a framework to ensure the optimum utilisation of resources by establishing priorities in relation to operational activity

(f) it should lead to a more logical and beneficial allocation of resources available to an organisation

(g) it can assist motivation of management at all levels

(h) it provides a plan to follow when more financial resources become available, establishing priorities

(i) it establishes minimum requirements from departments

(j) it can be done piecemeal, for example department by department

(k) it can be particularly effective as a means of preparing budgets for service departments – an activity which is more difficult than budgeting for manufacturing department, because of the lack of a visible product or output.

It does have some disadvantages namely:

(a)   it takes more management time than conventional systems, in part because managers need to learn what is required of them. As a consequence it is a more costly system to operate

(b)   there is a temptation to concentrate on short-term cost savings at the expense of longer-term benefits

it is difficult to rank competing projects presented by different managers for their particular area of responsibility

it may be difficult to develop decision packages for non-production departments.

Many managers use the term 'zero-based budgeting' to justify random large-scale cost-cutting exercises.

1.4   Application of ZBB

The following example is designed to show the mechanics of a ZBB system. You should note that the study guide for Paper 7 indicates that you will not be preparing a ZBB in your examination questions, but seeing how the system operates will help you with explanation and discussion questions in this area.

 Example

ZB Budgets Ltd has two service departments – material handling and maintenance, which are in competition for budget funds which must not exceed $925,000 in the coming year. A zero base budgeting approach will be used whereby each department is to be treated as a decision package and will submit a number of levels of operation showing the minimum level at which its service could be offered and two additional levels which would improve the quality of the service above the minimum level.

The following data have been prepared for each department showing the three possible operating levels for each:

Material handling department

Level 1. A squad of 30 labourers would work 40 hours per week for 48 weeks of the year. Each labourer would be paid a basic rate of $4 per hour for a 35-hour week. Overtime hours would attract a premium of 50% on the basic rate per hour. In addition, the company anticipates payments of 20% of gross wages in respect of employee benefits. Directly attributable variable overheads would be incurred at the rate of $0.12 per man hour. The squad would move 600,000 kilos per week to a warehouse at the end of the production process.

Level 2. In addition to the level 1 operation, the company would lease 10 fork lift trucks at a cost of $2,000 per truck per annum. This would provide a better service by enabling the same volume of output as for level 1 to be moved to a customer collection point which would be 400 metres closer to the main factory gate. Each truck would be manned by a driver working a 48-week year. Each driver would receive a fixed weekly wage of $155.

Directly attributable overheads of $150 per truck per week would be incurred.

Level 3. A computer could be leased to plan the work of the squad of labourers in order to reduce their total work hours. The main benefit would be improvement in safety through reduction in the time that work-in-progress would lie unattended. The computer leasing costs would be $20,000 for the first quarter (3 months), reducing by 10% per quarter cumulatively thereafter.

The computer data would result in a 10% reduction in labourer hours, half of this reduction being a saving in overtime hours.

Maintenance department

Level 1. Two engineers would each be paid a salary of $18,000 per annum and would arrange for repairs to be carried out by outside contractors at an annual cost of $250,000.

Level 2. The company would employ a squad of 10 fitters who would carry out breakdown repairs and routine maintenance as required by the engineers. The fitters would each be paid a salary of $11,000 per annum.

Maintenance materials would cost $48,000 per annum and would be used at a constant rate throughout the year.

Overheads directly related to the maintenance operation would be a fixed amount of $50,000 per annum.

In addition to the maintenance squad it is estimated that $160,000 of outside contractor work would still have to be paid for.

Level 3. The company could increase its maintenance squad to 16 fitters which would enable the service to be extended to include a series of major overhauls of machinery. The additional fitters would be paid at the same salary as the existing squad members.

Maintenance materials would now cost $96,000 per annum and would be used at a constant rate throughout the year.

Overheads directly related to the maintenance operation would increase by $20,000 from the level 2 figure.

It is estimated that $90,000 of outside contractor work would still have to be paid for.

Determine the incremental (extra) cost for each of levels 1, 2 and 3 in each department.

Solution

(a) *Material handling department*

Level 1: note that all the costs of level 1 are incremental – this is the lowest level of activity achievable

	$
Wages cost: 30 × 40 hours × 48 weeks × $4	230,400
30 × 5 hours × 48 weeks × $2	14,400
	244,800
Employee benefits	
20% × $244,800	48,960
Variable overhead	
30 × 40 hours × 48 weeks × $0.12	6,912
Incremental cost	**$300,672**

Level 2: note that the costs here are described as additional, therefore they are incremental

Leasing:	10 trucks @ $2,000	
	20,000	
Drivers' wages	10 drivers × 48 weeks × $155	74,400
Overhead	10 trucks × 48 weeks × $150	72,000
Incremental cost		**$166,400**

Level 3:

Additional costs incurred

Leasing:	
($20,000 + $18,000 + $16,200 + $14,580)	68,780

Less costs saved (Savings):
(30 men × 40 hours × 48 weeks × 10% = 5,760 hours)

Wages cost: 5,760 hours × $4	23,040
2,880 hours × $2	5,760
	28,800

Employee benefits		
20% × 28,800		5,760
Variable overhead	5,760 hours × $0.12	691
		(35,251)
Incremental cost		**$33,529**

Maintenance department

Level 1:

		$
Engineers' salaries	2 × $18,000	36,000
Outside contractors		250,000
Incremental cost		**$286,000**

Level 2:

Engineers' salaries	2 × $18,000	36,000
Fitters' salaries	10 × $11,000	110,000
Materials		48,000
Overheads		50,000
Outside contractors		160,000
		404,000
Less level one costs		(286,000)
Incremental cost		**$118,000**

Level 3:

Engineers' salaries	2 × $18,000	36,000
Fitters' salaries	16 × $11,000	176,000
Materials		96,000
Overheads		70,000
Outside contractors		90,000
		468,000
Less level two costs		(404,000)
Incremental cost		**$64,000**

In order to use ZBB fully, the company would also need to estimate the incremental benefits resulting at each level so that a rational decision can then be taken on whether operating Level 1, 2 or 3 is most profitable

1.5 The use of ZBB

In principle ZBB is a very sound tool of management, and the likely success of such a system depends very largely on commitment to it in terms of management time and effort. This type of analytical approach to budgeting can be very costly in terms of time and money, and there should be some attempt to measure the benefits that could be obtained.

Few, if any, large organisations in the UK have adopted ZBB for *all* their departments for *every* year, and it is doubtful whether this would ever be completely feasible. However, a selective approach as to which parts of the organisation are to be subjected to a ZBB procedure in any one year may be a practical compromise.

Research carried out by one of the major writers on management accounting systems, Charles Horngren generated the following summary of the uses of ZBB.

		Private sector	*Public sector*
(1)	Extent of use	The use of ZBB has spread rapidly in both sectors since the early 1970s. Furthermore, there is no indication that there is a levelling off of interest in ZBB or its use.	
(2)	Where and how it is primarily being used	As a management tool in planning for and controlling the staff and support functions. A ZBB review is normally conducted for a relatively small portion of a corporation's total budget.	As the main system of budget justification (and, in most cases, presentation) for all functions within an organisation.
(3)	Perceived effectiveness of ZBB as a tool in reducing costs/personnel and shifting resource allocations	There have been some examples of cost/personnel savings and shifts in resource allocation resulting from the use of ZBB, but these have not been widespread.	To date there have been no substantive examples of savings or shifts in resource allocation which resulted from the use of ZBB.

(4)	Most frequently mentioned benefit and problem associated with the use of ZBB	*Benefit* – Increased participation of managers in the budget preparation process. *Problem* – Time and effort required to develop, implement and operate the system.
(5)	Incidence of post audits of ZBB	Many user organisations in both sectors have conducted a review of the process at various stages in its implementation and use. However, these reviews tend to be informal, providing limited insight into the 'real' cost-effectiveness of the process.

2 Rolling budgets

2.1 The problem of change in budgeting

As we have seen already, budgeting involves forecasting which is always subject to a high degree of uncertainty because circumstances change. A budget prepared based on forecasts reflecting a given set of assumptions about, say, future price changes, exchange rates or tax rates, will not be valid if those factors change. Most of the changes companies are likely to be facing are environmental – they arise outside the organisation and are typically not something over which the organisation has control. Government action, competitors' behaviour or even the weather may affect the accuracy of forecasts.

Change is one of the major problems in budgeting – this is sometimes referred to as the problems of budgeting in a dynamic environment. This problem will become more significant the further ahead we try to budget. The time period for which a budget is prepared is known as the time horizon. Budgets prepared for a shorter time horizon (say three months or a year) are going to be more reliable than budgets prepared for a longer time horizon, say five years.

2.2 Techniques for dealing with change in budgeting

A number of options are available to management for dealing with the problem of change in the budgetary process. These include:

- continue with the original budget, making allowances as necessary
- adapt the original budget to reflect the changed circumstances

- re-budget from scratch
- adopt a 'rolling budget' or forecast revision approach.

Continue with the original budget

If environmental changes are not significant, it may be appropriate to retain the original budget and expect managers to adapt to the changed situation within the structure of the original budget. This policy will keep budgeting procedures as simple as possible and may be the most practical and economic approach.

Adapt the original budget to reflect the changed circumstances

If the changes relate to one or two key variables (such as interest rates and a certain material input inflation), it might be wise and feasible to **adapt the master budget to the new situation**, particularly if the budgetary data are held in a sophisticated computer financial model. As the revised budget would be based on the original budget it is more likely to be accepted by managers who would appreciate the need to reflect new conditions.

Re-budget from scratch

This is the most radical (and costly) approach which will involve re-working the entire budget preparation process building in the new information. As well as the time involved, it is also possible that there will be hidden costs here – managers will be presented with a revised set of budgets and will be expected to adjust their behaviour and activities accordingly – this could prove to be disruptive to the operations of the business.

Rolling budgets (and forecast revisions)

These are dealt with in detail below.

2.3 Rolling budgets and rolling forecasts

A **rolling budget** is a budget continuously updated by adding a further accounting period, (month or quarter) when the earliest accounting period has expired.

A **rolling forecast** is a continuously updated forecast whereby each time actual results are reported, a further period is added and intermediate period forecasts are updated.

Some organisations which work in a particularly dynamic environment may adopt a rolling approach as their normal budgeting system. The technique essentially attempts to keep budgets and forecasts up to date by revising figures as new information comes to light.

Steps in preparing a rolling budget

Typically a rolling budget is prepared as follows:

(a)   A budget is prepared for the coming year (say January to December 20X2) broken down into suitable, say quarterly, control periods.

(b)   At the end of the first control period (31 March 20X2) a comparison is made of that period's results against the budget. The conclusions drawn from this analysis are used to update the budgets for the remaining control periods and to add a budget for a further three months, so that the company once again has budgets available for the coming year (this time, April 20X2 to March 20X3).

(c)   This process is repeated at the end of each three-month control period.

Advantages of rolling budgets

- Budgets are more realistic and achievable since they are continuously revised to reflect changing circumstances.

- The disruption associated with the preparation of an annual budget is removed – the budgetary process is spread over the year.

- The pressures (and stress) placed on managers to achieve unrealistic budget targets are eased.

- Variance feedback (comparison of budget with actual data) is more meaningful.

- It reduces the rigidity of the budget system and builds unforeseen events and innovation into the budgetary process.

- The assessment of objectives and plans is continuous rather than being a one-off exercise.

- Without some form of budget revision, operational management may continue to invest and recruit, etc. with the belief that the original forecast remains valid – inappropriate decisions may be taken.

- It might help to increase management commitment to the budget.

- The arbitrary and artificial distinction drawn between one financial year and the next is removed, since budgets always extend for a year ahead.

Disadvantages of rolling budgets

- If it is difficult to plan ahead accurately once a year, how likely is it that managers can do the same forecasts more accurately every month or quarter when they are involved in other responsibilities?

- There is a danger that the rolling budget will become the last budget 'plus or minus a bit' and will be representative of absolutely nothing in terms of corporate objectives and meaningless for performance control purposes.

- Managers will be faced with a greater work load and additional staff may be required – extra time and cost could be incurred.

- Managers may devote insufficient attention to preparing budgets which they know will shortly be revised.

- The organisation might be required to operate annual budgets (such as enterprises operating in the public sector).

In conclusion it is worth noting that the development of computer budgeting 'models' using spreadsheets has increased the use of rolling budgets and similar concepts in organisations.

3 Use of computer models in budgeting and forecasting

3.1 Introduction

Most of the numerical forecasting and budgeting techniques studied here will be carried out far more efficiently with the help of computer software packages.

Packages may have specific statistical applications (index numbers, time series analysis, regression, etc.), or be of a more general nature, that can be used in a variety of areas, according to how they are set up by the user (e.g. spreadsheets and databases).

Spreadsheets, in particular, are of great use in budgeting and decision-making, due to the ability to manipulate a large amount of data very quickly to answer 'what-if' questions.

When producing a master budget manually the major problem is ensuring that any initial entry in the budget or any adjustment to a budget item is dealt with in **every** budget that is relevant – in effect, budgets need to comply with normal double entry principles to be consistent.

Suppose, for instance, that sales in the last month were expected to rise by $10,000, what adjustments would be necessary?

> The sales budget would need to be increased.
>
> ↓
>
> If receivables take more than one month to pay, year-end receivables would need to be increased.
>
> ↓
>
> Cost of sales would increase.
>
> ↓
>
> Purchases would need to be increased.
>
> ↓
>
> Either payables or cash payments would be increased.
>
> ↓
>
> Inventory at a month end may have to be increased, but not the final year-end inventory.
>
> ↓
>
> Profit would increase.

Performing all these adjustments by hand would be time consuming and the likelihood of error high.

Using computer programs, spreadsheets for example, all of the above adjustments could be processed automatically if the relevant formulae were set up properly. On adjusting month 12's sales; receivables, cost of sales, purchases, payables, cash, inventory and profit could change instantly.

3.2 Spreadsheets

A spreadsheet is a computer package which stores data in a matrix format where the intersection of each row and column is referred to as a cell. Columns are referenced alphabetically and rows numerically with the result that a cell reference is a combination of these. This is illustrated below:

	A	B	C	D	E
1					
2					
3		▨			
4	.				
5					

The reference of the shaded cell is B3 because it is the intersection of column B and row 3.

Each cell within a spreadsheet may be used to store:

- a label (description) e.g. the title of the spreadsheet
- a value
- a formula.

The formula is used to carry out calculations on values entered in other parts of the spreadsheet. The spreadsheet can be used to make large numbers of calculations based on the data contained in other cells of the same or another spreadsheet, or using values incorporated within the formulae.

So, changes to any of the data within the spreadsheet will automatically revise the values contained in any formula related cells – clearly this is very useful in the budgeting situation above where we need to recognise the knock on effect of a change in a sales forecast.

The simple example of a cash flow model which follows shows how this linking of cells is used. In this example, the cash flow data has been simplified to show only balance brought forward, receipts and payments, without giving detailed analysis:

	A	B	C	D	E
1		Jan	Feb	Mar	April
2					
3	Opening balance	1,000	1,100	1,000	550
4	Add: Receipts	700	800	500	850
5	Less: Payments	600	900	950	400
6					
7	Closing balance	1,100	1,000	550	1,000
8					

The great advantage of spreadsheets results from the fact that the cells showing balances, such as B7, contain relationships. This is the result of applying formulae, as we can see below:

	A	B	C	D	E
1		Jan	Feb	Mar	April
2					
3	Opening balance	1,000	=B7	=C7	550
4	Add: Receipts	700	800	500	850
5	Less: Payments	600	900	950	400
6					
7	Closing balance	=B3+B4-B5	=C3+C4-C5	=D3+D4-D5	=E3+E4-E5
8					

The opening balance for every month except January equals the previous month's closing balance. Similarly the closing balance is the Opening balance + Receipts – Payments.

Advantages of spreadsheets

The great advantage of this approach becomes apparent when applied to a large and complex problem:

- a typical spreadsheet can handle approximately 8,000 rows and over 200 columns, enough to accommodate a very complex model

- if any figure is amended, all the figures will be immediately recalculated

- the results can be printed out without going through a separate typing phase

- most programs can also represent the results graphically e.g. the above balances can be shown in a bar chart:

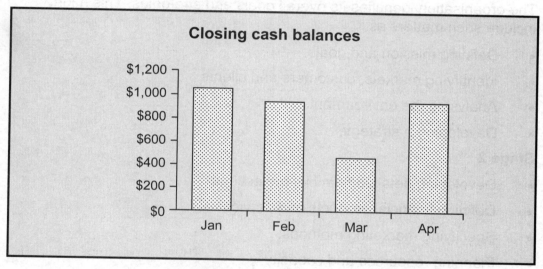

Disadvantages of spreadsheets

- Spreadsheets for a particular budgeting application will take time to build up and develop. There is no benefit in taking many hours to develop a spreadsheet which is then only used occasionally to complete a task which could easily be done efficiently using a manual method.

- Data can be accidentally changed (or deleted) without the user being aware of this occurring.

- Errors in design, particularly in the use of formulae, can produce invalid output. Due to the complexity of the model, these design errors may be difficult to locate.

- The manipulation of the data using such a mathematical approach may lead to the loss of the original concepts, these being replaced with a seemingly accurate set of output reports. In the context of budgets and forecasts it must be remembered that such output is based on data which are estimates and which may therefore be incorrect.

3.3 Financial modelling software

Many software houses have developed their own financial modelling software programs. Most of these are based on modified spreadsheets and many of them allow an organisation to build up an overall financial plan including a detailed set of budgets.

Each of these models will, of course have their own specific features, but a typical approach taken is outlined below:

Stage 1

The organisation identifies its overall goals and strategies. This might include such matters as:

- Defining mission and goals.
- Identifying markets, customers and clients.
- Analysing the environment.
- Developing a strategy.

Stage 2

- Developing detailed financial projections.
- Defining financial products and services.
- Specifying marketing methods.
- Planning resources and capacity.
- Developing a financing strategy.
- Analysing financial projections and indicators.

It should be noted that these models will be expensive to buy or develop and so their use if often limited to larger organisations. It will also be necessary for management and accountants to develop skills and experience to enable them to use the models effectively.

3.4 What-if analysis

'What-if' analysis is a form of sensitivity analysis, which allows the effects of changing one or more data values to be quickly recalculated.

Most decisions are made under conditions of uncertainty where the majority of input values are estimated. These input values are combined to produce an output value which appears to be mathematically accurate, but such accuracy may be misleading.

Most decisions are quite complex, involving a range of different input values. What-if analysis enables each of these to be changed both individually and in combination to see the effects on the final results. An example to illustrate this is shown below.

 Example

PH Ltd is considering a new product and has estimated the following details:

Selling price/unit	$5.00
Monthly sales volume	1,000 units
Variable cost/unit	$2.00
Monthly fixed cost	$2,000

Assuming that the production and sales volumes are always equal, the profit based upon this data is:

$$[1,000 \times (\$5.00 - \$2.00)] - \$2,000 = \$1,000 \text{ PROFIT}$$

If the volume is reduced by 20% the effect on profit is:

$$[800 \times (\$5.00 - \$2.00)] - \$2,000 = \$400 \text{ PROFIT}$$

---

 4   **Budgets and control and motivation**

4.1 Introduction

In addition to asking you to analyse and explain variances, examinations frequently require a discussion on whether the budgeting procedures used within an organisation are likely to achieve their aims.

These aims, and the methods used to achieve them, can be broadly categorised as follows:

- efficient management – management by exception;

- motivation of workforce – responsibility accounting.

4.2 Management by exception

The features of this method of reporting are that:

(a) attention is drawn only to areas where operations are seen to be 'out of control';

(b) this may be achieved by identifying those variances that are deemed to be 'exceptional';

(c) only these variances will be investigated and (where possible) corrected;

(d) management time and expertise are utilised where it can be most effective in improving the efficiency of future operations.

For it to be effective, it is important that:

* exceptional variances are correctly isolated;

* only such variances owing to factors capable of correction be considered for investigation;

* costs and benefits of investigation are assessed.

4.3 Responsibility accounting

The aim of a responsibility accounting system is to motivate management at all levels to work towards the company's objectives with the minimum of direction.

What is involved?

(a) The use of budgets as 'targets' against which management performance may be measured and (often) rewarded.

(b) The presentation of 'performance reports' relating to particular responsibility centres. These centres fall into three categories as follows.

    (i) **Cost centre** or **expense centre** where a manager is held responsible for control of expenditure.

    (ii) **Profit centre** where a manager is held responsible for control of sales revenue and expenditure.

    (iii) **Investment centre** where a manager is held responsible for investment decisions as well as the control of sales revenue and expenditure.

(c) The requirement that the person deemed responsible for that area should give explanations of significant variances shown therein.

Examinations on this subject tend to concentrate on a practical application of the principles necessary for a system of responsibility accounting to work effectively, and often require the preparation of a draft performance report, or the criticism of such a report. An in-depth theoretical knowledge of the work carried out in this field is not needed; a commonsense approach to a practical problem suffices.

4.4 Budgets and motivation

Motivation is the drive or urge to achieve an end result. Motivation can be as a force operating within an individual which drives that individual on to attain some goals or objectives. The word motivation comes from the Latin word meaning to move – this shows the key idea involved. An individual is motivated if they are moving forward to achieving goals or objectives.

Motivation may affect many aspects of the life of an individual. You have to be motivated to pass your examinations and to gain a recognised accounting qualification. At work you are motivated to achieve promotion and to gain a position of greater authority and responsibility within the organisation.

In a business context, if employees and managers are not motivated, they will lack the drive or urge to improve their performance and to help the organisation to achieve its goals and move forward. This is the importance of motivation in a business.

Three main areas need to be examined in relation to the use of budgets in responsibility accounting:

(a)   participation in budget setting;

(b)   budgets as motivational targets;

(c)   performance evaluation and reward.

The conclusions under each of these headings are largely common sense – you should try to think up practical examples in relation to your own position in study or at work to help you remember them.

4.5 Participation in budget setting

Conventional wisdom suggests that managers should be encouraged to participate in the budget setting process and that the budget should be built up from the lower rungs of management ('bottom up' budgeting) rather than imposed from above ('top down' budgeting).These are the advantages:

- Managers will then feel that they 'own' the budget and will therefore be more committed to the targets and motivated to achieve them.

- Operating managers are often the only people with sufficient detailed knowledge to develop a meaningful budget.

4.6 Disadvantages of participation

However, there are disadvantages to participation.

- The objectives of the managers and the objectives of the organisation may not be the same. 'Goal congruence' does not automatically result from empowering managers to develop their own budgets.

- Operating management may use their knowledge to manipulate the budget. They may deliberately set targets that they cannot fail to achieve, particularly if bonuses are awarded for meeting the budget.

- Managers may not wish to participate in the budget setting process. This may be because:

    (i)   they simply want to know what their targets are;

    (ii) they do not have the technical expertise to participate in budget setting;

    (iii) they do not have the necessary commitment to the organisation;

    (iv) they feel that the budget will be 'used against them'.

4.7 Budgets as motivational targets

In general, it is accepted that corporate objectives are more likely to be met if they are expressed as quantified targets, often in the form of budgets.

If a target is to have any influence on performance:

- the recipient must be aware of its existence and feel committed to achieving it;

- it must be set at the right level of difficulty to act as a motivator; both unrealistic and over-generous targets will be demotivational.

In theory, there may be a need for two budgets to be prepared for the same area.

- One should be a challenging (aspirations) budget to motivate the manager.

- The second should be a lower, and more realistic, expectations budget for planning and decision purposes.

Care should be taken to reward success as well as penalising failure, in order that a benefit is perceived in bettering rather than just achieving the target.

Budgets become stronger motivators as they become tighter up to a point, but thereafter motivation declines. The optimal degree of tightness depends on both the situation and the personality of the individuals concerned.

Empirical evidence suggests that if a budget target is set that is too easy, then actual performance will be a little better than the budget but it will not be optimised. In other words, managers do not usually work to their full potential if they know that a lower level of performance will still meet the budget – human behaviour will tend to lead to individuals putting in the minimum possible effort to achieve a set target. If greater effort were applied, a higher target may be achieved.

On the other hand, if the budget is too difficult, because it is based on ideal levels of performance, managers become discouraged at what they regard as an unattainable standard. This may de-motivate and as a result, actual performance falls short of what might reasonably have been expected.

You can apply these points to your own position in the context of examinations. If the pass mark for an examination is very low – say 10% – you know you can pass with little effort and you will (perhaps) not work to your full potential. On the other hand, if the pass mark were 99% you would, probably, view that as impossible to achieve and decide not to try at all!

The aim should be to agree a budget that falls between these two extremes and therefore incorporates just the right degree of difficulty which will lead to the optimal level of performance. At this level the budget should be challenging enough to motivate a manager to optimise his performance without being too ambitious. Authors writing on this subject have used the phrase 'tough but attainable' targets should be set.

The right level of difficulty is that which is acceptable to that individual manager. This level of acceptability will differ from manager to manager, as each individual behaves and reacts in a different way in similar circumstances.

This concept of budget difficulty can be demonstrated diagrammatically as follows:

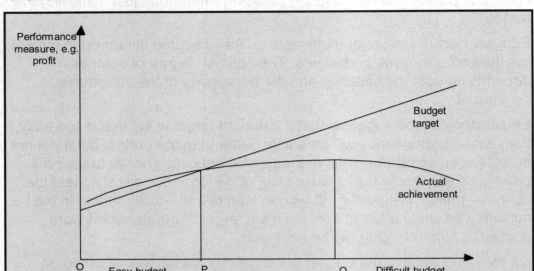

- A budget set at the degree of difficulty represented by point P is referred to as an 'expectations budget' as budget target and actual achievement are likely to coincide. The target level of performance has been met.

- However, a relatively easy-to-achieve budget, (set to the left of point P), is likely to lead to sub-optimal actual performance in that, although the budget has been met, the ACTUAL performance is at a relatively low level.

- In order to achieve a higher actual performance a more difficult budget needs to be set (an 'aspirations budget') at some point between P and Q. A budget set where point Q represents the degree of difficulty should lead to optimal performance (highest point on the 'actual' performance curve). However, it should be noted that this would give rise to an adverse variance compared with budget. If this target is set, senior management should not penalise the manager for the adverse variance, which may be unavoidable.

The diagram brings out one of the most fundamental points in budgeting: How the degree of difficulty, represented by point Q, is determined is not at all easy in practice because it involves a knowledge of how each individual manager will react and behave. Attempts to quantify the degree of difficulty using work study assessments are a highly simplified approach to a very complex problem.

Furthermore, attempts to use the budget as a motivating tool in the manner described may in fact lead to the need for two budgets.

- One is the total of what all the individual managers have agreed to achieve (with the different degrees of budget difficulty incorporated into them).

- The second may recognise that actual performance is likely to fall short of aspiration and is, therefore, a more realistic basis for planning purposes.

4.8 Performance evaluation and reward

Managers should only be held accountable for items over which they have control, and measures of performance should be devised that promote decisions in line with corporate objectives.

Thus a manager of a profit centre may be judged by variances affecting sales and direct costs (before allocated fixed costs); the performance of the centre itself will be measured by direct controllable contribution (having accounted for costs that are directly attributable to that centre, but not necessarily all controlled by the manager).

There are three main styles of management in the use of budget performance reports:

(a) The budget-constrained style, which lays particular emphasis on results being closely in accordance with the budget plan;

(b) The profit-conscious style, which is less concerned with current deviations from budget than with a manager's ability to achieve a trend of results which is acceptable in relation to changing conditions;

(c) The non-accounting style, which tends to disregard accounting reports as a means of measuring management performance and instead looks at factors such as:

- the number of customer complaints or substandard items produced;

- staff turnover;

- morale in the department;

- other qualitative measures.

Of the three styles, the middle is probably the most successful in achieving the company's long-term goals. The first creates good cost consciousness but also a great deal of tension between a manager and his subordinates, and manipulation of accounting information. The last promotes general good morale, but managers have a low involvement with costs.

Managers may receive financial rewards (for example, bonuses) and non-financial rewards (for example, promotion or greater responsibility) based on their ability to meet budget targets.

In the previous section the motivating effect of budgets was considered, but it should be remembered that the budgets by themselves have a limited motivational effect. It is the reward structure that is linked to achieving the budget requirements, or lack of reward for non-achievement, which provides the real underlying motivational potential of budgets.

A manager will need to regard the reward as being worthwhile if his behaviour is to be influenced so that he/she strives actively towards the achievement of the budget.

It is a common practice to attempt to assess the performance of a manager by a comparison of budgeted and actual results for his area of responsibility in the organisation. The choice of which particular measures to use is important to ensure that the individual manager sees the attainment of his targets as worthwhile for himself and at the same time in the best interests of the organisation as a whole – this is the concept of goal congruence which we saw in the chapter on responsibility accounting and which we shall cover again later in this chapter. In practice, conflicts can and often do arise between individual managers' personal objectives and those of the organisation as a whole.

The way in which the information in budget reports is used in the assessment of managerial performance has to be considered. Different degrees of emphasis on the results of budget versus actual comparisons can lead to different attitudes and feelings among managers. There is a need to achieve the correct balance between on the one extreme, an over-emphasis on results leading to pressure and feelings of injustice from the system; and on the other, too little stress on results leading to a budget irrelevancy attitude and low morale.

In general, we can summarise the characteristics of a sound employee reward system as follows:

- Fairness – the system should reward effort which helps the organisation achieve its objectives.

- Motivational – it should motivate the managers and employees to behave congruently i.e. in a way which assists the organisation to achieve its objectives.

- Understandability – the system should be such that it is clear to managers what they need to do to achieve the rewards. Unduly complex reward systems, perhaps based on complex bonus formulae are unlikely to be effective in generating improved performance.

- Consistently applied – the system should operate in the same way for all employees or, if not possible, for all employees at a given level in the organisation.

- Objective – the system should be based on measurable criteria with a minimum of subjectivity. It should also be such that it is not open to manipulation by managers in their own interests.

- Universal – all employees and managers at all levels in the organisation should be subject to an appraisal and reward system.

5 Participation in budget setting

5.1 The top down approach to budgeting

The top down approach is where budgets are set by higher levels of management and then communicated to the lower levels of management to whose areas of responsibility they relate. This is also known as an imposed budget.

In this approach lower-level managers are not allowed to participate in the budget-setting process.

The main problem with this approach is that those responsible for operating the budget will see it as something in which they have had no say. They lack ownership of the budget and as such they will be reluctant to take responsibility for it. It is unlikely to motivate the employees to achieve the budgetary targets set for them.

However, it can be argued that this top down approach may be the only approach to budgeting which is feasible if:

- lower level employees have no interest in participating in the process

- they are not technically capable of participating in budget setting

- only top level management have access to information which is necessary for budgeting purposes – perhaps information which is commercially sensitive.

5.2 The bottom up approach to budgeting

The bottom approach to budgeting is where lower level managers are involved in setting budget targets. This is known as a participative budget.

The more that individual managers are involved in setting budget targets, the more likely it is that they will accept those targets and strive actively towards the attainment of them. Employees are more likely to internalise the budget – accept it as part of themselves.

In this way actual performances should be improved by the motivational impact of budgets.

The main problem is:

- If budgets are used both in a motivational role and for the evaluation of managerial performance, then the problem of budgetary bias may arise.

Budgetary bias is where a manager deliberately sets a lower revenue target or a higher cost target.

By lowering the standard in the budget the target will be easier to achieve and performance will appear to be better. There is evidence to show that this tends to occur where a manager is actively seeking progression within an organisation or where financial rewards are based on ability to beat the budget. The effects of this sort of bias can be minimised by careful control, at the budget setting stage, and over any changes in the budget from one year to the next which are not due to external factors.

- Some people in organisations, by the very nature of their personality, do not wish to participate in the wider aspects of their jobs. They prefer an authoritarian style of leadership and do not strive for independence. Participative approaches to budget-setting will be very limited in their effect in such circumstances.

- Participation will be less effective in organisational situations where a manager or employee feels that he has little scope to influence the actual results for the budgeted area of responsibility. The lower down in the organisation structure the budget holder is, the more constrained is he by factors imposed from above. For example, objectives, strategies and policies, as well as the sales forecast and budget, limit the extent that a subordinate manager in the production function has for real participation in the setting of the budget for his area of responsibility.

- An important point to recognise is the difference between actual and perceived participation. It is the extent to which an individual manager perceives that he has influenced the budget that is crucial in that manager's acceptance of it.

An extension of this bottom up approach is the concept of budget challenging – employees are given the chance to question a budget presented to them (in a positive way!) before it is finalised.

5.3 Goal congruence

The principle of goal congruence involves ensuring that all members of the organisation pull in the same direction towards helping the organisation to achieve its overall goals and objectives.

If individuals in an organisation fail to demonstrate congruent behaviour, decisions taken may benefit that individual personally or the division which that individual woks for, but it may not benefit the organisation as a whole – this is known as dysfunctional behaviour.

We saw in the earlier chapter that an appropriate choice of performance evaluation methods is important in this context. The way the budgetary control system is operated can also be significant.

There may be a general fear and misunderstanding about the purpose of budgetary control. It is often regarded as a penny-pinching exercise by top management rather than recognised as a tool of management at all levels in an organisation structure. If this tends to be the attitude, a carefully planned campaign of education and training should be undertaken. Managers should be encouraged to discover how the budgetary control system can be of benefit to them personally as well as how it may benefit the organisation.

Employees may become united against management and devote their energies to finding excuses for not meeting targets. Targets that are realistic, and are seen by the employees as being realistic, are what is required. Good communications involving consultation and participation should help to minimise this problem.

One of the key roles in any organisation is at the supervisor/foreman level where the continual interface between management and employees exists. The leadership and motivational function of a supervisor or foreman is very important if the work is to be done and targets are to be achieved.

Conclusion

Most organisations use a conventional incremental approach to budgeting – essentially basing this period's budget on information relating to the previous period. Zero-based budgeting (ZBB) is designed to avoid the problem of the conventional budgeting approach of inaccuracies and inefficiencies being carried forward from previous period's budgets. ZBB requires managers to start budgeting for each activity from a fresh start and justify increases in expenditure in terms of the generation of extra benefits.

Rolling budgets are developed as a technique to keep budgets up to date where an organisation is operating in a rapidly changing environment.

The mechanics of budget preparation can be made quicker and more efficient by the use of a number of modern computer-based techniques. Spreadsheets are the main technique involved, but these can be developed into more sophisticated packages such as financial modelling programs. These in turn can be used as part of a scenario building exercise as part of the forecasting and planning process.

It is important that you appreciate that the budgetary control system which operates within an organisation may have a significant effect on the people who work within that organisation. This important fact must always be born in mind when designing or commenting on such a system.

The main point to appreciate is that a budgetary control system should have the effect of motivating employees to work in the best interests of the organisation as a whole – the concept of goal congruence.

Participation (the bottom up approach, and education play important roles in encouraging a positive approach to budgeting in the mind of employees.

6 Test your knowledge

 Workbook Activity 1

You are the Assistant Budget Accountant of Brunel Plc and have recently attended a conference on alternative approaches to Budgeting. Upon your return, you are asked to write an email to the Finance Director that :

(a) Briefly describes zero-based budgeting, how it might be implemented in an organisation and the benefits that should result.

(b) Explains what is meant by a rolling budget and what advantages and disadvantages can be claimed for this type of budget compared with a periodic budgeting system.

(c) Explains what is meant by 'what if' analysis, describe the action that management might take in response to the information provided and state any limitations of the analysis.

To : Finance Director

Date : (Today)

From : Assistant Budget Accountant

Subject : Alternative approaches to budgeting

(a) Zero-based budgeting

(b) Rolling budgets

(c) What-if analysis

 Workbook Activity 2

Trygon Limited

Six months ago, Parmod plc established a new subsidiary, Trygon Limited. Trygon was formed to assemble and sell computers direct to the public. Its annual budget was drawn up by Mike Barratt, Parmod's Finance Director. Trygon's plant was capable of producing 150,000 computers per year although the budget for the first year was only 80% of this amount. Factory overheads – defined as all factory fixed costs other than labour – were to be charged to finished stocks at all times on the basis of this 80% activity, irrespective of actual activity.

Trygon had entered into an agreement with the employees whereby their wages were guaranteed provided the employees made themselves available to produce 120,000 computers per year. Because of this agreement, the labour element in finished stocks was always to be based on the production level of 120,000 computers. If output exceeded the 120,000 units, additional overtime equivalent to £70 per extra computer would be paid. Managers were also to be given a bonus of £15 per computer produced in excess of 120,000 units in the year.

At the beginning of the year, Mike had given all the managers a financial statement showing the annual budget (based on 80% activity) and the effect of operating at only half the planned activity level. This is reproduced below.

Trygon Limited budgeted profit for the year to 31 December 20X6

Activity	Annual budget (80%)	40%
	£	£
Direct materials	24,000,000	12,000,000
Direct labour	7,200,000	7,200,000
Light, heat and power	4,000,000	2,200,000
Production management salaries	1,500,000	1,500,000
Factory rent, rates and insurance	9,400,000	9,400,000
Depreciation of factory machinery	5,500,000	5,500,000
National advertising	20,000,000	20,000,000
Marketing and administration	2,300,000	2,300,000
Delivery costs	2,400,000	1,200,000
Total costs	76,300,000	61,300,000
Sales revenue	84,000,000	42,000,000
Operating profit/(loss)	7,700,000	(19,300,000)

In preparing the financial statement, Mike Barratt had made the following assumptions:

(a) (i) Unit selling prices were the same over the different activity levels.

(ii) No quantity discounts or other similar efficiencies had been assumed for purchases.

(b) Production fixed overheads comprised the depreciation of the machinery, the rent, rates and insurance, the production management salaries (other than any possible bonus) and part of the cost of light, heat and power.

Six months after Mike Barratt had issued the statement, you are called to a meeting of the directors of Trygon Limited. Anne Darcy, the managing director, tells you that production and sales for the year are likely to be 112,500 computers.

Required:

(a) You are the Management Accountant to Trygon. Anne Darcy asks you to prepare a flexible budget for the year using the data given by Mike Barratt and assuming 112,500 computers are produced and sold. She also asks you to identity the budgeted profit.

Further data

On receiving your flexible budget, Anne Darcy reminds her fellow directors that Trygon plans a major marketing campaign at the beginning of the next financial year and this will require a building up of stocks in preparation for the campaign. The production director, Alan Williams believes it is feasible to increase production close to capacity without increasing any of the fixed costs. As a result, the Board agrees to budget for sales of 112,500 units by the year end but to produce at 95% capacity.

A discussion then followed about the role of budgeting in Trygon Limited *'I do not know why we should take up all this time discussing* budgets' said Anne Darcy. *'They are not my* figures. I *had no say in their* preparation. Let *Mike Barratt take responsibility for them – after all, it was his budget – and let us get on with the job of building up a* business.'

'I agree,' Alan Williams said. 'I *wish Mike would make up his mind what we are supposed to be doing. Are we just concerned with making short-term* profits *or are we supposed to be building up a quality product? Just what are our objectives when budgeting? Besides, you can prove anything with* figures. Just *look at the budget prepared by the Management Accountant compared with the annual budget prepared by Mike* Barratt.'

Anne Darcy then turns to you. 'We *need to resolve these* issues. *Will you please write a short report to the Board members giving us your advice.'*

Required:

(b) In response to Anne Darcy's request, you are required to write a short report drawing on the information given above. The report should:

(i)   recalculate the flexible budget based on production at 95% capacity assuming fixed overheads in finished stock are based on 80% activity;

(ii) explain why the revised flexible budget may differ from the one prepared in (a);

(iii) answer the issues raised by Alan Williams regarding the two different budget statements, the uncertainty about budgetary objectives and the manipulation of budget data;

(iv) briefly discuss whether or not Anne Darcy should have been responsible for preparing the original budget.

Workbook Activity 3

World History Museum (AAT CA J94)

The World History Museum has an Education Department which specialises in running courses in various subjects. The courses are run on premises which the museum rents for the purpose and they are presented by freelance expert speakers. Each course is of standard type and format and can therefore be treated alike for budgetary control purposes.

The museum currently uses fixed budgets to control expenditure. The following data shows the actual costs of the Education Department for the month of April compared with the budgeted figures.

Education Department – April

	Actual	Budget	Variance
Number of courses run	5	6	(1)
	£	£	£
Expenditure			
Speakers' fees	2,500	3,180	680
Hire of premises	1,500	1,500	–
Depreciation of equipment	200	180	(20)
Stationery	530	600	70
Catering	1,500	1,750	250
Insurance	700	820	120
Administration	1,650	1,620	(30)
	8,580	9,650	1,070

You have recently started work as the assistant management accountant for the museum. During a discussion with Chris Brooks, the general manager, she expresses to you some doubt about the usefulness of the above statement in providing control information for the Education Department manager.

Chris is interested in the possibility of using flexible budgets to control the activities of the Education Department. You therefore spend some time analysing the behaviour patterns of the costs incurred in the Education Department. Your findings can be summarised as follows:

1 Depreciation of equipment is a fixed cost.

2 Administration is a fixed cost.

3   The budget figures for the catering costs and insurance costs include a fixed element as follows:

Catering   £250

Insurance   £100

The remaining elements of the catering and insurance costs follow linear variable patterns.

4   All other costs follow linear variable patterns.

Required:

(a) Use the above information to produce a budgetary control statement for April, based on a flexible budget for the actual number of courses run.

(b) Calculate the revised variances based on your flexible budget.

(c) Chris Brooks' interest in the control aspects of budgeting has been sparked by her attendance on a course entitled 'Budgetary control for managers'. She has shown you the following extract from the course notes she was given:

'A system of participative budgeting involves managers in the process of setting their own budgets. Participative systems are likely to be more successful in planning and controlling the activities of an organisation.'

Write a brief memo to Chris Brooks which explains the advantages and disadvantages of participative budgeting as a part of the budgetary planning and control process.

WORKBOOK ACTIVITIES
ANSWERS

Workbook Activities Answers

1 Forecasting and planning

Workbook Activity 1

Data	Source
TV Licence fee	BBC website
Cost of electricity (wind power)	The Environment agency
Inflation trend in the UK	Office for National Statistics

Workbook Activity 2

Who would you contact in each of the following situations?

- You want to identify the production capacity of the firm: Production Planning Manager

- You want to forecast the price of raw materials: Buyer

- The draft budget is ready for final approval: Board of Directors

Workbook Activity 3

Regression line

(a) In the formula y represents total cost (the dependent variable), x represents the units of activity (the independent variable), 192 represents the fixed cost element (£), 2.40 represents the variable cost per unit (£).

The formula is estimating a linear relationship between activity level and total cost.

(b) (i)   x   =   500

y   =   192 + 2.40 (500)

=   £1,392

(ii) x   =   1,500

y   =   192 + 2.40 (1,500)

=   £3,792

 Workbook Activity 4

Income forecast

The forecast should be revised to **£5,800,000**

Working :

Remove the 3% increase in selling price from forecast data :

£5,974,000 ÷ 103 = £5,800,000

Workbook Activity 5

Next year's sales = £1,325,000 × (1 +2%)
Next year's sales = £1,351,500
Next year quarterly sales = £1,351,500 ÷ 4 = £337,875 per quarter

- Quarter 1   sales : £337,875 + £12,000 = £349,875
- Quarter 2   sales : £337,875 + £18,000 = £355,875
- Quarter 3   sales : £337,875 - £25,000 = £312,875
- Quarter 4   sales : £337,875 - £5,000 = £332,875

Quarter	£
1	£349,875
2	£355,875
3	£312,875
4	£332,875
Year	£1,351,500

 Workbook Activity 6

Price indices

Simple price index $= \dfrac{P_1}{P_0} \times 100$

$= \dfrac{13.65}{12.50} \times 100$

$= 1.092 \times 100$

$= 109.2$

This means that the price has increased by 9.2% of its base year price of £12.50.

Workbook Activity 7

2001	Q1	Q2	Q3	Q4
Actual price per tonne	£40	£44	£64	£76
Seasonal variation	− £4	− £8	+ £4	+ £8
Trend	£44	£52	£60	£68
2002				
Trend (+ £8 per quarter)	£76	£84	£92	£100
Seasonal variation	− £4	− £8	+ £4	+ £8
Forecast price per tonne	£72	£76	£96	£108

Workbook Activity 8

(a)

Year	Quarter	Actual	4 quarter total	4 quarter average	Centred trend	Seasonal variation
1997	3	142				
	4	142				
			584	146		
1998	1	150			146	4
			584	146		
	2	150			148	2
			600	150		
	3	142			150	-8
			600	150		
	4	158			152	6
			616	154		
1999	1	150			154	-4
			616	154		
	2	166			156	10
			632	158		
	3	142			158	−16
			632	158		
	4	174			160	14
			648	162		
2000	1	150				
	2	182				

(b)   Analysis of seasonal variations

	Quarter 1	Quarter 2	Quarter 3	Quarter 4	Residual
1998	4	2	− 8	6	
1999	− 4	10	− 16	14	
Total	0	12	− 24	20	
Average	0	6	− 12	10	4
Adjustment for residual	− 1	− 1	− 1	− 1	− 4
Seasonal variations	− 1	5	− 13	9	0

(c)   Forecast demand for quarter 2:

Trend	164
Seasonal variation	5
	———
Forecast	169
Actual (estimate)	182
Residual	13
	———

(d) Suggest **TWO** reasons why there might be a difference between the forecast figure calculated in (c) and the result given in the data.

Reason 1	Possibility of random errors.
Reason 2	Seasonal variations might not be additive.
Reason 3	The original actual data was only an estimate.
Reason 4	The sales volume data ignores some factors which might influence demand, e.g. price changes

 Workbook Activity 9

The 4% increase in energy consumption should be revised and reduced by 10% instead of increased by 4%.

(£2,970,000 ÷1.04) × (1 − 10%) = **£ 2,570,192**

2 Dealing with fixed overheads

Workbook Activity 1

Overhead recovery rates for each cost centre:

Machining $\dfrac{£36,000}{4,000 \text{ machine hours}}$ = £9.00 per machine hour

Fabrication $\dfrac{£41,600}{5,200 \text{ machine hours}}$ = £8.00 per machine hour

Outside contract work $\dfrac{£28,600}{1,950 \text{ labour hours}}$ = £14.67 per direct labour hr

Production cost of contract:		£
Direct material		3,100
Direct labour:		
Machining	12 hours	
Fabrication	8 hours	
Outside work	6 hours	
	26 hours × £7.50	195
Overheads:		
Machining	12 hours × £9.00	108
Fabrication	8 hours × £8.00	64
Outside work	6 hours × £14.67	88
Production cost		3,555
Add 10% for admin, selling and distribution		356
		£3,911

Selling price/contract price (£3,911/75) ×100 =	**£5,215**

Check:	£
Contract price/selling price	5,215
Cost	3,911
Profit	£1,304

Profit = 25% of selling price as required.

Workbook Activity 2

Overhead absorption rate	£
Building occupancy	9,100
Telephone, postage and stationery	4,700
Other overheads	11,200
Administrator's salary	14,500
Total Overheads	39,500

Number of labour hours	9,400

£39,500/9,400

Overhead absorption rate per labour hour	4.20

		£	
Partner's labour charge-out rate £30,000/1,880	=	15.96	per hour
Qualified senior £18,500/1,880	=	9.84	per hour
Trainee (1) £10,500/1,880	=	5.59	per hour
Trainee (2) £12,000/1,880	=	6.38	per hour

White Rose Hotel Estimated fee

		£
Direct labour		
Partners : 5 hours x £15.96	=	£79.80
Qualified seniors : 12 hrs × £9.84	=	£118.08
Trainee (1) : 3 hrs × £5.59	=	£16.77
Trainee (2) : 3 hrs × £6.38	=	£19.14
Total Direct Labour		233.79
Overheads		
Total Overhead cost 23 hrs × £4.20		£96.60
Total Cost		£330.39
Thus charge to client		£471.99

Workbook Activity 3

Task

(a) **Sandsend Engineers Ltd overhead recovered:**

		£
Machining	4,250 machine hours × £9.00	38,250
Fabrication	5,300 machine hours × £8.00	42,400
Outside work	1,975 labour hours × £14.67	28,973
		£109,623

(b)

Overhead control account

	£		£
Actual:		*Recovered in work-in-progress*	
Machining	37,800	Machining	32,250
Fabrication	42,000	Fabrication	42,400
Outside work	29,100	Outside work	28,973
Over-recovered P/L account (bal)	723		
	109,623		109,623

Workbook Activity 4

		£
Direct labour	4.5 hours × £8.50	38.25
Direct material	1.1 tonnes × £25	27.50
Variable overhead	£378,000/12,000 tonnes	31.50
Marginal cost = Total variable costs per tonne		£97.25

Contribution / tonne = = Selling Price – Variable Cost
= £132 – £97.25
= £34.75

Workbook Activity 5

(a) **Cost driver rates:**

Activity	Cost pool £	Cost driver volume	Cost driver rate
Process set up	260,000	200 set ups	£1,300 / set up
Material procurement	74,000	50 purchase orders	£1,480 per purchase order
Maintenance	64,000	12 maintenance plans	£5,333 per plan
Material handling	120,000	2,500 material movements	£48 per movement
Quality costs	80,000	200 inspections	£400 per inspection
Order processing	30,000	1,000 customers	£30 per customer

(b) Using the ABC method, the following overhead would be recovered for each 1,000 tonnes of output:

			£
17 set ups	×	£1,300	22,100
4 purchase orders	×	£1,480	5,920
1 maintenance plan	×	£5,333	5,333
210 material movements	×	£48	10,080
16 inspections	×	£400	6,400
80 customers	×	£30	2,400
			£52,233

Thus the overhead cost per tonne of product would be:

£52,233/1,000 = £52.23 per tonne

Workbook Activity 6

Situation	Answer
Redesign of the website	Allocate to marketing overheads
Holiday pay for operatives on the production line	Charge to production in a labour hour overhead rate
Material wastage in the production process	Direct cost
Administrative wages	Allocate to administrative overheads
Machinery maintenance services	Charge to production in a machine hour overhead rate
Production equipment cleaning	Charge to production in a machine hour overhead rate
Depreciation of machinery	Charge to production in a machine hour overhead rate
Cost of Purchasing Department	Activity based charge to production cost centres.

3 Preparing budgets

 Workbook Activity 1

Your organisation

MEMORANDUM

To: Marketing Manager

From: Assistant Management Accountant

Date: 12 December 20X4

Subject: Budgetary planning process

As requested, I provide below answers to your queries about the budgetary planning process.

(a) **The key factor**

Otherwise known as the principal budget factor or limiting factor, the key factor is the factor which limits the activity of an organisation. In our organisation it is sales volume, since there is a limit to how much we can sell. However, it is possible for other factors to be key factors, especially in the short term. Examples could be cash, machine capacity or skilled labour.

The determination of the key factor is important in the budgetary process because this is the budget which must be prepared first. Then all other budgets can be co-ordinated to this budget.

For example, once the sales budget has been determined, this will provide the basis for the production budget and for other budgets such as the purchasing budget and the cash budget.

(b) A number of steps can be taken to achieve co-ordination in the budgetary planning process, including the following:

(i) Set up a budget committee which consists of representatives from all parts of the organisation. Regular meetings of this committee should ensure that each part of the organisation is aware of what all other parts are doing.

(ii) Give one person the overall responsibility for ensuring that budgets are prepared on time and that they take into account all relevant factors. This person is often called the budget officer and will usually chair the budget committee.

(iii) Provide a timetable to all those involved in the budgetary process, detailing who is responsible for preparing each budget and when it must be prepared. This should reduce the risk of bottlenecks in the budgetary process and will co-ordinate the order of budget preparation.

(iv) Provide a budget manual to all those involved in the budgetary process. The contents of the budget manual would include the budget timetable mentioned above, instructions on completing the budget planning forms, details on key assumptions to be made in the planning process (such as the inflation rate and exchange rate), and so on.

(v) Provide regular feedback on the progress of budget preparation.

The key to co-ordinated budget preparation is communication.

Workbook Activity 2

			Alpha	Beta
(a)	Production budget – no shortage		*units*	*units*
	Sales volume		2,000	3,000
	Add closing stock		500	595
	Less opening stock		(300)	(297)
			———	———
	Production		2,200	3,298
			———	———

				Metres
(b)	(i)	**Material available for production**		
		Maximum purchases possible		61,580
		Add opening stock		8,750
		Less closing stock		(15,530)
				———
		Material available for production		54,800
				———

				Metres
	(ii)	**Material required for Beta production**		
		Net material required for Beta production		
		(3,298 × 12)		39,576
		Faulty (3/97 × 39,576)		1,224
				———
		Gross material required for Beta production		40,800

(iii)	**Material available for Alpha production**	*Metres*
	Material available for production	54,800
	Gross material required for Beta production	40,800
	Gross material available for Alpha production	14,000

(iv)	**Production of Alphas**	*Metres*
	Gross material available for Alpha production	14,000
	Wastage (3/100 × 14,000)	420
	Net material available for Alpha production	13,580
	Alphas produced (13,580/10)	1,358 units

(v)	**Labour hours to be worked**	*Hours*
	Alpha production (1,358 units × 1.15 hours)	1,561.70
	Beta production (3,298 units × 1.38 hours)	4,551.24
		6,112.94

(vi)	**Cost of labour budget**	
	Labour hours available (46 employees × 35 hours × 4 weeks)	6,440.00
	Cost of labour (46 employees × £210 per week × 4 weeks)*	£38,640

*As employees are guaranteed a 35-hour week, the labour cost will be based on the contracted amount and not the hours worked.

(c)	**Revised budgeted sales volumes**	*Units*
	Production of Alphas	1,358
	Add opening stock	300
	Less closing stock	(500)
	Sales volume – Alphas	1,158
	Sales volume – Betas (contracted volume)	3,000

	A	B
1	Selling price per unit	£140
2	Variable cost per unit	£70
3	Fixed costs per 4 week period	£40,000
4	Volume per period	1,000
5	4 weeks ending	1 February 2002
6	Turnover	= B1 × B4
7	Total variable cost	= B2 × B4
8	Contribution	= B6 – B7
9	Fixed costs	= B3
10	Operating profit	= B8 – B9

Workbook Activity 3

(a) **Production budget in units**

	Period 1	Period 2	Period 3	Period 4	Period 5
Demand	5,700	5,700	6,840	6,460	6,080
Less Opening stock	(1,330)	(855)	(1,026)	(969)	(912)
Add Closing stock	855	1,026	969	912	
Production	5,225	5,871	6,783	6,403	

(b)   Material purchases budget (litres)

		Period 1	Period 2	Period 3	Period 4
Production (units)		5,225	5,871	6,783	6,403
Material required (production × 6 litres)	(i)	31,350	35,226	40,698	38,418
Maximum material available	(ii)		34,000	34,000	34,000
Shortfall of material available (i – ii)				6,698	4,418
Reschedule purchases		1,226	1,226 −1,226		
Material purchases from Contrax plc	(iii)	32,576	34,000	34,000	34,000
Material purchases from outside supplier	(iv)			6,698	4,418

(c)   Material purchases budget (£)

	Period 1 £	Period 2 £	Period3 £	Period 4 £
Material purchases from Contrax plc (c) × £8	260,608	272,000	272,000	272,000
Material purchases from outside supplier (d) × £12			80,376	53,016
	260,608	272,000	352,376	325,016

(d)   Labour hours budget

	Period 1	Period 2	Period 3	Period 4
Production (units of Omega)	5,225	5,871	6,783	6,403
Standard hours required (units × 2 hours)	10,450	11,742	13,566	12,806
Inefficiency (5/95 × standard hours)	550	618	714	674
Total labour hours required	11,000	12,360	14,280	13,480
Basic hours (78 employees × 4 weeks × 40 hours)	12,480	12,480	12,480	12,480
Overtime	Nil	Nil	1,800	1,000

(e) **Labour budget (£)**

	Period 1	Period 2	Period 3	Period 4
Basic wage (£160 × 78 employees × 4 weeks)	49,920	49,920	49,920	49,920
Overtime (Overtime hours × £6)			10,800	6,000
	49,920	49,920	60,720	55,920

MEMO

To: Adrian Jones

From: Management Accountant

Date: X-X-XX

Subject: Cost savings

Following our recent discussions and your observations regarding the level of overtime and the material supplier, I list my comments below.

(a) **Immediate cost savings**

The material available in period 1 is 34,000 litres, whereas our requirement is 32,576 litres. A further 1,424 litres is available from Contrax and could result in a saving in one of two ways.

(b) By bringing production forward to period 1, there would be a saving of £5,696 because of the reduction in purchases, at a later date, from the alternative supplier – 1,424 litres × £4 = £5,696.

The same saving is possible by simply buying the 1,424 litres in advance to be used in a later period.

(c) **Continuing difficulties**

If minimum demand for the product continues at 5,700 per four-week period, the material requirements will be 34,200 litres per period, which suggests that the material constraint is a longer term problem.

The planned labour hours for minimum demand would be 12,000 per period, even if the inefficiency problem continues. However, with 12,480 hours available each period, this constraint is considered short-term.

(d) **Possible long-term cost savings**

In the longer term it may be possible to renegotiate the stock requirements with Advanced Industries. This would allow a lower investment in finished stocks.

However, we would need to satisfy them that we could supply them on time if their forecast requirement were inaccurate. One way of dealing with this would be flexible working, whereby excess demand was met by working unpaid overtime and allowing time off, paid in lieu, when demand was low.

Workbook Activity 4

(a) **Closing stocks quarter 3**

Delta

3,300 boxes × (6/60)   330 boxes

Omega   2,640 boxes × (8/60)

352 boxes

(b) **Labour hours available**

52 employees × 36 hours × 12 weeks   22,464 hours

(c) **Production budget**

	Delta	Omega
Sales demand quarter 3	3,000	2,400
Add Closing stocks	330	352
Less Opening stocks (given)	(630)	(502)
Good production	2,700	2,250
Add Scrap (1/9)	300	250
Total production (boxes)	3,000	2,500

(d) Material purchases budget

		kg
Material for *Delta* production	12 kg × 3,000 boxes	36,000
Material for *Omega* production	15 kg × 2,500 boxes	37,500
Material used in production		73,500
Add Closing stock		21,340
Less Opening stock		(13,560)
Material purchases		81,280
Cost of purchases	£7 × 81,280	£568,960

(e) Labour budget

		Hours
Labour hours for Delta production	3 hours × 3,000 boxes	9,000
Labour hours for Omega production	6 hours × 2,500 boxes	15,000
Labour hours required		24,000
Labour hours before overtime		22,464
Overtime hours		1,536
Cost of labour Wages	£180 × 52 employees × 12 weeks	£112,320
Overtime	£7.50 × 1,536 hours	£11,520
		£123,840

Workbook Activity 5

(a) (i) Number of production days in quarter 1:

12 weeks × 5 days   = 60 days

(ii) Units of closing finished stock:

Exe 930 × $\dfrac{8}{60}$ = 124 units

Wye 1,320 × $\dfrac{9}{60}$ = 198 units

(iii) Labour hours in the period before overtime:

12 weeks × 35 hours × 46 employees   = 19,320 hours

(b) (i) **Production budget for the 12 weeks ending 24 March 2000**

		Exe	Wye
Budgeted sales (units)		930	1,320
Add	Closing stocks	124	198
Less	Opening stocks	(172)	(257)
Production of good units		882	1,261
Faulty production (Exe = 2/98 × 882, Wye = 3/97 × 1,261)		18	39
Gross production before faults		900	1,300

(ii) **Material purchases budget for the 12 weeks ending 24 March 2000**

	Litres
Material requirement for Exe production (6 litres × 900 Exe)	5,400
Material requirement for Wye production (9 litres × 1,300 Wye)	11,700
Total material required for production	17,100

Add Closing raw material stock (5 days/60 days × 17,100 litres) 1,425

Less Opening raw material stock	(1,878)
Material purchases (litres)	16,647
Total material cost (16,647 × £15)	£249,705

(iii) **Production labour budget for the 12 weeks ending 24 March 2000**

	Hours
Budgeted hours required for Exe production (12 hours × 900)	10,800
Budgeted hours required for Wye production (7 hours × 1,300)	9,100
Total planned labour hours	19,900
Hours available before overtime	19,320
Overtime hours	580
Cost of normal hours (19,320 × £6)	£115,920
Cost of overtime (580 × £6 × 130%)	£4,524
Total labour cost	£120,444

Finance and other savings per quarter		£192
Exe	([172 – 124] × £4)	
Wye	([257 – 198] × £5)	£295
Raw material	([1,878 – 1,425] × £1)	£453
		£940

Workbook Activity 6

(a) Production budget – quarter ended 17 September 1999

	Alphas (units)	Betas (units)
Budgeted sales	2,000	2,400
Add: Closing stock (see Note 1)	200	480
Less: Opening stock	(500)	(600)
Production (finished units)	1,700	2,280

Note 1	Alphas	Betas
Sales this quarter 3	2,000	2,400
Add 20% seasonal variation	400	480
Budgeted sales next quarter 4	2,400	2,880
Closing stock (5/60 × 2,400 = 200) (10/60 × 2,880 = 480)	200	480

(b) Material purchases budget – quarter ended 17 September 1999

	Kilograms
Usage – Alpha production (8 kg × 1,700)	13,600
Usage – Beta production (12 kg × 2,280)	27,360
	40,960
Add Closing material stock (see Note 2)	16,384
Less Opening material stock	(12,000)
Purchases of material	45,344

Note 2	
Closing stock of materials:	
Usage this period	40,960
Add 20%	8,192
Material required for production next period	49,152
Stock required (20/60 × 49,152)	16,384

(c) Cost of purchases

(45,344 kg × £10)   £453,440

(d) Labour budget – quarter ended 17 September 1999

	Hours
Labour hours required for Alpha production (3 hours × 1,700)	5,100
Labour hours required for Beta production (6 hours × 2,280)	13,680
Total hours required before efficiency adjustment	18,780
Efficiency adjustment (20% / 80%)	4,695
Gross labour hours	23,475
Normal hours (50 employees × 35 hours × 12 weeks)	21,000
Overtime hours required	2,475

(e)

Normal hours (50 employees × 12 weeks × £210)	£126,000
Overtime (2,475 hours × £9)	£22,275
Direct labour cost	£148,275

Workbook Activity 7

(a) **Production budget (units)**	*Exe*	*Wye*
Sales volume	8,820	5,800
Add closing finished stocks (W)	5,292	3,016
Less opening finished stocks	(4,410)	(2,320)
Planned production	9,702	6,496

Working

Closing stocks

	Exe	Wye
Sales in period 1	8,820	5,800
Sales in period 2 (20% / 30% higher)	8,820 × 1.20	5,800 ×1.30
Closing stock = 10/8 days sales	$8,820 \times 1.2 \times \dfrac{10}{20}$	$5,800 \times 1.3 \times \dfrac{8}{20}$

(b) **Materials purchase budget** (square metres)

Production – Exe: 9,702 × 5 sq m	48,510
Production – Wye: 6,496 × 7 sq m	45,472
	93,982
Wastage (W)	1,918
Gross material issued to production	95,900
Add closing material stock	18,000
Less opening material stock	(16,950)
Purchase (square metres)	96,950

Good production	98	93,982
Waste	2	?
Input material	100	?

Therefore waste = $\dfrac{93,982}{98} \times 2 = 1,918$

(c) **Cost of purchases budget**

96,850 × £2.00	£193,900

(d) **Labour hours worked budget**

Exe: 9,702/6	1,617
Wye: 6,496/4	1,624
	3,241
Basic hours available: 22 × 35 × 4	3,080
Overtime	161

(e) **Cost of labour budget**

Basic hours: 3,080 × £8.00	£24,640
Overtime: 161 × £12.00	£1,932
	———
	£26,572
	———

(f) **Cost of production budget by product**

	Exe £	*Wye* £
Materials issued to production (W1)	99,000	92,800
Labour (W2)	12,936	12,992
Production overhead (W3)	19,404	19,488
	———	———
	131,340	125,280
	———	———

Workings

1 Materials
   Exe: 48,510 × 100/98 × £2.00 = £99,000
   Wye: 45,472 × 100/98 × £2.00 = £92,800
2 Labour
   Exe: 1,617 × £8.00 = £12,936
   Wye: 1,624 × £8.00 = £12,992
3 Production overhead
   Exe: 1,617 × £12.00 = £19,404
   Wye: 1,624 × £12.00 = £19,488

Note that it is a coincidence that the production overhead rate of £12 per hour equals the overtime rate. 161 hours of overtime at £4 per hour (£644) is charged to the production overhead account, along with the other (unspecified) overheads. These are all then charged to production at £12 per hour.

MEMO

To: Susan Fellows

From: Management Accountant

Date: 4 December 2003

Subject: Production constraints period 2

(a) Extra possible production of Exe

The calculations to determine whether materials or labour are the constraint are as follows:

	Material	Labour
Available resource	2,000 sq m	88 hours
Waste (2,000 × 2%) =	40 sq m	–
	1,960 sq m	88 hours
Possible production	1,960 ÷ 5 = 392	88 × 6 = 528

Material is, therefore, the effective constraint in period 1 if extra production is required, and 392 extra units of Exe can be produced.

(b) Revised production budget for period 1

With no extra production of Wye, the revised production budget will be as follows:

	Exe	Wye
Original production budget	9,702	6,496
Add additional production	392	
Revised Production budget	10,094	6,496

(c) Other ways of overcoming the constraint in period 2

There are several possible short-term solutions. The company should consider:

- holding less raw material stock: this will reduce the material constraint identified above

- holding less finished stock, which would release Exes and Wyes for sale

- sub-contracting out extra production

Workbook Activity 8

Tutorial note: Stock is used up by material usage, and by closing stock. This usage Is made up partly from opening stock. The balance must be made up from purchases.

	June £	July £	August £
Material usage	8,000	9,000	10,000
Closing stock	3,500	6,000	4,000
	11,500	15,000	14,000
Less: Opening stock	5,000	3,500	6,000
Purchases	6,500	11,500	8,000

(a) ***Tutorial note:*** The main points to watch out for are sales receipts and overheads. Tackle sales receipts by calculating separate figures for cash sales (10%of total sales, received in the month of sale) and credit sales (90% of last month's sales). For overheads, remember that depreciation is not a cash expense and must therefore be stripped out of the overheads cash cost.

Cash budgets, June – August

	June £	July £	August £
Receipts of cash			
Cash sales	4,500	5,000	6,000
Credit sales	29,500	40,500	45,000
	34,000	45,500	51,000
Cash payments			
Wages	12,000	13,000	14,500
Overheads	6,500	7,000	8,000
Direct materials	6,500	11,500	8,000
Taxation	–	25,000	–
	25,000	56,500	30,500

Surplus/(deficit) for month	9,000	(11,000)	20,500
Opening balance	11,750	20,750	9,750
Closing balance	20,750	9,750	30,250

(b) Cash budgets are an important part of business planning. They highlight future surpluses of cash (enabling managers to make appropriate plans for investing the surplus) and shortfalls of cash (enabling managers to take appropriate action in advance, perhaps by advising their bank of overdraft requirements or raising funds from other sources.)

Workbook Activity 9

	Sept £	Oct £	Nov £	Dec £	Jan £	Feb £
Receipts						
Cash sales (W1)	18,240	15,200	17,100	16,720	15,960	19,000
Credit sales (W2)	30,000	28,800	24,000	27,000	26,400	25,200
Capital		8,000				
	48,240	52,000	41,100	43,720	42,360	44,200
Payments						
Purchases (W3)	18,800	19,600	17,600	17,000	19,800	17,200
Wages (W4)	6,800	6,000	6,500	6,400	6,200	7,000
Fixed costs (W5)	6,000	6,000	6,000	6,000	6,000	6,000
Capital	15,000		10,000			4,000
Corporation tax			44,000			
	46,600	31,600	84,100	29,400	32,000	34,200
Surplus/(Deficit)	1,640	20,400	(43,000)	14,320	10,360	10,000
Balance b/f	5,000	6,640	27,040	(15,960)	(1,640)	8,720
Balance c/f	6,640	27,040	(15,960)	(1,640)	8,720	18,720

Workings

(W1) Since 60% of sales are credit sales, 40% are cash sales, e.g.,

	£
September cash sales = £48,000 × 40% =	19,200
5% discount on £19,200	960
	18,240

(W2) August credit sales are paid in September, and so on.

Credit sales = 60% so the September receipt = 60% × £50,000 = £30,000

(W3)

	July	Aug	Sept	Oct	Nov	Dec
Sales:						
Stock used (40% of sales)	17,600	20,000	19,200	16,000	18,000	17,600
Opening stock (50% of 40% of sales)	(8,800)	(10,000)	(9,600)	(8,000)	(9,000)	(8,800)
Closing stock (50% of 40% of next month's sales)	10,000	9,600	8,000	9,000	8,800	8,400
Extra stock					2,000	
PURCHASES	18,800	19,600	17,600	17,000	19,800	17,200
Paid in	Sept	Oct	Nov	Dec	Jan	Feb

(W4) 10% of sales + £2,000

e.g., September:

(10% × £48,000) + £2,000 = £6,800

(W5) £7,500 − £1,500 Depreciation: £6,000

Workbook Activity 10

Prepare a cash forecast for May from the following budget data

Budget data	March £	April £	May £	June £
Invoiced sales	2,500	3,000	2,800	4,000
Purchases	900	1,300	1,250	1,200
Wages	500	510	520	480
Other overheads	600	660	620	630
Capital expenditure	–	1,200	–	–

Average terms

Half of customers take 1 month to pay. Half take 2 months.

Purchases paid for after 2 months

Wages paid in the current month

Other overheads paid after one month

Capital expenditure paid in the current month

Cash forecast	May £
Opening Cash balance	(500)
Customer receipts	2,750
Payments	
For purchases	900
For wages	520
For overheads	660
For capital expenditure	0
Total	2,080
Closing cash balance	1,170

Workbook Activity 11

You are required to complete the working schedules and Operating Budget below. In the Exam, the shaded cells will be completed for you.

Working schedules

Materials	Kg	£
Opening stock	2,100	2,000
Purchases	15,500	27,125
Sub-total	17,600	29,125
Used	16,400	27,025
Closing stock	1200	2,100

Closing stock to be valued at budgeted purchase price

Labour	Hours	£
Basic time at £12 per hour	1,600	19,200
Overtime	400	7,200
Total	2,000	26,400

It takes 4 minutes to make each item

8 staff work 200 basic hours each

Overtime is paid at time and a half (50% above basic rate)

Overhead	Hours	£
Variable at £1.50 per hour	2,000	3,000
Fixed		3500
Total		6,500

Variable overhead recovered on total labour hours

Operating budgets

		Units	£
Sales revenue at	£2.50 each	29,000	72,500
Opening stock of finished goods		4,000	7,000
Cost of production		30,000	
Materials			27,025
Labour			26,400
Overhead			6,500
Total			59,925
Closing stock of finished goods		5000	9,987.5
valued at budgeted production cost per unit			
Cost of goods sold			56,938
Gross Profit			15,562.50

Overheads

	£
Administration	2,780
Marketing	2,500
Total	5,280
Operating profit	10,282.50

4 Budgetary control – flexing budgets

Workbook Activity 1

(a) **Budgeted data**

   (i)   Budgeted cost of material per unit of Delta:

      £600,000/100,000 Deltas   =   £6.00

   (ii)   Budgeted variable cost of light, heat and power per Delta:

      (£200,000 – £40,000)/100,000   =   £1.60

   (iii)   Number of budgeted production employees:

      £120,000/£12,000   =   10 employees

(b) **Flexible budgetary control statement for the year ended 30 November 2000**

	Flexible budget	Actual results	Variance
Volume (number of Deltas)	125,000	125,000	Nil
	£000	£000	£000
Turnover (@ £20)	2,500	2,250	250 (A)
Material (W1)	750	800	50 (A)
Light, heat and power (W2)	240	265	25 (A)
Production labour (W3)	156	156	0
Rent, rates and depreciation	140	175	35 (A)
Administrative expenses	110	110	0
Profit	1,104	744	360 (A)

Key:

A = Adverse

F = Favourable

Workings for flexed budget

(W1) Material   125,000 units × £6.00 = £750,000

(W2) Light, heat and power £40,000 + (125,000 × £1.60) = £240,000

(W3) Labour   13 employees × £12,000 = £156,000

REPORT
THE ROLE OF BUDGETS, FORECASTING AND VARIANCES
AT PARKSIDE MANUFACTURING LTD

To: Judith Green
Prepared by: Management Accountant
Date: X-X-XX Introduction

The purpose of this report is to provide a background and prior briefing on planning to be discussed at the Board meeting.

(a) **Budgets used at Parkside**

There are two types of budget used in the company. A fixed budget is one which is essentially a planning device and sets a target to which management are in the short-run committed. A flexible budget, however, is a control device. It is principally a revision of the original plan, whereby allowances are given for both cost and revenue, to match the level of activity actually achieved.

This enables a 'like with like' comparison to be made – the flexed budget v the actual results.

From this comparison meaningful variances can be reported, on which a measure of control can focus.

(b) **Factors to take into account before investigating variances**

It is not practicable to investigate all variances. Because of this, exception techniques are used by applying both a minimum absolute value and a minimum percentage variance before investigation is recommended.

A variance may be investigated if it is an element of a continuing trend.

Variances would not be investigated if the cause is a factor, of which management are aware. It is also not worth investigating variances if they are not controllable, e.g. insurances.

It is essential that the benefits of investigation, at all times, outweigh the cost.

(c) **Limitations of linear regression techniques**

- Assumption of linearity whereas sales volume might not follow that pattern.

- Use of historical data; past performance is not always a good guide to the future.

- Does not account for the effects of a product life cycle.

Workbook Activity 2

(a) Revised budgeted selling price:
(£1,760,000/11,000)   £160

(b) Material cost per unit in revised budget:
(£396,000/11,000)   £36

(c) Variable cost of production and administrative labour – high/low method:

Increase in budgeted labour cost (£630,000 – £580,000)	£50,000
Increase in budgeted volume (11,000 – 10,000)	1,000
Variable cost of labour per unit (£50,000/1,000)	£50

(d) Fixed cost of production and administrative labour:

Total budgeted cost of labour for 11,000 units	£630,000
Variable cost of labour (11,000 × £50)	£550,000
Budgeted fixed cost of labour	£80,000

(e) Variable cost of light, heat and power – high/low method:

Increase in budgeted light, heat and power (£164,000 – £160,000)	£4,000
Increase in budgeted volume	1,000
Budgeted variable cost of light, heat and power per unit (£4,000/1,000)	£4

(f) Fixed cost of light, heat and power:

Total budgeted cost of light, heat and power for 11,000 units	£164,000
Variable cost of light, heat and power (11,000 × £4)	£44,000
Budgeted fixed cost of light, heat and power	£120,000

MEMO

To:	Mike Green
From:	Management Accountant
Date:	22 June 2000
Subject:	Motivation and performance

I attach a budgetary control statement for Visiguard based on the flexible budget technique and wish to make the following observations.

(a) **Visiguard Ltd – Flexible budgetary control statement for the year ended 31 May 2000**

	Flexed budget	Actual results	Variances
Sales and production volume (units)	11,600	11,600	Nil
	£	£	£
Turnover (£160 × 11,600)	1,856,000	1,844,400	11,600 (A)
Variable materials (£36 × 11,600)	417,600	440,800	23,200 (A)
Production and administrative labour (£80,000 + [£50 × 11,600])	660,000	677,600	17,600 (A)
Light, heat and power 120,000 + [4 × 11,600]	166,400	136,400	30,000 (F)
Fixed overheads	240,000	259,600	19,600 (A)
Profit	372,000	330,000	42,000 (A)

(b) There is an assumption that a participative approach to budgets and budgetary control will improve management motivation and results. However, there are a number of situations where imposed budgets may be more effective than participative budgets. These include:

- Managers' objectives may not be those of the organisation as a whole.

- Managers do not have the training, skill or technical knowledge to set budgets.

- Managers would prefer not to set their own targets.

- Time constraint whereby full participation is not practicable.

(c) Setting of budgetary targets that are not achievable can be demotivating. If managers recognise this they are likely not even to attempt to achieve the target. Impossible targets can also bring into disrepute the whole planning process; and managers may question the validity and usefulness of the budgetary process.

This might have been the case in terms of the request to reduce material costs. If Visiguard do not have an alternative supplier, the managers may have little control over material prices.

(d) It does not always follow that improved performance compared to the original budget is because managers were motivated by the budget revision.

- Actual activity was greater than the agreed revision. This may have been due to the increased energy and motivation of managers. However, there may have been, outside the control of managers, a general increase in demand for the product.

- The only cost less than planned in the budget is light, heat and power. This may have been an inaccurate forecast or because weather conditions have been milder, thus reducing heating costs. It is unlikely that the power supplier has reduced costs.

Workbook Activity 3

(a) Calculation of unit variable costs – high/low method

	High original budget	Low revised budget	Range	Variable unit cost
Fasta units	24,000	20,000	4,000	
Variable costs	£	£	£	
Material	216,000	180,000	36,000	£9
Labour	288,000	240,000	48,000	£12
Semi-variable costs				
Heat, light and power	31,000	27,000	£4,000	£1

Analysis of heat, light and power

Variable cost (£1/unit)	£24,000	£20,000
Total cost	£31,000	£27,000
Fixed cost	£7,000	£7,000

Analysis of heat, light and power

Variable cost (£1/unit)	£24,000	£20,000
Total cost	£31,000	£27,000
Fixed cost	£7,000	£7,000

(b) **Rivermede Ltd**

Flexible budgetary control statement for the year ended 31 May 1999

	Revised budget	Actual results	Adjustment	Revised actual	Variance
Production and sales (units)	22,000	22,000		22,000	
	£	£	£	£	£
Variable costs					
Material (W1)	198,000	206,800	7,520	214,320	16,320 (A)
Labour (W2)	264,000	255,200		255,200	8,800 (F)
Semi-variable costs					
Heat, light and power (W3)	29,000	33,400	(7,520)	25,880	3,120 (F)
Fixed costs					
Rent, rates and depreciation	40,000	38,000		38,000	2,000 (F)
	531,000	533,400		533,400	2,400 (A)

Workings for flexed budget:

(W1) Material $22,000 \times £9$

(W2) Labour $22,000 \times £12$

(W3) Heat, light and power $(22,000 \times £1) + £7,000$

MEMO

To: Steven Jones

From: Management Accountant

Date: 16 June 1999

Subject: Flexible budgetary control

(a) The original operating statement compares an actual level of activity of 22,000 units with a revised forecast of 20,000 units. This is not a 'like with like' comparison and is of little use for management control purposes.

The flexible budget, however, informs on a 'like with like' comparison by giving an allowance for costs and revenue in relation to the actual level of activity achieved. The variances reported are therefore smaller and also are more meaningful. The reduction in these variances is not attributable to participative budgeting.

(b) There are a number of reasons why favourable cost variances may arise other than with the introduction of participative budgeting.

- A favourable variance may arise for a reason outside management's span of control.

  The variance on fixed expenditure relates to rent, rates and depreciation which are costs that are not controllable.

  A further example is that the fixed charge for heat, light and power may be different from planned.

- Managers may have inflated costs in the budget as a result of their participation.

(c) Similar reasons could be argued for the increase in sales volume.

- There could have been a general increase in demand without extra sales effort.

- The revision to the budget may have been too low. This may have been a genuine concern that the original target was not achievable. However, it may have been intentional, since by understating forecast demand, the actual performance looks better.

We should continue with participative budgeting but based on the flexible budgetary control technique.

Workbook Activity 4

(a)	**Budgeted unit selling price:** £4,800,000/120,000	£40.00

(b) **Budgeted variable cost of material**

(i)	**A:** £480,000/120,000	£4.00
(ii)	**B:** £840,000/120,000	£7.00
(iii)	**C:** £360,000/120,000	£3.00

(c) (i) **Budgeted fixed cost of light, heat and power**

Total budgeted cost	£290,000
Variable cost: £2 × 120,000	£240,000
	£50,000

(ii) Budgeted variable cost of water

Budgeted total cost	£212,000
Budgeted fixed cost	£20,000
Total variable cost	£192,000
Unit variable cost (£192,000/120,000)	£1.60

(d) **Shifnal Ltd: Flexible budget statement year ended 30 November 2003**

Omegas produced and sold	Flexed budget 95,000	Actual 95,000	Variance	
	£000	£000	£000	
Turnover (95,000 × £40)	3,800	3,990	190	(F)
Material A (95,000 × £4)	380	456	76	(A)
Material B (95,000 × £7)	665	665	–	(A)
Material C (95,000 × £3)	285	266	19	(F)
Light, heat and power (W1)	240	249	9	(A)
Water (W2)	172	182	10	(A)
Labour (W3)	160	168	8	(A)
Maintenance (W4)	50	54	4	(A)
Rent and rates	360	355	5	(F)
Distribution expenses	600	620	20	(A)
Administrative expenses	300	280	20	(F)
Operating profit	588	695	107	(F)

Workings

1 £50,000 + (£2.00 × 95,000) = £240,000

2 £20,000 + (£1.60 × 95,000) = £172,000

3 Up to 3,000 units cost £5,000 of labour

   95,000 units require $\frac{95,000}{3,000}$ = 31.67 'groups' of labour 3,000

   This is rounded to 32 as it is a stepped cost and you cannot employ part of a 'group'. Cost of labour = 32 × £5,000 = £160,000

4 95,000/20,000 = 4.75. Round up, therefore cost is 5 × £10,000 = £50,000

5 Investigating and reporting variances

Workbook Activity 1

Excelsior Manufacturing Company

(a)

	Production level (units)				
	4,000	5,000	6,000	7,000	8,000
	£	£	£	£	£
Direct materials	80,000	100,000	120,000	140,000	160,000
Indirect materials	12,000	14,000	16,000	18,000	20,000
Direct labour	50,000	62,500	75,000	87,500	100,000
Power	18,000	18,000	18,000	21,000	24,000
Repairs	20,000	22,500	25,000	27,500	30,000
Supervision	20,000	20,000	36,000	36,000	36,000
Rent, insurance and rates	9,000	9,000	9,000	9,000	9,000
Total cost					
	209,000	246,000	299,000	339,000	379,000

(b)

	Budget	Actual	Variance
	£	£	£
Direct materials	100,000	110,000	10,000 (A)
Indirect materials	14,000	14,000	–
Direct labour	62,500	70,000	7,500 (A)
Power	18,000	18,000	–
Repairs	22,500	30,000	7,500 (A)
Supervision	20,000	20,000	–
Rent, insurance and rates	9,000	8,000	1,000 (F)
Total cost			
	246,000	270,000	24,000 (A)

Comments on variances

- Direct materials: more was used than expected. Possibly waste in production, poor quality materials, operatives need more training. Is a particular department or machine at fault?

- Direct labour: again more was used than expected. Investigate reasons. Excessive overtime (should not be needed at a low level of production)?

- Repairs: needs investigation. Possible exceptional item. Do some pieces of capital equipment need replacing?

- Rent, insurance and rates: this is probably a price variance. Is this a one-off item or does the budget need to be altered in future?

 Workbook Activity 2

WH Limited

(a) – (c)

WH Limited

MEMORANDUM

To: Production Manager

From: Assistant Accountant
Date: 12 December 20X4
Subject: Direct cost variances for November

As requested I detail below explanations of the direct cost variances and possible suggestions as to their cause in November. Page 1 of 3

(a)   *The meaning of the variances*

Direct material price variance

This variance shows the saving or overspending which resulted from paying a lower or higher price than standard for the direct material used in the period. The favourable variance indicates that a lower than standard price was paid.

Direct material usage variance

This variance shows the saving or overspending, at standard prices, which resulted from using less or more material than standard to manufacture the production for the period. The adverse variance indicates that more material was used than standard.

Direct labour rate variance

This variance shows the saving or overspending which resulted from paying a lower or higher hourly rate than standard for the hours worked in the period. The adverse variance indicates that a higher than standard hourly rate was paid.

Direct labour efficiency variance

This variance shows the saving or overspending, at standard rates, which resulted from working less or more hours than standard to manufacture the production for the period. The favourable variance indicates that less hours were worked than standard.

(b) *Possible causes of the variances*

Favourable direct material price variance

Bulk discounts were received which were not allowed for in the standard. The standard price of material was set too high. A lower quality material was purchased, at a lower price than standard. Effective negotiations by the buyer secured a price lower than the standard.

Adverse direct material usage variance

Material wastage was higher than allowed in the standard. The standard usage was set too low. There was a higher than standard level of rejects. Theft of material.

Adverse direct labour rate variance

High levels of overtime were paid for compared with the standard allowance. The standard wage rate was set too low.

A higher grade of labour was used.

Bonus payments were higher than standard.

Favourable direct labour efficiency variance

Employees were working faster than standard. More skilled employees were used.

There were savings through the learning effect.

The standard labour time was set too high.

The material was easy to process, leading to savings against the standard time.

(c) Two examples of interdependence, where one variance can be related to others, could include the following.

The savings made on material price (favourable material price variance) may indicate that poor quality material was purchased, leading to high wastage, rejects and an adverse usage variance.

Bulk discounts may have resulted in the saving on material price. However, the consequent excessive stocks may have led to deterioration and write-offs, hence the adverse usage variance.

Direct workers may have been of a higher grade than standard, resulting in higher hourly rates and the adverse rate variance. However, the higher skill level may have led to time savings and the favourable efficiency variance.

Higher than standard bonus payments may have caused the adverse labour rate variance, but the bonuses may have resulted from faster working and hence the favourable efficiency variance.

Faster working resulted in the favourable efficiency variance, but less care may have been taken over weighing and handling the material, hence the adverse material usage variance.

Workbook Activity 3

Revamp Furniture Limited

(a)   Reconciliation for Period 1 (see workings)

	£	£	£
Flexed budgeted cost (W1)			34,840
Cost variances			
Materials (W2)			
Price	270		
Usage		400	
Labour (W3)			
Rate of pay		1,412	
Efficiency	512		
Fixed overhead (W4)			
Expenditure		50	
Efficiency	80		
Capacity	20		
	882	1,862	980
Actual cost (W5)			35,820

(b)   (i)   Although standard costing has, as one of its purposes, the allocation of responsibility for cost variances, it is often found in practice that the analysis of variances is merely the beginning of a further task of investigation before ultimate responsibility can be fairly assigned.

On the operating statement submitted for part (a) of this question there is disclosed a favourable material price variance and an adverse usage variance. Theoretically this should indicate that the buyer is operating efficiently and the production manager inefficiently. This need not necessarily be true, however. The buyer could have taken advantage of a special offer of material at less than standard price, not appreciating that the material was slightly below standard quality. It is very likely that the inferior material would give rise to production problems of machining, handling and possibly others which could well result in excess usage; hence the adverse usage variance.

(ii) As regards labour, the payment of higher than standard rates (suggested by the adverse rate of pay variance in the operating statement) may well have had the effect of providing greater motivation, and hence speedier work, which is reflected in the favourable efficiency variance.

There may well be interdependence between the material and labour cost variances; for instance, the speedier work suggested by the favourable labour efficiency variance may have been accomplished by disregarding material usage standards.

From the foregoing it will be seen that not only is there possible interdependence between the variances of each element of cost, but also cross-interdependence between the elements of cost.

Workings

1   *Standard cost per unit*

	£
Materials (6 × 50p)	3.00
Labour (2 × £1.60)	3.20
Fixed overhead $\frac{£30,000}{120,000}$ = 25p per hour × 2 hours	0.50
	6.70

Flexed budgeted cost 5,200 × £6.70   £34,840

(Fixed overhead is budgeted to be absorbed over (60,000 × 2 hours) = 120,000 hours

2   Materials

   (i)   Price variance

	£
Actual cost of 32,000 lb (5,880 + 6,790 + 3,060)	15,730
Standard cost	16,000
	———
	270 (F)
	———

   (ii)   Usage variance

	lb
Expected usage for 5,200 chairs (5,200 x 6)	31,200
Actual usage	32,000
	———
Excessive usage	800
	———
@ 50p per lb	£400 (A)
	———

3   Labour

   (i)   Rate of pay

	£
Actual cost of 10,080 hours	17,540
Standard cost (10,080 × £1.60)	16,128
	———
	1,412 (A)
	———

   (iii)   Efficiency

	Hrs
Standard time for 5,200 chairs	10,400
Actual time taken	10,080
	———
Hours gained through efficiency	320
	———
@ 160p per hour	512 (F)
	———

4   *Fixed overhead*

(i)   *Expenditure variance*

                                                                £
Budgeted cost (30,000 x 20/240)   2,500
Actual cost   2,550
                                                        _____

                                                          50 (A)
                                                        _____

(ii)   *Efficiency variance*

320 hours @ 25p   80 (F)
                                                        _____

(The absorption rate is calculated by dividing the budgeted cost by
the budgeted number of hours to be worked: £30,000/(60,000 × 2
hours) = 25p.)

(iii)   *Capacity variance*

                                                                £
Actual hours worked   10,080
Budgeted 20/240 × 120,000   10,000
                                                        _____

                                                           80
                                                        _____

@ 25p per hour   20 (F)
                                                        _____

5   *Actual cost statement*

                                                                £
Materials (5,880 + 6,790 + 3,060)   15,730
Labour   17,540
Fixed overhead   2,550
                                                        _____

                                                        35,820
                                                        _____

6 Performance indicators

 Workbook Activity 1

Barwin

(a) Financial performance per sales area

Note that gross profit margins are given in the question. Gross profit can therefore be found by multiplying the sales revenue by the relevant margin.

		Northern Region $000	Southern Region $000
Gross profit per customer size			
Large	10%	200	400
Medium	20%	240	460
Large	30%	510	300
Gross profit per region		950	1,160
Less			
Sales representatives : Salaries		180	171
Overall expenses			
fixed		72	54
variable		36	21
Sales manager's salary		32	34
		320	280
Profit after charging sales expenses		630	880

(b) Performance measures

		North	South
(1)	Sales expenses: Gross profit		
	(i) Sales expenses % of GP	34%	24%
	(ii) Gross profit per $ of sales expenses	$2.97	$4.14
	(iii) Sales per $ of sales expenses	$15.31	$26.07
(2)	Average gross margin	19%	16%
(3)	% gross profit per customer category to total gross profit		
	Large	21%	34%
	Medium	25%	40%
	Small	54%	26%
(4)	Gross profit per region as % of total company gross profit	45%	55%
(5)	Sales per company representative	$408,000	$811,000
(6)	Gross profit per representative	$79,000	$127,000
(7)	Profit after sales expenses as % of total for company	42%	58%

(c) Notes on performance of the two sales areas

The representatives in the Southern area out-perform their colleagues in the North as is highlighted by the performance measures sales and profit per employee. Also gross expenses as a % of GP is much lower.

The Southern team also performs better when focusing on cancelled orders, however in the North there is a higher % of new business, with the South concentrating on repeat business.

The North has lower total sales than the South, the North is concentrating on business in the small category customer band, giving a good margin but costly in terms of sales expenses.

The Northern region is undergoing a period of growth – new business. The South may well have to improve after sales service to attract new business.

Perhaps the future varies according to geography and concentration of business as indicated by total distance travelled in North compared to South.

The task of selling seems to be easier in the South than the North. It may be that the sales reps in the South are better trained and that the company should consider a staff development programme for the Northern Region.

Workbook Activity 2

Hotel Departments

(a) **Catering Department – net profit**

Income

Restaurant meals (2,140 × $12.60)	26,964
Provision of food	4,620
Beverages	18,610
	50,194

Costs
Direct

Food/beverages	16,188
Staff	11,784
Other	2,640
	30,612

Contribution   19,582   (39.0%)

Apportioned costs

General occupancy costs	4,732	
Household and Admin	12,994	
		17,726
Net profit	**1,856**	(3.7%)

The department has not achieved its target profit margin (net of direct costs) of 40%, being 1% below this at 39%. Its net profit after apportioned cost is $1,856, 3.7% of sales.

(b) (i) The Catering Department is likely to be run as a profit centre, being responsible for both income and costs, but not capital investment.

(ii) The Administration Department is likely to be a cost centre as it has no revenue income.

(iii) The Hotel will be treated as an investment centre, being accountable for costs, revenues and capital investment decisions.

(c) (i) (ii)

(*Tutorial note:* Only ONE measure for each category is required.)

Department	Financial	Non-financial
Accommodation	Sales revenue per bed-night	
		Occupancy rates (bed/meeting room)
	Letting income (per meeting-room hr)	
Household	Cost per bed-night	Hours worked: hours available
	Cost per customer stay	Customer complaint rate

(d) Difficulties that may be encountered in performance measurement in the hotel group include:

External (uncontrollable) factors – when comparing one hotel with another, it is difficult to take account of differences in location (e.g. rural/urban), size, local competition, changes in tourist attractiveness (e.g. building work nearby, threats of terrorism, local disease outbreak), etc.

Interdependence – when comparing departments within a hotel, it must be recognised that actions taken by one departmental manager can impact on the performance of other departments – for example, the number of rooms, meeting rooms let by the accommodation department will impact on the income of the catering department.

Workbook Activity 3

Nicholson

(a) **Nicholson ratios and statistics**

Return on capital employed

$$\frac{\text{Profit before interest and tax}}{\text{Capital employed}} \times 100\% = \frac{\$48m}{\$192m} = 25\%$$

Return on sales

$$\frac{\text{Profit before interest and tax}}{\text{Sales revenue}} \times 100\% = \frac{\$48m}{\$480m} = 10\%$$

Asset turnover

$$\frac{\text{Sales revenue}}{\text{Capital employed}} = \frac{\$480m}{\$192m} = 2.5 \text{ times}$$

Annual number of complaints per 1,000 customers

$$\frac{\text{Number of customer complaints}}{\text{Average number of customers (in thousands)}} = \frac{21,600}{1,960} = 11$$

Percentage of customers lost per annum

$$\frac{\text{Number of customers lost}}{\text{Average number of customers}} \times 100\% = \frac{117,600}{1,960,000} = 6\%$$

Average time to resolve billing queries

$$\frac{\text{Average number of bill queries unresolved at the end of each day}}{\text{Total bill queries}} \times 365 = \frac{118}{12,000} = 3.6 \text{ days}$$

Average wait for a telephone repair

$$\frac{\text{Average number of telephones unrepaired at the end of each day}}{\text{Number of telephones returned for repair}} \times 365 = \frac{804}{10,000} \times 365 = 29.3 \text{ days}$$

Percentage of sales attributable to new products

$$\frac{\text{Sales turnover attributable to new products}}{\text{Total sales turnover}} = \frac{\$8m}{\$480m} = 1.7\%$$

(b) **Discussion of performance**

(i) **Financial success**

Nicholson's return on capital employed at 25% is much higher than the industry average and this indicates that it is generating a good return on the money invested in it. This is largely explained by a return on sales of 10%, exactly double that of the industry average company. This could be due to higher prices, lower costs, or both. The only financial weakness apparent is that Nicholson does not enjoy as high a sales per $ of capital employed as its competitors. Overall the company appears to have performed well financially.

(ii) **Customer satisfaction**

Nicholson does not perform as well as the industry average in this area. It is losing customers at twice the rate of the industry average company. It is often much easier to retain existing customers than to win new ones. The level of customer complaints is also much higher than average. These factors will result in lost sales. They should be seen as leading indicators of future financial problems.

(iii) **Process efficiency**

The two processes that appear in the statistics are telephone repair and bill enquiries. On both counts Nicholson performs badly. Telephone repair appears to take an average of nearly 30 days (as compared to a two day industry average). This will prove annoying to customers and will probably result in lost sales (customers cannot make calls without telephones). Similarly delays in processing bill enquiries will eventually result in dissatisfied customers and poor financial results.

(iv) **Organisational learning and growth**

Less than 2% of Nicholson's income comes from new products, as compared to 20% for the industry average company. In a sector characterised by changing technology and product innovation this is very poor. Failing to innovate is a failing to compete. Eventually this will result in lost sales and profits.

In conclusion the company's financial results have been good in the past year, but the prospects for the future appear poor unless improvements are made to customer service, process efficiency and innovation.

7 Budgeting – other considerations

Workbook Activity 1

To : Finance Director

Date : (Today)

From : Assistant Budget Accountant

Subject : Alternative approaches to budgeting

(a) **Zero-based budgeting** (ZBB) is an approach to budgeting which, instead of building on the previous year's budget as a base, requires justification of all expenditure from scratch. This technique would not suit expenditure planning in all areas, for example in the line departments of a manufacturing company, because here there will be clear relationships of input and output which are defined by standard values. In less clearly defined areas such as service departments or not for profit businesses ZBB might have some value if it is applied selectively.

ZBB would involve describing all of the organisation's activities in a series of decision packages. The decision package for each activity describes the activity, analyses its costs and benefits and identifies alternative methods of achieving the same purpose. The packages can then be evaluated and ranked: what is essential, what is highly desirable, what is desirable and so on. The available resources would then be allocated according to the packages selected. Once the budget is set the packages are adopted up to the spending level indicated, which represents the cut-off point.

ZBB may not be easy to install because it could be expensive in time and effort to analyse all expenditure and difficult to establish priorities for the activities or decision packages. However a number of benefits may be derived from the system.

It is possible that economies and increased efficiency could result if departments were to justify all expenditure, not just the incremental expenditure. It is argued that if expenditure were examined on a cost/benefit basis, a more rational allocation of resources would take place. Such an approach would force managers to make plans and prioritise their activities before committing themselves to the budget. It should achieve a more structured involvement of departmental management and should improve the quality of decisions and management information, enabling such questions to be asked as: Should this be done? At what quality/quantity? Should it be done in this way? What should it cost?

(b) A **rolling budget** is a continuously updated budget whereby a further period's budget is added at the end of the budget when the earliest period has expired. The remainder of the budget might also be updated at this point. For example if rolling budgets are prepared quarterly, four quarter's rolling budgets will be available at any one time. As each quarter comes to an end, a new quarter is added at the end of the budget, to replace the current quarter just ending.

Advantages of this approach are as follows:

- Managers always have available a full year's plan. This will emphasise a longer term approach to planning.

- Managers will be constantly planning for the future and considering the validity of these plans.

- When conditions are subject to change, actual performance is compared with a more realistic target than if the budget were prepared on a fixed basis only once a year.

- Uncertainty is reduced in the planning process.

Disadvantages of a rolling budget system are as follows:

- Preparing new budgets on a regular basis can be time consuming.

- It can be difficult to communicate frequent budget changes.

(c) **'What if' analysis** is used in the context of budgetary planning. A budgetary plan is based on a large number of forecasts and assumptions about the future. For example in preparing the sales budget for the forthcoming period forecasts will be made concerning variables such as the selling price of the products or services and the sales volume that will be achieved at this price. These forecasts are likely to be inaccurate, to a greater or lesser degree.

'What if' analysis investigates what the budgeted results would be if certain variables in the budget were different from forecast. The variable is altered by a given amount to investigate what the budgeted outcome would be if the variable were to change by that amount.

For example a 'what if' analysis might be carried out to ask the question: 'What if sales volume is 5% lower than budgeted?' or 'What if sales volume is 5% higher than budgeted?'. The analysis would calculate the impact on the budgetary plans, including the effect each time on the master profit and loss account and balance sheet.

This would enable managers to see the potential impact of changes in forecast variables. They can then consider what measures should be taken, if any, to avoid exposure to unfavourable results or to capitalise on opportunities to achieve more favourable results.

Limitations of the analysis include the following:

- The amount by which the variables is adjusted is subjective.

The analysis does not indicate the probability of the calculated outcome arising.

Workbook Activity 2

Trygon Limited

(a) *Trygon Limited: Flexible budget at 75% activity*

Sales and production (units)	(80%) 120,000	(40%) 60,000	Variable cost/revenue per unit	(75%) 112,500
	£	£	£	£
Direct materials	24,000,000	12,000,000	200	22,500,000
Direct labour	7,200,000	7,200,000		7,200,000
Light, heat and power*	4,000,000	2,200,000	30	3,775,000
Production management salaries	1,500,000	1,500,000		1,500,000
Factory rent, rates and insurance	9,400,000	9,400,000		9,400,000
Depreciation of factory machinery	5,500,000	5,500,000		5,500,000
National advertising	20,000,000	20,000,000		20,000,000
Marketing and administration	2,300,000	2,300,000		2,300,000
Delivery costs	2,400,000	1,200,000	20	2,250,000
Total costs	76,300,000	61,300,000		74,425,000
Sales revenue	84,000,000	42,000,000	700	78,750,000
Operating profit				
				4,325,000

*Variable cost for 120,000 units = £3,600,000 to give fixed costs of £400,000.

(b)

REPORT

To:	The Board of Directors
From:	The Management Accountant
Date:	X June 20X6
Subject:	Budgeting within Trygon Limited

Following the instructions from the Group Finance Director, finished stocks are to be valued as material and labour plus an appropriate proportion of factory overheads based on normal activity. Each unsold computer will therefore be valued at £430 and comprise the following costs:

Valuation of closing stock

	£
Production management salaries	1,500,000
Factory rent, rates and insurance	9,400,000
Depreciation of factory machinery	5,500,000
Fixed element of light, heat and power	400,000
	_____
Total fixed overheads	16,800,000
	_____
Unit fixed cost based on normal activity – £16,800,000/120,000	140
Unit direct costs	
Light, heat and power	30
Direct materials	200
Direct labour £7,200,000/120,000	60
	_____
Unit cost for stock valuation	430
	_____

Closing stock $= (150,000 \times 0.95) - 112,500$

$$= 142,500 - 112,500 = 30,000 \text{ units}$$

With each unit of closing stock valued at £430, the total closing stock will be valued at £12,900,000 to give an operating profit of £8.4 million. The revised budget is reproduced below.

(i),(ii) *Trygon* Limited: *flexible budget at 75% sales activity but 95% production activity*

	£
Direct material – 142,500 × £200	28,500,000
Direct labour – £7,200,000 + (£70 × 22,500)	8,775,000
Light, heat and power – £400,000 + (£30 × 142,500)	4,675,000
Production management salaries – £1,500,000 + (£15 × 22,500)	1,837,500
Factory rent, rates and insurance	9,400,000
Depreciation of factory machinery	5,500,000
Factory cost of production	58,687,500
Less closing stock – 30,000 × £430	12,900,000
Factory cost of sales	45,787,500
Marketing, administration and distribution expenses	
National advertising	20,000,000
Marketing and administration	2,300,000
Delivery costs – 112,500 × £20	2,250,000
Total expenses	70,337,500
Sales turnover – 112,500 × £700	78,750,000
Operating profit	8,412,500

The reason for this increase in budgeted profit from £4,325,000 to £8,412,500 despite the additional costs of overtime and bonus payments is mainly due to the treatment of overheads. Fixed costs are essentially time-based but by using absorption costing some of these are carried forward in the value of unsold stocks. With no opening stocks and production equalling sales, all overheads are charged to the current period, even under an absorption costing system. With production being greater than sales volume and with overheads being based on normal activity, the difference in profit can be explained in terms of the treatment of fixed costs and the additional payments resulting from production being greater than the budgeted activity.

KAPLAN PUBLISHING

(iii)   *Fixed and flexible budgets*

The original budget prepared by the group director was a fixed budget. Fixed budgets are designed to remain unaltered. Their primary uses are for planning and co-ordinating. Prior to commencing sales and production activity, the enterprise needs to know what is possible and what is achievable. The co-ordination role of budgeting helps to identify possible bottlenecks and to resolve them before production and selling commences. The planning role is concerned with where the enterprise wants to be at the end of the budget period and provides a target and a commitment to that target.

The flexible budgets I prepared serve two purposes. First, they help to show likely outcomes as conditions change. Secondly, they help managers to control the business by identifying what expenses and turnover should be at different levels of activity. The flexible budget can then be compared with the actual results which enables meaningful variances to be produced. This a flexible budget does by recognising (i) that fixed costs are unlikely to change as a matter of course over a range of activity levels and (ii) that variable costs, by their nature, will increase in proportion to increases in volume.

Budgetary objectives

For a budget to have meaning, there has to be a clear, unambiguous objective. Traditionally, this has involved the key or principal budget factor being identified, that is the factor which will limit the possible achievements for the period. Normally, this is sales although it could be production if there is a shortage of inputs or limited capacity. Being asked to both maximise sales and develop a long-term market position may not be compatible.

Confusion about the company's objectives or how those objectives can be achieved can lead to difficulties for the managers of Trygon. This might lead you to attempt to achieve the budget – but not in the way anticipated. For Trygon, it is clear that we are unlikely to achieve the budget target set at the beginning of the year. However, if Parmod plc is only concerned with profits, the directors of Trygon are more than able to meet the original profit target, not by actually selling more but by manipulating the results. This we can do by simply producing more. As a consequence, some of the fixed costs are carried forward to another period. The outcome is that we will have appeared to have achieved the target. The reality is we will have caused an increase in costs such as storekeeping costs which do not directly appear in the budget or the actual results.

(iv) *Participation in budgets*

Turning to the issue raised by Anne Darcy, conventional wisdom suggests that managers should be encouraged to participate in the budget process and that the budget should be built up from the lower rungs of management rather than imposed from the top. The belief is that managers will then feel they have ownership of the budget and this will encourage commitment and motivation. More than that it is argued that the operating managers are the only ones with sufficient detailed knowledge to develop a meaningful budget.

Unfortunately, the budget process is not always as simple as that. First, the objectives of the managers and the objectives of the organisation may not be the same.

There is a need for a similarity of goals – goal congruence – and this does not automatically result from empowering managers to develop their own budgets. Secondly, the operating management may have detailed knowledge but they might use this to their own benefits – as with the current plan to build up stocks and so manipulate the budget. Thirdly the managers may not wish to participate in the budget setting process. This may be because of some psychological fear resulting in managers simply wanting to be told what their targets are; it might be because they do not have the technical knowledge to participate in budget setting; or it might be that they either do not have the necessary degree of commitment to the organisation or they feel that the budgetary control system will be used against them. Because of this, it is not self-evident that participation will always help managers and the organisation.

Workbook Activity 3

World History Museum

(a)/(b) Analysis of budgeted costs

Fixed cost Variable cost Variable cost per course

	Fixed cost	Variable cost	Variable cost per course
	£	£	£
Speakers' fees	–	3,180	530
Hire of premises	–	1,500	250
Depreciation of equipment	180	–	–
Stationery	–	600	100
Catering	250	1,500	250
Insurance	100	720	120
Administration	1,620	–	–

Flexible budget control statement for April – 5 courses

Expenditure	Fixed cost budget	Variable cost budget	Total cost budget	Actual cost	Variance
	£	£	£	£	£
Speakers' fees	–	2,650	2,650	2,500	150
Hire of premises	–	1,250	1,250	1,500	(250)
Depreciation of equipment	180	–	180	200	(20)
Stationery	–	500	500	530	(30)
Catering	250	1,250	1,500	1,500	–
Insurance	100	600	700	700	–
Administration	1,620	–	1,620	1,650	(30)
	2,150	6,250	8,400	8,580	(180)

(c)

MEMORANDUM

To:	Chris Brooks
From:	Assistant Management Accountant
Date:	13 June 20X4
Subject:	Participative budgeting

As requested, I enclose brief explanations of the advantages and disadvantages of participative budgeting.

Advantages

(i) Managers are likely to be demotivated if budgets are imposed on them without any prior consultation. If they are consulted, they are more likely to accept the budgets as realistic targets.

(ii) If managers are consulted, then the budgets are more likely to take account of their own aspiration levels. Aspiration levels are personal targets which individuals or departments set for themselves. If budget targets exceed aspiration levels, then the budgets can have a negative motivational impact because they will be perceived as unachievable. However, if the targets fall too far below aspiration levels, then the performance of the individuals or departments may be lower than might otherwise have been achieved.

(iii) Managers who are consulted may be motivated by the feeling that their views are valuable to senior management.

(iv) Managers who are closely involved with the day to day running of operations may be able to give very valuable input to the forecasting and planning process.

Disadvantages

(i) If too many people are involved in budgetary planning, it can make the process very slow and difficult to manage.

(ii) Senior managers may need to overrule decisions made by local managers. This can be demotivating if it is not dealt with correctly.

(iii) The participative process may not be genuine. Managers must feel that their participation is really valued by senior management. A false attempt to appear to be interested in their views can be even more demotivating than a system of imposed budgets.

(iv) Managers may attempt to include excess expenditure in their budgets, due to 'empire-building' or to a desire to guard against unforeseen circumstances.

MOCK ASSESSMENT

1 Mock Assessment Questions

SECTION 1

Task 1.1 A

Match the data in the first column with the most appropriate source in the second column.

Data	Source
Global Economic Trends	Washington Post
Likely future government policy	World Bank, International Monetary Fund
UK Inflation Trends	Market Research
Office for National Statistics	SWOT Analysis
	Political consultancies / commentators

Task 1.1 B

Who would you contact in each of the following situations?

Situation	Pick from
You want to know plans to disrupt the firms' operations	Firms' customers
You want to identify the firm's production capacity	Suppliers
You want to check the availability of a raw material	Competitors' price lists
	Pressure groups
	Production planning manager

Task 1.1 C

Drag each item of revenue or cost in the list below and drop it into its appropriate budget:

Cost
Factory extension
Raw material usage
Production wages
Printing employee opinion survey results
Billboard advertising
Spare parts for production machines
New delivery van

Capital expenditure	Marketing

Personnel	Cost of Production

Maintenance

Task 1.1 D

Select the most appropriate accounting treatment for each of the following costs.

- Ingredients wastage in the production process
- Administrative wages
- Holiday pay for production workers
- Direct marketing costs
- Depreciation of equipment located in the materials store.
- Office stationery
- Basic pay for production workers

Options available against each item are:

- Allocate to marketing overheads
- Allocate to administrative overheads
- Direct cost
- Charge to production in a machine hour overhead rate
- Charge to production in a labour hour overhead rate

Task 1.1 E

Calculate the appropriate budgeted overhead recovery rate for the following production department. The department's annual budget for indirect costs is:

	£
Indirect labour	6,250
Supervisor wages	29,000
Depreciation of equipment	35,000
Machine maintenance	4,000
Canteen subsidy	9,750
Total	**84,000**

Notes: The budgeted production of 1,000 units will require 25,000 machine hours and 35,000 direct labour hours.

Answer: Overhead recovery should be based on _____.
The recovery rate will be £_____ per _____.

The first blank is a drop down box containing Labour hours, Machine hours and Units produced. The second box is a numeric gap fill (2dp). The third box is free text.

Task 1.2 A

Complete the following production forecast for product Mauve.

Units of product Mauve

	Week 1	Week 2	Week 3	Week 4	Week 5
Opening stock	1,000				
Production					
Sub-total					
Sales	7,000	8,000	7,500	7,000	8,000
Closing stock					

Closing stock should be 25% of the following week's forecast sales,

(All gaps are numeric. Allow 2 dp)

Task 1.2 B

The quarterly production requirements for product B are shown below.
3% of production fails the quality checks and must be scrapped.
How many items of product B must be manufactured to allow for waste?

	Month 1	Month 2	Month 3
Required units	50,600	49,500	49,800
Manufactured units			

(Round **up** to nearest whole unit)

Task 1.2 C

Raw Material purchases

50,000 items of product G are to be manufactured in April.

Each requires 1.5 metres of raw material.

20% of raw material is wasted during manufacture.

The opening stock will be 10,000 metres.

The closing stock will be 11,000 metres.

How much material must be purchased?

Select from

94,750m;   94,550m   94,900m;   95,000m;   96,750m

Task 1.2 D

Labour hours

114,000 units of product X are to be manufactured in May.

Each one takes 2 minutes to produce.

20 staff will each work 160 hours basic time.

How many overtime hours must be worked to complete the production?

Select from

600;   200;   360;   300;   3,800

Task 1.2 E

Department C manufactures three products, D, E and F.

Calculate the machine hours required to manufacture these in November.

Product	Units	Hours per unit	Hours required
D	50	1.5	
E	130	2.0	
F	250	2.5	
Total hours for department X			

There are seven machines in the department.

Each machine can be used for 120 hours in November. Additional machines can be hired if required.

How many additional machines should be hired?

Task 1.3

You are required to complete the workings schedules and Operating Budget below.

The shaded cells will be completed for you.

Workings schedules

Materials

	Kg	£
Opening stock	3,600	8,000
Purchases	28,000	56,000
Sub-total	31,600	64,000
Used		
Closing stock	7,000	

Closing stock to be valued at budgeted purchase price

Labour

	Hours	£
Basic time @ £16 per hour		
Overtime		
Total		

It takes 5 minutes to make each item

5 staff work 500 basic hours each

Overtime is paid time and a half (50% above basic rate)

Overhead

	Hours	£
Variable @ £8 per hour		
Fixed		67,000
Total		

Variable overhead recovered on total labour hours

Operating budget

	Units	£
Sales revenue @ £10.5 each	34,000	
Opening stock of finished goods	9,000	5,500
Cost of production	35,500	
Materials		
Labour		
Overhead		
Total		
Closing stock of finished goods*	10,500	

*Valued at budgeted production cost per unit

Cost of goods sold	
Gross profit	

Overheads

	£
Administration	52,000
Marketing	104,000
Total	156,000
Operating profit	

Task 1.4 A

This year sales are £500,000.

Analysis of recent years shows a growth trend of 25% per annum.

The seasonal variation has been:

- quarter 1   +£15,000
- quarter 2   +£20,000
- quarter 3   –£10,000
- quarter 4   –£25,000

Forecast the income for each quarter of **next year**.

Quarter	£
1	
2	
3	
4	
Year	

Task 1.4 B

Calculate these sales and cost budgets for July

	Budget for the year	Budget for July
Units sold	60,000	6,000
Units produced	55,000	6,500

	£	£
Sales	924,000	
Materials used	825,000	
Labour	222,000	
Variable production overhead	68,750	
Fixed overhead	3,600	

Each unit is made from 3 kg of material costing £5 per kg

It takes 15 minutes to make each item.

750 hours of basic time is available in the month. Any extra hours must be worked in overtime.

The basic rate is £12 per hour. Overtime is paid at double time (100% more than basic rate.)

Variable overhead relates to labour hours, including overtime.

Fixed overhead costs are incurred evenly through the year.

Task 1.4 C

Prepare a cash forecast for November from the following budget data:

Budget data	Aug £	Sep £	Oct £	Nov £	Cash Forecast	Nov £
Invoiced sales	27,000	29,000	32,000	33,000	Opening cash balance	–1,000
Purchases	20,000	21,700	22,700	24,300	Customer receipts	
Wages	5000	5500	5600	5400		
Other overheads	700	760	750	810	Payments	
Capital expenditure	0	0	0	2000	For purchases	
					For wages	
Average terms					For overheads	

70% of customers pay in the current month, the remainder take 1 month   For capital exp.

Purchases paid for after one month   Total

Wages paid in the current month

Other overheads paid after three months   Closing cash balance

Capital expenditure paid in the current month

Show payments and receipts as plus figures.

Negative balance = overdrawn

Task 1.5

You have prepared a draft budget for direct labour costs. It is based on this year's costs plus an expected pay rise and increased staffing.

- The manager of human resources has forecast the pay rise.
- You have calculated the required staffing from the agreed production budget.
- Major labour shortages have required salaries to increase significantly.
- Senior management require increased productivity.
- You have been asked to suggest appropriate performance measures that would assist managers to monitor direct labour performance against budget.

Direct Labour Budget	Current Year	Next Year
Production Units	1,400,000	1,700,000
Minutes per unit	15	14
Labour hours	350,000	396,667
Annual hrs per staff member	4,650	4,650
Number of staff	76	86
Average salary pa	£40,000	£45,000
Direct Labour Cost	£3,040,000	£3,870,000

Write an email to the Production Director:

(a) Explaining the calculations and assumptions and requesting his approval

(b) Suggesting appropriate direct labour performance indicators for this department

To: Production Director

Date: (Today)

From: Budget Accountant

Subject: Review of operation statement

(a)   Budget submission

(b)   Performance indicators

Task 1.6 A

The company has budgeted to make and sell 600,000 units in the coming year.

Each unit takes 5 labour hours to make and requires 4kg of raw material. The quality control department can test 40,000 units each month. A contract has been placed to purchase 2,200,000kg of raw material at an agreed price. Further supplies can be obtained on the open market but the price is likely to be much higher. The company employs 1,250 production workers. Each worker works 2,000 hours in a year in normal time.

Complete the following analysis.

There is labour available to make _____ units in normal time. Therefore, _____ hours of overtime will be needed.

The raw material contract will provide enough material to make _____ units. Therefore, _____ kg will have to be purchased on the open market.

Quality control can test _____ units in the year. It will be necessary to make alternative arrangements for _____ units.

Task 1.6 B

From the following data revise the income forecast.

Next year income is forecast at £6,037,500. This assumes a 5% increase in selling price.

In the light of increasing competition the marketing manager has decided not to make the increase.

The forecast should be revised to _____

Select from

£5,735,625   £5,750,000   £6,037,500   £6,339,375

Task 1.6 C

From the following data revise the forecast for energy costs.

Next year energy costs are forecast at £180,285. This assumes a 2% increase in energy consumption and a 1% increase in gas and electricity tariffs.

However, due to a reduction in global oil prices, gas and electricity tariffs should be reduced by 1%.

The energy budget should be £_____

Select from

£170,000   £176,715   £178,482   £178,500

SECTION 2

Task 2.1

A monthly operating statement is shown below with some explanatory notes. You are required to flex the budget, calculate variances and show whether each variance is favourable or adverse.

Monthly Operating Statement

	Budget	Actual
Volume	36,000	33,000
	£	£
Turnover	396,000	371,250
Costs		
Material	99,000	89,900
Labour	54,000	50,750
Distribution	1800	1,550
Energy	37,400	35,830
Equipment hire	480	455
Depreciation	21,000	21,000
Marketing	30,000	28,000
Administration	45,000	47,350
Total	288,680	274,835
Operating Profit	107,320	96,415

Monthly Operating Statement

Volume 33,000

	Flexed budget £	Actual £	Variance Fav/(Adv) £
Turnover		371,250	
Costs			
Material		89,900	
Labour		50,750	
Distribution		1,550	
Energy		35,830	
Equipment hire		455	
Depreciation		21,000	
Marketing		28,000	
Administration		47,350	
Total		274,835	
Operating Profit		96,415	

Enter adverse variances as minus

Notes

Material, labour and distribution costs are variable.

The budget for energy is semi-variable. The variable element is £0.90 per unit.

The budget for equipment hire is stepped, increasing at every 5,000 units of monthly production.

Depreciation, marketing and administration costs are fixed.

Task 2.2

You are asked to review the Operating Statement shown below, and the background information provided, and to make recommendations.

Operating Statement for May 2011

Turnover (units)   2,600,000

	Budget	Actual	Variance Fav/(Adverse)
	£000	£000	£000
Turnover	13,000	14,300	1,300
Variable Costs			
Material	2,080	1,950	130
Labour	2,340	2,392	(52)
Transport	1,430	1,410	20
Power	1,300	1,352	(52)
Storage	416	416	–
	7,566	7,520	46
Contribution	5,434	6,780	1,346
Fixed costs			
Power	390	390	-
Storage	550	576	(26)
Depreciation	970	960	10
Maintenance	770	790	(20)
Administration	650	658	(8)
	3,330	3,374	(44)
Operating Profit	2,104	3,406	1,302

The budget has been flexed to the actual number of units produced and sold. The original budget had been drawn up by the Chief Executive and communicated to senior managers by email.

Storage is a semi-variable cost and has been split between its fixed and variable elements.

Transport is a stepped cost. For every £130,000 spent on transport, the company can carry 250,000 units.

Write an email to the Chief Executive in which you:

(a) Suggest ONE possible reason for each of the following variances:

    (a) Turnover

    (b) Materials

    (c) Labour

    (d) Power

    (e) Storage

    (f) Transport.

(b) Explain TWO methods of assisting departmental managers to be more involved in preparing the budgets.

To:	Chief Executive
Date:	(Today)
From:	Budget Accountant
Subject:	Review of operating statement

(a) Reasons for variances

(b) Two steps to assist departmental managers to be more involved in preparing the budgets:

2 Mock Assessment Answers

SECTION 1

Task 1.1 A

Data	Answer
Data	*Answer*
Global Economic Trends	World Bank, International Monetary Fund
Likely future government policy	Political consultancies / commentators
UK Inflation Trends	Office for National Statistics

Task 1.1 B

Situation	Answer
Situation	*Answer*
You want to know plans to disrupt the firms' operations	Pressure groups
You want to identify the firm's production capacity of the firm	Production planning manager
You want to check the availability of a raw material	Suppliers

Task 1.1 C

Capital expenditure Factory extension New delivery van	*Marketing* Billboard advertising
Personnel Printing employee opinion survey results	*Cost of production* Production wages Raw material usage
Maintenance Spare parts for production machines	

Task 1.1 D

• Ingredients wastage in the production process	Direct cost
• Administrative wages	Allocate to administrative overheads
• Holiday pay for production workers	Charge to production in a labour hour overhead rate
• Direct marketing costs	Allocate to marketing overheads
• Depreciation of equipment located in the material store	Charge to production in a machine hour overhead rate
• Office stationery	Allocate to administrative overheads
• Basic pay for production workers	Direct cost

Task 1.1 E

Overhead recovery should be based on **Labour hours**. The recovery rate will be **£2 .40 per hour.**

Task 1.2 A

Units of product A

	Week 1	Week 2	Week 3	Week 4	Week 5
Opening stock	1,000	2,000	1,875	1,750	2,000
Production	8,000	7,875	7,375	7,250	
Sub-total	9,000	9,875	9,250	9,000	
Sales	7,000	8,000	7,500	7,000	8,000
Closing stock	2,000	1,875	1,750	2,000	

Task 1.2 B

	Month 1	Month 2	Month 3
Required units	50,600	49,500	49,800
Manufactured units	52,165	51,031	51,340

(Round **up** to nearest whole unit)

Task 1.2 C

94,750m

Working

50,000 items @ 1.5 metres = 75,000 metres.

75,000m × 100 / 80 (wastage) = 93,750m

Plus 11,000m closing stock less 10,000m = 94,750m

Task 1.2 D

600

Working

114,000 × 2/60 = 3,800 hrs required.

3,800 – (20 × 160) = 600 hrs overtime needed.

Task 1.2 E

Product	Units	Hours per unit	Hours required
D	50	1.5	75
E	130	2.0	260
F	250	2.5	625
Total			960

How many additional machines should be hired? | 1 |

Task 1.3

Workings schedules			Operating budget		

Workings schedules

Materials	Kg	£
Opening stock	3,600	8,000
Purchases	28,000	56,000
Sub-total	31,600	64,000
Used	24,600	50,000
Closing stock	7,000	14,000

Closing stock to be valued at budgeted purchase price

Labour	Hours	£
Basic time @ £16 per hour	2,500	40,000
Overtime	458	11,000
Total	2,958	51,000

It takes 5 minutes to make each item

5 staff work 500 basic hours each

Overtime is paid time and a half (50% above basic rate)

Overhead	Hours	£
Variable @ £8 per hour	2,958	23,667
Fixed		67,000
Total		90,667

Operating budget

	Units	£
Sales revenue @ £10.5 each	34,000	357,000
Opening stock of finished goods	9,000	5,500
Cost of production	35,500	
Materials		50,000
Labour		51,000
Overhead		90,667
Total		191,667
Closing stock of finished goods*	10,500	56,690

*Valued at budgeted production cost per unit

		£
Cost of goods sold		140,477
Gross profit		216,523

Overheads

	£
Administration	52,000
Marketing	104,000
Total	156,000
Operating profit	60,523

Task 1.4 A

Quarter	£
1	171,250
2	176,250
3	146,250
4	131,250

Task 1.4 B

	Budget for July
Units sold	6,000
Units produced	6,500
	£
Sales	92,400
Materials used	97,500
Labour	30,000
Variable production overhead	8,126
Fixed overhead	300

Task 1.4 C

Cash Forecast	Nov
	£
Opening cash balance	−1,000
Customer receipts	32,700
Payments	
For purchases	22,700
For wages	5,400
For overheads	700
For capital exp.	2,000
Total	30,800
Closing cash balance	900

Task 1.5

To:	Production Director
From:	Accounting Technician
Date:	xx/xx/xxxx
Subject:	Direct Labour Budget

Budget submission

I attach the proposed direct labour budget for next year for your consideration and approval.

The agreed production plan indicates an increase in volume to 1,700,000 units next year. An increase in productivity has been assumed from 15 minutes per unit to 14 minutes per unit. Overall the staffing level needs to increase by 10 to 86.

The manager of human resources estimates that average pay will increase by 12.5% next year to £45,000. This reflects labour shortages.

Please let me know if you need any further information.

Performance indicators

There is a range of useful measures to monitor cost, efficiency, effectiveness and employee satisfaction. Staff hours and output data should be available on a daily basis. Labour rates are reviewed periodically. However employee satisfaction is probably best canvassed once or twice a year. I recommend that we conduct a weekly review of performance based on:

- Minutes per unit
- Hours of overtime
- Percentage of good output (or similar quality measure)
- Average hourly rate

We should also commission a confidential employee satisfaction and involvement questionnaire.

A Technician

Task 1.6 A

There is labour available to make 500,000 units in normal time. Therefore, 500,000 hours of overtime will be needed.

The raw material contract will provide enough material to make 550,000 units. Therefore, 200,000 kg will have to be purchased on the open market.

Quality control can test 480,000 units in the year. It will be necessary to make alternative arrangements for 120,000 units.

Task 1.6 B

Next year's income forecast assumes a 5% increase in selling price. So:

Forecast without the increase × (1 + 5%) = £6,037,500

Therefore, forecast without the increase = $\dfrac{£6,037,500}{1.05}$

Forecast without the increase = £5,750,000

Task 1.6 C

Answer : £176,715

The 2% increase in energy consumption should be left untouched – it is not revised in the question.

The 1% increase in electricity tariffs should be stripped out of next year's energy forecast :

Therefore, forecast without the increase = $\dfrac{£180,285}{1.01}$

Forecast without the increase = £178,500

This in turn should benefit from a reduction of 1% in gas and electricity tariffs :

£178,500 × (1 – 1%) = **£176,715**

SECTION 2

Task 2.1

Monthly Operating Statement

Volume   33,000

	Flexed budget £	Actual £	Variance Fav/(Adv) £
Turnover	363,000	371,250	8,250
Costs			
Material	90,750	89,900	850
Labour	49,500	50,750	(1,250)
Distribution	1,650	1,550	100
Energy	34,700	35,830	(1,130)
Equipment hire	420	455	(35)
Depreciation	21,000	21,000	–
Marketing	30,000	28,000	2,000
Administration	45,000	47,350	(2,350)
Total	273,020	274,835	(1,815)
Operating Profit	89,980	96,415	6,435

Task 2.2

To	**Chief Executive**
Date	**(Today)**
From	**Budget Accountant**
Subject	**Review of Operation Statement**

(a) **Reasons for variances**

Turnover

The favourable turnover variance is due to an increased selling price which could have arisen due to increased demand for the product.

Materials

The favourable material variance is due to a lower price being paid for materials. This could be because of an overall reduction in prices due to fall in demand for the material or other economic factors or to better buying techniques.

Labour

The adverse labour variance could have arisen because of using less (or more) skilled staff or incurring higher overtime than expected.

Power

The adverse power variance is due to the increase in price per unit. This could reflect the increase in demand for this resource or it could be due to prices rises being higher than the expected level of inflation.

Storage

The adverse storage variance is due to an increased fixed cost which could have been caused by rises in underlying costs such as business rates or the rents charged by landlords..

Transport

The favourable transport variance arises because the budgeted stepped cost rises by fixed amounts whereas actual costs can vary because of differences in costs for such things as fuel , maintenance or improved usage.

(b) **Two steps to assist departmental managers to be more involved in preparing the budgets**

The accounts staff can give advice and support to the department or cost centre managers and in the process can ensure consistency in approach whilst not reducing their responsibility for the preparation of the budgets.

Strategic plans and goals must be made clear by senior management and then communicated to the departmental managers both before the budgets are prepared and part of the feedback process after the budgets have been co-ordinated and reviewed.

INDEX

A

ABC system, 60
    mechanics, 57

Absorption, 50, 54
    costing, 49

Acid test, 184, 209

Activity levels, 117, 124, 127, 139

Activity-based costing, 56

Actual
    activity level, 92
    costs, 150

Additive model, 22

Allocation, 49, 50

Apportionment, 49, 50

Appraisal costs, 203, 205

Asset turnover, 180, 183, 184

Average capital employed, 181

B

Balanced scorecard, 205, 206

Bases
    of absorption, 54
    of apportionment, 51

Behaviour, 117

Benchmarking, 208

Bottom up budgeting, 241

Budget, 6
    committee, 14
    manual, 15
    preparation, 73, 75, 77, 83, 93

Budgetary
    bias, 242
    control statement, 134

Budgeted
    activity level, 91
    profit and loss account, 86

Business environment, 1

C

Capital expenditure budget, 93

Cash budget, 94, 95

Census, 35

Classification of costs, 124

Cluster sampling, 37

Communication, 91

Consumer price index, 39

Control, 5

Co-ordination, 99, 100

Corporate
    objectives, 4
    planning, 3

Cost
    allocation, 51
    apportionment, 51
    behaviour, 123
    budgets, 88
    centre, 119, 120, 124, 139
    classification, 120
    control,, 207
    drivers, 57
    elements, 117
    estimation, 127
    of quality, 202
    per unit, 123
    pools, 57
    reduction, 207
    reduction programme, 207
    reduction techniques, 208

Creditor days, 186

Current ratio, 184, 185, 209

Cyclical variations, 22, 23

D

Debtor days, 186

Decision making, 117

Dependent variable, 29

Direct costs, 49, 50, 121

E

Effectiveness, 176, 195, 199, 200, 201

Efficiency, 176, 191, 192

Exception reporting, 150

Exchange rates, 168

Expectations budget, 238

External
    failure costs, 203, 205
    information, 16
    sources of information, 1

Extrapolation., 35

F

Failure costs, 202

Financial modelling software, 232

Fixed
    costs, 124, 125
    production overhead, 155

Flexed budgets, 130

Flexible budgetary control, 129

Fluctuating variances, 157

Forecast balance sheet, 94

Forecasting with time series analysis, 30

Functional budgets, 83, 84, 87, 94

G

Goal congruence, 243

Graph, 21

Gross profit margin, 184

H

High/low method, 127, 129

Historical data, 1, 20

Horizontal x axis, 21

I

Independent variable, 29

Index numbers, 38

Indices, 39

Indirect
    costs, 49, 50, 122
    production costs, 49

Inflation, 39, 40

Innovation, 194

Interdependence of variances, 166

Interest receivable, 182

Internal failure costs, 202, 205

Investigation of variances, 161

L

Labour
    activity ratio, 191
    budget, 78, 80, 86
    capacity ratio, 191
    efficiency ratios, 191

Limiting factors, 75

Line of best fit, 29

Linear regression, 24, 29, 30

Liquidity, 184, 188, 209
    ratios, 177

M

Management
    accounting, 1
    by exception, 234

Manufacturing industries, 190

Marginal costing, 155

Master budget, 94

Materials
    budget with losses, 80
    price variance, 156

Measurement errors, 161

Mission, 3

Mixed costs, 125

Motivation, 117, 135, 233, 235, 237, 241

Moving averages, 24, 25, 27, 28

Multiplicative model, 34

Multi-stage sampling, 37

KAPLAN PUBLISHING

N

Nature of costs, 123

Non-production costs, 49, 122

Non-random sampling, 37

O

OAR, 91, 92

Objectives, 3

Operating plans, 5

Operational
    causes, 161
    causes of variances, 162

Over-absorption, 55

Overheads, 120, 122, 139
    budget, 78

P

Participation, 235

Performance
    evaluation, 239
    indicators, 176, 189, 196, 197, 198, 201, 205, 206, 208, 209

Planning, 117
    errors, 161
    process, 6

Plotting, 21

Population, 35

Prevention costs, 203

Price
    adjusted figure, 39
    variances, 168

Principal budgetary factor, 10, 75

Production budget, 78
    with losses, 81

Productivity, 190, 191, 198

Profit
    centres, 120
    margin, 180, 182, 184

Profitability, 180, 189, 199, 209
    ratios, 175, 176, 177, 182, 184, 188, 198, 199

Q

Qualitative performance indicators, 176

Quality, 194, 200, 202, 203
    circles, 202

Quantitative performance indicators, 176

Quick ratio, 184, 185

Quota sampling, 37

R

Random
    factors, 161
    sampling, 36
    variations, 23

Ratio analysis, 177

Ratios, 175, 176, 177, 178, 182, 184, 185, 187, 188, 189, 191, 192, 194, 195, 199, 200, 205, 209

Raw materials purchases, 78

Reconciliation, 150

Regression
    analysis, 29
    line, 43

Resource utilisation, 194

Responsibility accounting, 166, 234

Retail price index, 39

Return on capital employed (ROCE), 180, 199, 209

Rolling
    budgets, 225, 226
    forecasts, 226

S

Sales budget, 77, 78, 79, 82, 84, 85, 87, 90

Sampling, 35

Scattergraph;, 24

Seasonal
    adjustments, 35
    variations, 1, 21, 22, 23, 25, 30, 33, 34, 35, 41

Secondary cost apportionment, 53

Semi-variable, 125, 126
    costs, 50

Service
   departments, 195
   sectors, 197

Significance of variances, 157, 170

Spreadsheets, 170, 229

Stages in the budgetary process, 12

Standard costs, 150

Stepped costs, 125, 126

Stock days, 185

Strategy, 3

Stratified sampling, 37

SWOT analysis, 20

Systematic sampling, 36

T

Target costing, 208

Time series, 1, 20, 22, 35
   analysis, 41

Top down budgeting, 241

Total quality management (TQM), 201, 202

Trend, 20, 21, 22, 23, 24, 25, 26, 27, 28, 29, 30, 31, 32, 33, 34, 35, 38

U

Under-absorption, 55

Unit costs, 194, 198

V

Value
   added, 192, 193
   engineering, 208
   enhancement, 207, 208

Variable
   and fixed costs, 129
   costs, 123, 124, 125

Variance analysis, 165

Variances, 117, 134, 135, 150, 233, 234, 239, 250

Variations, 22

W

What if? analysis, 189, 232

Why prepare budgets?, 9

X

X axis, 21

Z

Zero-based budgeting (ZBB), 218

KAPLAN
PUBLISHING

Kaplan Publishing are constantly finding new ways to make a difference to your studies and our exciting online resources really do offer something different to AAT students looking for exam success.

FOR THE FIRST TIME, KAPLAN'S AAT TEXTS COME WITH FREE EN-gage ONLINE RESOURCES SO THAT YOU CAN STUDY ANYTIME, ANYWHERE

Having purchased this Kaplan Text, you have access to the following online study materials:

- An online version of the Text
- Fixed Online Tests with instant answers

How to access your online resources

- **Kaplan Financial students** will already have a Kaplan EN-gage account and these extra resources will be available to you online. You do not need to register again, as this process was completed when you enrolled. If you are having problems accessing online materials, please ask your course administrator.
- **If you purchased through Kaplan Flexible Learning or via the Kaplan Publishing website** you will automatically receive an e-mail invitation to Kaplan EN-gage online. Please register your details using this e-mail to gain access to your content. If you do not receive the e-mail or book content, please contact Kaplan Flexible Learning.
- **If you are already a registered Kaplan EN-gage user** go to www.EN-gage.co.uk and log in. Select the 'add a book' feature and enter the ISBN number of this book and the unique pass key at the bottom of this card. Then click 'finished' or 'add another book'. You may add as many books as you have purchased from this screen.
- **If you are a new Kaplan EN-gage user** register at www.EN-gage.co.uk and click on the link contained in the e-mail we sent you to activate your account. Then select the 'add a book' feature, enter the ISBN number of this book and the unique pass key at the bottom of this card. Then click 'finished' or 'add another book'.

Your Code and Information

This code can only be used once for the registration of one book online. This registration will expire when the final sittings for the examinations covered by this book have taken place. Please allow one hour from the time you submitted your book details for us to process your request.

Please scratch the film to access your engage code.

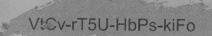

VtCv-rT5U-HbPs-kiFo

Please be aware that this code is case-sensitive and you will need to include the dashes within the passcode, but not when entering the ISBN. For further technical support, please visit www.EN-gage.co.uk